PICCADILLY

PICCADILLY

LONDON'S WEST END AND THE PURSUIT OF PLEASURE

STEPHEN HOARE

In loving memory of Don and Marjorie.

First published 2021

The History Press
97 St George's Place, Cheltenham,
Gloucestershire, GL50 3QB
www.thehistorypress.co.uk

© Stephen Hoare, 2021

The right of Stephen Hoare to be identified as the Author
of this work has been asserted in accordance with the
Copyright, Designs and Patents Act 1988.

British Library Cataloguing in Publication Data.
A catalogue record for this book is available from the British Library.

ISBN 978 0 7509 9565 8

Typesetting and origination by The History Press
Printed and bound in Great Britain by TJ Books Limited, Padstow, Cornwall.

Trees for LYfe

CONTENTS

Acknowledgements   11
Introduction   15

1   A Circus to the World   19
    Introduction   19
    Anteros   20
    Paving the Way for Pleasure   21
    Ghosts of the Past   23
    Change and Development – Market Forces   24
    Advertising   26
    Piccadilly at Night   27
    A Focus for Celebrations   29
    The Circus Goes Underground   30
    The Interwar Years   32
    War Looms   33
    War Comes to Piccadilly   34
    Surviving the Blitz   37
    A Time to Celebrate   38

2   Aristocratic Pleasures   39
    A Local Economy   39
    A Green Park   40
    The May Fair   41
    A Magnificent Palace   42
    Noble Developers   43

St James's Church, Piccadilly	44
Burlington House – A Grander Vision	45
The Elgin Marbles	46
The Balloonist of Burlington House	46
The Socialite and the Statesman	48
Grafton Street and the American War of Independence	49
Fox and his Courtesan	51
Albany	52
Albany's Literary Sensation	54
Number One London	55
Triumphal Arches	57
Past Glory	58
3 Inns, Clubs and Hotels	59
A Tourist Destination	59
Early Coaching Inns	60
The Royal Mail	61
The Broadband of the Georgian Era	62
An Industry is Born	63
The Old White Horse Cellar	64
The Gloucester Coffee House	65
New White Horse Cellar and Hatchett's Hotel	67
The Family Hotel	69
Members' Clubs	72
Rosa Lewis and the Cavendish Hotel	73
The Ritz and the Savoy	74
Building the Ritz	76
Escoffier	76
The Hospitality Industry	77
4 Popular Entertainments	79
Piccadilly – The 'Magic Mile'	79
From Sawdust Ring to Circus	80
Winstanley's Water Theatre	81
Museums and Attractions	82
William Bullock and the Liverpool Museum	83
The Egyptian Hall	84
'Mummy' Pettigrew	86

The 'Freak Show' 88

The 'Hottentot Venus' 90

High Art and Low Culture 91

General Tom Thumb 92

The Greatest Show on Earth 94

Magic, Illusion and Automata 95

England's Home of Mystery 96

Moving Pictures 98

Birth of the Leisure and Entertainments Industry 100

5 The West End Shops 101

A Nation of Shopkeepers 101

A Cornucopia of Small Businesses 102

Tea, Coffee and Spices 103

Reading for Pleasure 104

Polemicists and Pamphleteers 105

A 'Literary Coffee House' 106

Burlington Arcade 107

By Royal Appointment 109

Mr Fortnum and Mr Mason 110

The Fortnum Hamper 112

The 'Expeditions Department' 113

Conquering Everest on Pâté de Foie Gras 114

A Consumer Revolution 115

The Department Store 116

Selfridges – The First Modern Department Store 117

Simpson's of Piccadilly 118

Luxury Brands 120

6 Eating Out 139

A Taste for High Living 139

Street Food 140

The Rise of the West End Restaurant 142

Fine Dining Comes of Age 143

The Monico 145

Café Society 146

Paradise in the Strand 148

A Cultural Melting Pot 150

	Bentley's Oyster Bar	152
	Catering for the Masses	153
	Corner Houses	155
	What Makes the West End?	155
7	Nightlife	157
	Attempts at Regulation	157
	Sodom and Gomorrah	158
	Evans's Song and Supper Rooms	159
	Dinner and Dance	161
	Haunts of the Rich and Famous	162
	Hollywood Comes to London	163
	Chez Victor	165
	Bottle Parties	166
	The Queen of Clubs	167
	London's Jazz Hotspot	169
	A Warm Welcome for Black Servicemen	171
	The Gay Scene	172
	High Bohemia	174
	A Crucible of Creativity	176
8	The Theatre	177
	The Restoration	177
	The Italian Opera	178
	Diva Wars	180
	Masquerade	181
	The Final Years of Italian Opera	181
	No Leg to Stand On	183
	David Garrick, Inventor of Modern Theatre	184
	The Dark Charisma of Henry Irving	186
	The Criterion Puts Piccadilly Centre Stage	188
	Oscar Wilde and the *Vision of Salome*	189
	There is Nothing Like a Dame	191
	A Financial Lifeline	193
	Surviving the Great Depression	194
9	Show Time!	197
	Popular Culture	197

Penny Gaffs, Popular Entertainments and the London
    Pavilion Music Hall   198
Minstrel Shows   200
An Entertainments Hub   201
Cultivating Respectability   203
The Gaiety Theatre   204
Gaiety Girls   206
Breaking Down Barriers   207
Gertie Millar   209
Leg Shows and Censorship   210
Cultural Transformation   211
C.B. Cochran and the London Pavilion   213
Mrs Henderson Presents   214
World War Rude   215

10 The Business of Pleasure   219
Austerity Bites   219
A Bigger Vision   220
Let the Good Times Roll   221
The Circus   223
Sex and the Swinging Sixties   224
The King of Soho   225
Fast Food and Chain Restaurants   228
La Dolce Vita   229
Chinatown   231
Fine Dining   232
Clubland's Shifting Axis   233
Annabel's – Celebrity Meets Royalty   235
Film Premieres   236
Angry Young Men   237
Musicals   238
Green Shoots   240

Notes   243
Bibliography   247
Index   251

ACKNOWLEDGEMENTS

My previous book, *Palaces of Power*, covered the history of the members' clubs of St James's and Pall Mall. But that story would not be complete without an overview of London's West End. How did it evolve? Why did it coalesce around Piccadilly? And what drove London's economy?

The story is complex and involves piecing together an interlocking urban jigsaw. I conceived and began my research when London's West End economy was in full swing. But within months of starting my writing, the Covid-19 pandemic hit. This immediately prompted sober reflection. Pre-lockdown Piccadilly might itself become history – an unfamiliar social construct in need of recording while the memory is still fresh.

I have combined my own lifetime memories of the West End with previous writings, histories and contemporary accounts and ephemera. The West End may be timeless, but it will re-emerge adapted to changed circumstances, as it has always done. The pursuit of pleasure is hardwired into people's being.

I began my journey at the start of 2020 with a London Underground 'Hidden London' guided tour of the closed-off foot tunnels of Piccadilly Circus Station, the epicentre of the past I wanted to explore and where so many Londoners had sheltered during the Blitz.

I would like to thank all those who work in and around Piccadilly for their active participation in the book. First and foremost, to the staff of the London Library in St James's Square who ensured the collection was accessible right through the pandemic, reorganising services to meet members' needs, even to the extent of posting books when the library was locked down.

Special thanks is due to my library researcher and archivist Yvette Dickerson who responded enthusiastically to my requests for information on West End institutions, and the colourful characters whose stories she helped me bring to light. No subject was too obscure and I am grateful for the sheer volume of newspaper articles, advertisements, playbills and ephemera she managed to turn up.

I must also acknowledge individuals with a personal connection to the West End. Thanks are due to David and Pauline Bentley for their unique insights into the history of Bentley's Oyster Bar, Swallow Street, and allowing me access to family documents. Dr Andrea Tanner, Fortnum and Mason's in-house historian, shed light on aspects of the store's rich history and the previous owner's enthusiasm for automata, as well as the store's important role during the Georgian era as a post office regulated by the Royal Mail. I am grateful to Francis Beckett for sharing with me his father John Beckett MP's unpublished memoir, which chronicled the time he spent as manager of the Strand Theatre during the 1930s.

In the book's early stages, Francis Cleverdon, manager of Hatchards, was a source of inspiration and encouragement, leading me to focus on the bookshop's role as a 'literary coffee house'. Martin Price, a fellow member of the Long Eighteenth Century Group at Senate House, University of London, alerted me to the role played by Caroline Howe in brokering peace negotiations between the government of Lord North and the American colonists. Martin sent me his unpublished research on Mrs Howe and the special status of Grafton Street, Piccadilly. I should also like to thank the Geological Society for granting me behind-the-scenes access to their library in Piccadilly, which gave me a better understanding of the historic role and function of Burlington House as a centre of arts and scholarship.

This book depends for its appeal on insights and conversations with fellow pleasure seekers. In particular, I am grateful to Miranda Levy and Sarah Minxie Mann Yeager for sharing their memories of the idiosyncratic Won Kei Restaurant in Chinatown and Dr Keith C. Marshall of the Anthony Powell Society for giving background information on the location of the novel *Casanova's Chinese Restaurant*.

I would also thank my editor Mark Beynon for his unflagging enthusiasm and support for this project. Exploring London's past uncovers countless moral dilemmas that our more sensitive age would rather prefer to pretend did not happen. Mark's experienced eye and his good humour have been a reassuring presence and has made sure nothing has been lost in the telling.

Writing needs a sympathetic ear and so finally I should like to thank my wife Pauline whose encouragement and support helped keep me focused, especially during the torrid days of lockdown. During the early days of the pandemic, we rode our bicycles around the almost deserted streets of Piccadilly. The absence of crowds enabled us to study the buildings and to read in them the history of London's West End. We know the good times will return.

London, March 2021

INTRODUCTION

Of the fields, meadows and open countryside cut through by the mile-long highway formerly known as the Reading Road and later named Piccadilly, there is now no trace. This was once the western gateway to London where stage coaches from Reading, Bath, Bristol, Plymouth and beyond terminated or set off from Piccadilly's bustling coaching inns. The outer reaches of London became a resort of pleasure.

Coffee houses, theatres, fairgrounds, dance halls and opera houses sprang up. Hotels and clubs clustered around the Court of St James's. For more than three centuries the West End has created entertainments for the wealthy few and for the masses. It has provided employment for legions of makers and entrepreneurs, for actors and theatre managers, restaurateurs and waiters, shopkeepers and shop assistants.

The drivers that have caused this transformation have been many and various. The pursuit of pleasure is a 24-hours-a-day, 365-days-a-year obsession that has driven the economy of what was once the world's largest city, creating a unique urban environment.

The focus of all this activity is Piccadilly Circus. If you imagine London's hub as a giant ant hill, you will find not one square inch of original ground that has been left undisturbed by successive cycles of building, demolition, burrowing, tunnelling, bomb damage, fire and redevelopment.

This volume traces the social history of entertainment and pleasure in London's West End. Painting a broad-brush picture, I have focused on major themes and highlighted just a few of the colourful characters who emerged as influential. Readers will find themselves transported back in time to a world that is at once familiar and at the same time profoundly alien. The liberal values that underpin our modern society were noticeably absent in the grotesque entertainments and freak shows of Georgian Piccadilly. Sadly, the role of women was all too often relegated to subservience, sexual display or exploitation.

Piccadilly and the West End were an important crucible of enterprise that created and sustained globally recognised luxury brands like Fortnum and Mason, Floris, Ritz Hotels, Alfred Dunhill, Hatchards, Liberty's and many more. Often, establishments can trace their origins to humble beginnings like the royal footman Charles Fortnum, who in 1690, with his partner Mr Mason, made a respectable living selling ends of high-quality wax candles discarded by the Court of St James's.

Yet certain key elements of the pursuit of pleasure have remained constant and are likely to challenge our thinking. The West End's culture is overwhelmingly cosmopolitan, whose vibrant economy was augmented by foreign migrants and refugees. Successive waves of migration from Europe and from all four corners of the world created restaurants, clubs, hotels and an international cuisine that established London's position as a world city. It is easy to ignore the fact that the Ritz – the name most associated with luxury – was founded by the poor but ambitious son of a Swiss farmer, César Ritz.

What emerges from this history are the close links that evolved with the USA spanning tourism, entertainment and culture. Dating from the 1770s, when America was a British colony, Piccadilly booksellers published and exported pamphlets and books that supported the colonists' cause and especially the 'universal rights of man'. When in England, Benjamin Franklin and John Quincy Adams befriended radical booksellers like John Almon of Piccadilly.

The growth and success of the West End's music and entertainment sector shares a common history with New York's Broadway. When P.T. Barnum, 'the greatest showman on earth', arrived with his tiny sensation General Tom Thumb in tow, he played to packed audiences at Piccadilly's Egyptian Hall. The dwarf was such a consummate entertainer that advertisements suggesting that he had performed to 'the crowned heads of Europe' were no exaggeration. A private performance was even arranged for Queen Victoria who, one gathers, was 'amused'.

Barnum was no one-off. The Christy Minstrels who performed nightly at St James's Hall, Piccadilly and the African American dancers who arrived from Broadway to star in the musical *Blackbirds* took Britain by storm. So too did the jazz music which provided the backdrop to the upper-class din-ner–dance restaurants and nightclubs of the 'roaring twenties' through to the music counterculture of freestyle jazz or bebop that permeated Soho's black basement clubs like the Shim Sham and the Blue Lagoon.

The giant neon advertising hoardings of Piccadilly Circus are a tangible link to the West End's Edwardian heyday. The history of the nation can be viewed through the lens of the consumer. From the very first electric signage featuring Mellin's infant food supplement, the products say something about our values, lifestyle choices and disposable income, from Guinness, Sandeman's Port and Wrigley's Chewing Gum to Coca-Cola, TDK and Sanyo.

As fashions have changed or economic crisis has hit, the West End has reinvented itself time after time. It is and always has been in a state of dynamic flux.

1

A CIRCUS TO
THE WORLD

The Circus is full of the flashing and twinkling of multitudinous lights of hurrying hansoms, of many carriages speeding home to supper, of streams of people, men and women, mostly in evening dress, walking along, smiling and jesting.

Robert Machray, *The Night Side of London*

INTRODUCTION

Piccadilly is the centre of London's bustling West End – an entertainment and shopping district that encompasses the Strand, Charing Cross Road, Leicester Square, Haymarket, Regent Street, Oxford Street and Bond Street. Piccadilly is the hub of theatre-land. Piccadilly Circus is dead centre – of London ... of England ... of the United Kingdom ... possibly of the world? It is a curious and eclectic blend of the international scene and a small village where everyone knows everyone else.

It once marked the western extent of London and acquired its name from the word 'piccadill'. This is the ruff adorning the collar of an Elizabethan gentleman's coat. For a brief time during the late seventeenth and early eighteenth century, the eastern end of Piccadilly, the most built-up part closest to the Court of St James's, had been officially named Portugal Street in honour of Charles II's Portuguese consort, Catherine of Braganza. The links to the royal family of the time provided a driver for the cosmopolitan, entrepreneurial Piccadilly, and its entertainment hub.

If we could journey back in time, the 1890s would have been the moment when Piccadilly and its traffic circus with its famous statue came to symbolise Britain's vibrant capital city with all its confidence and charisma. It became one of the great streets of the world like New York's Times Square, Paris's Champs-Élysées, Rome's Via del Corso and Berlin's Unter den Linden.

Piccadilly Circus was not only the hub of an empire but a focal point for the West End with its luxury shops, hotels, restaurants and theatres. It has always been a surprisingly close-knit community in terms of the people who live locally, who operate businesses, both local and global, or who come to Piccadilly for entertainment and pleasure.

ANTEROS

The iconic Shaftesbury Memorial Fountain and its statue was erected in 1893 in honour of Anthony Ashley Cooper, 7th Earl of Shaftesbury, and stands in the middle of Piccadilly Circus. This centrepiece of the Circus somehow represents the contradictions and contrasts that are characteristic of the area.

Lord Shaftesbury, a parliamentarian, philanthropist and social reformer, had died in 1885 and a public subscription was raised to build a public monument. Where better than the vacant site in the middle of Piccadilly Circus? But it took considerable time for the charitable committee to decide on what form the memorial should take. In the end it was thought that a drinking fountain would be most appropriate.

The memorial fountain would be topped by a sculpture. Sculptor Alfred Gilbert was commissioned to design the winged figure of Anteros, the brother of Eros and known in classical mythology as the god of selfless love. Gilbert modelled the figure on his 16-year-old studio assistant Angelo Colarossi. After creating a clay model of the subject, the statue was cast in aluminium – the first time this soft metal had been used to create a sculpture. The statue stood atop the memorial's substantial bronze fountain.

Even now, people confuse the winged youth taking aim with a bow and arrow with Eros, mischievous god of love. Anteros was intended to represent Shaftesbury's selfless sacrifice, but people associated the statue with the sex trade around Piccadilly Circus and nearby Soho, the theatres, music halls and nightclubs and the pursuit of pleasure. The earl's worthy mission to help the poor was soon forgotten.

The steps at the base of the fountain were home to half a dozen cock-ney flower sellers who used the running water to keep their blooms fresh.

Despite being conceived as a public drinking fountain, the Shaftesbury Memorial Fountain was never used as such. The bronze drinking cups tethered to the fountain by chain were stolen within weeks. The flower sellers in their fringed shawls moved in and were a fixture of London street life right up to and throughout the Second World War and provided a vignette and the opportunity for song and dance for cockney flower sellers in the musical *My Fair Lady*.

PAVING THE WAY FOR PLEASURE

The word 'circus' has ancient origins. Rome's Circo Massimo (Circus Maximus) was originally built for the Emperor Vespasian: a gigantic oval circuit where crowds of spectators could watch chariot races and military parades. Piccadilly Circus may not have much in common with its Roman namesake, but it was an equally bold idea to enable traffic to move freely and to promote trade and business locally. Not quite the 'bread and circuses' of the Roman Empire but providing a similar opportunity for ease of movement to facilitate relaxation and 'letting off steam'.

The name was borrowed from classical antecedents by architect John Nash when planning Regent Street in the early 1800s. Stretching from Regent's Park in the north to St James's Park in the south, Regent Street was conceived as an ambitious residential and commercial development whose buildings would showcase Nash's classical style. Properties along the route were acquired by the Crown and demolished to help create a street that would be as wide and straight as possible. Apart from a kink in the road skirting around All Saints, Langham Place and the Quadrant, a curved section of colonnaded arcade where Regent Street feeds into Piccadilly Circus, Nash's route is remarkably straight.

Three large circular roundabouts, Regent's Circus, Oxford Circus and Piccadilly Circus, were planned to be built where Regent Street cut across existing roads. In the event, Regent's Circus was only half completed and became a crescent. Oxford Circus was shrunk in size so that today it appears as a simple road junction, and Piccadilly Circus, the only part of Nash's road plan to survive, was built in 1816.

Widening Regent Street to create a 'circus' roundabout where the street crossed bustling Piccadilly was the only way of avoiding arguments over rights of way. Horse-drawn traffic quickly adapted to the new rule of moving clockwise around the new Piccadilly Circus. Nash's solution to a potential traffic hazard was the first of its kind in England and became a model that was used in later centuries to replace busy crossroads or simplify awkward road junctions.

However, Piccadilly Circus had yet to achieve its present form. Shaftesbury Avenue was built between 1877 and 1886 by architect George Vulliamy and engineer Joseph Bazalgette to create a north–south artery linking Regent Street with Charing Cross. A key feature of the planned route was that it would spearhead a slum clearance scheme to eradicate notorious centres of poverty, such as the 'rookeries' of St Giles, and improve parts of Soho.

The new road, which was to sweep away so much poverty and human misery (or possibly relocate it in less salubrious areas of town), was named in honour of the same Lord Shaftesbury commemorated by the Shaftesbury Memorial Fountain in Piccadilly Circus. Among his many achievements were the protection of children who worked as chimney sweeps and the Factories Act of 1847.

Leading from New Oxford Street and cutting through the Charing Cross Road at Cambridge Circus, Shaftesbury Avenue linked with London's thriving West End, necessitating an enlarged road layout and the creation of a hub at Piccadilly Circus whose spokes were Tichborne Street, Shaftesbury Avenue, Coventry Street, Haymarket, Upper and Lower Regent's Street and Piccadilly. The completion of Shaftesbury Avenue in 1885 added six well-appointed theatres including the London Pavilion, the Trocadero, the Lyric, the Apollo, the Palace Theatre on Cambridge Circus, which opened briefly as Richard D'Oyly Carte's Royal English Opera House, and the New Prince's Theatre, since renamed the Shaftesbury Theatre. These palaces of pleasure helped cement the growing appeal of the West End's diverse theatreland. It was the expansion and improvement of the road network that enabled this development of the performing arts.

Modern road improvements set the perimeter of Soho, an enclave of original Hogarthian London whose densely populated grid pattern of grimy and dilapidated Georgian streets and alleyways was home to a thriving cosmopolitan community composed of virtually every nation on earth. A large Jewish community supported a garment industry based around small sweatshops. This later developed into the 'rag trade' located in and around Berwick Street, as well as Berwick Street Market. The need for theatrical costumiers drove this development in Piccadilly.

Soho's highly resourceful Italian, French and German communities gave birth to the West End's 'pleasure zone' – running the luxury hotels, the plethora of restaurants both large and small offering a wide variety of regional and gourmet cuisine, and the smart, moderately priced cafés that boosted international tourism. At the same time, a growing black diaspora contributed to a lively arts scene and provided the musical spark that lit up the West End's jazz-age nightclubs.

Redevelopment included the construction of Kingsway, a major road scheme that cut through in a straight line to Aldwych and linked with the Strand near Waterloo Bridge. Electric trams ran down Kingsway from Euston using shallow cut-and-cover tunnels at Holborn and the Strand, enabling trams to run beneath the streets and emerge onto the Thames Embankment at the foot of Waterloo Bridge, adding to the West End's accessibility. Modern London was taking shape. These works represented the final opening up of the West End for development and they rationalised the transport networks, increasing access for theatregoers and diners.

GHOSTS OF THE PAST

Far from sounding the death knell for Piccadilly's coaching inns, the coming of the railways fuelled demand from a younger generation eager to experience the romance of stage coaches before they were swept away forever. This wave of nostalgia is evidenced by the popularity of novels such as Charles Dickens's *Pickwick Papers* whose plot lines are derived from scenes of life observed in coaching inns. The experience of a bumpy ride along the open road in a stage coach was recreated by a group of aristocratic enthusiasts driving horses 'four in hand', who saved many mail coaches from the breaker's yard and invested their own money in maintaining the London to Brighton stage coach.

As recently as 1870, the White Bear coaching inn occupied the site where the Criterion Theatre now stands at Piccadilly Circus. Set back slightly from Nash's Regent Street, the inn was a throwback to a different age due to its imposing classical architecture. Built in the seventeenth century to serve the old Bath Road mail route, its busy coach yard looked out onto a contemporary streetscape: hawkers, hustlers and perhaps the occasional drove of bullocks on their way to slaughter at Smithfield Market to provide the raw materials for local restaurants and eateries.

Losing its passenger trade to the White Horse Cellar and the Gloucester Coffee House further down Piccadilly, the old White Bear hung on long past the heyday of the stage coach as a parcel depot and a clearing house for goods transported by road.

Even as late as the early 1900s, the West End was dominated by horse-drawn traffic. It was not just stage coaches and horse-drawn vans or carts on their way in or out of London: much of the traffic was generated by privately owned vehicles – phaetons, chariots, chaises, landaus, hackney carriages belonging to the aristocratic denizens of Piccadilly and the rising middle classes. The amount of horse dung deposited as a result was immense. Neat sellers collected and sold this useful resource for the leather trade, providing gainful employment for many.

Public transport was a relatively late arrival, starting with George Shillibeer's 'Omnibus', an enclosed carriage seating fifteen to eighteen people, which made its debut in July 1829 offering a service to fare-paying passengers between Paddington and the Bank of England. The idea caught the public imagination and served a real need. By the 1840s, Piccadilly was crowded with buses, the earliest type being a box-like affair drawn by a pair of horses with seating inside and a bench seat on the roof, which became known as 'garden seat' buses. Buses served the rising lower middle classes and provided an alternative to the expensive hackney carriages and four-wheeled 'growlers'. Despite the improvements to the network, the rapid rise of traffic meant the average speed of carriages hovered at around 5mph in central London.

This equestrian economy included not just the coaching inns and their stables but also riding clothes and schools, harness makers and saddlers. Tattersall's horse auction house stood on the south side of Hyde Park Corner, more or less opposite Apsley House.

At the lowest level, crossing sweepers, an industrious underclass of young urchins, enthusiastic beggars – 'sturdy imposters' – or former soldiers fallen on hard times kept the roads clear of horse droppings, surviving only on the tips they were given by a grateful public. Some achieved local fame as well-loved members of the urban communities they served. William Tomlins, a crossing sweeper who stood at Albemarle and St James's Streets, was pictured in an engraving dated 1816 wielding a besom broom and wearing a top hat, breeches and gaiters. A contemporary treatise on London beggars describes him as being 'alive to the receipt of every penny and will not suffer himself by any means to be diverted from his solicitations'.[1]

CHANGE AND DEVELOPMENT – MARKET FORCES

By the beginning of the twentieth century, Piccadilly's Georgian streetscape looked remarkably unchanged, with Nash's landmark buildings on Regent

Street, the ducal palaces of Piccadilly such as Albany, Burlington House and Devonshire House, and Cambridge House still being occupied by their aristocratic owners. Many palaces had been demolished to open up Mayfair, creating new streets to the north of Piccadilly. Some changes had been made in order to rationalise the road network; others were driven by market forces.

The construction of Shaftesbury Avenue and the widening of Piccadilly Circus brought modernity and rapid progress. An inn that had stood for 200 years was demolished and replaced by the Criterion Theatre and Restaurant, which in turn became an institution in its own right. The Shaftesbury Memorial Fountain came to symbolise a new era.

Opposite the Criterion stood a popular theatre and music hall, the London Pavilion. On the other side of the road, where Shaftesbury Avenue meets Piccadilly Circus, two enterprising brothers, Giacomo and Battista Monico set up the Monico Café and Restaurant in 1877, the same year as work on constructing Shaftesbury Avenue began. Over almost a century, the Monico was one of the West End's most popular restaurants.

Where Regent Street joins Piccadilly Circus is a curved section known as the Quadrant. At the turn of the twentieth century, this was still the colonnaded walkway designed by John Nash. On the Circus, the department store Swan and Edgar also had an entrance on Regent Street. On the opposite side of the Quadrant stood the County Fire Office, and a few doors down, on the Circus itself, were the Monico Café and its next-door neighbour, the jewellers Saqui and Lawrence.

Further along Regent Street from Swan and Edgar, where the colonnade starts, was another famous landmark, St James's Hall. Opened on 25 March 1858, the concert hall occupied an entire block with entrances in Piccadilly and Regent Street. Designed in the Moorish style in imitation of the Alhambra in Grenada, St James's Hall was a huge complex that included a restaurant, café, large concert hall for classical music concerts and two smaller halls on the ground floor suitable for popular entertainments and recitals. Among those recitals were dramatic readings of extracts from popular novels *Pickwick Papers* and *Oliver Twist*, staged from October to early December 1868 by the author Charles Dickens.

Popularly known as 'Jimmy's', the St James's Hall restaurant fronted onto Regent Street on the first floor above the colonnade. The area beneath its canopy was notorious as a night haunt for high-class prostitutes. The restaurant was a well-known place of assignation where wealthy men might meet and entertain their mistresses. It served a luxurious continental cuisine.

St James's Hall was London's only major concert hall, until superseded by the Royal Albert Hall in 1871. The construction of St James's Hall was financed by music publishers Chappell and Co. and Cramer and provided a massive boost to classical music, encouraging guest appearances by world-famous composers and touring orchestras. In 1893, for example, Tchaikovsky conducted the London premiere of his Fourth Symphony, and from 1875 the hall was home to the Bach Choir.

St James's Hall was demolished in February 1905 to make way for the redevelopment of Regent Street and Piccadilly. The Piccadilly Hotel, now the Le Méridien Hotel, was built on the site. Once the ninety-nine-year Crown leases expired on the properties in Regent Street, the busy shopping area was progressively demolished and redeveloped, widening the street and adding two more storeys to create unified Portland-stone frontages of seven storeys. With its notorious colonnade now gone, the columns were echoed in the massive stone pillars and balconies of the new stores.

Around Piccadilly Circus, the streets were a cacophony of sound – the clatter of horse-drawn traffic from two-wheeled hansom cabs and the large numbers of 'knife board' buses whose open upper decks were packed with passengers seated back to back on a wooden bench. The level of noise reflected the press of trade and business in the area.

ADVERTISING

By the early 1900s there were already large advertising billboards on many of the buildings on Piccadilly Circus. In 1904, the first electric sign spelled out 'Mellin's Food' in 6ft-high letters above Mellin's Pharmacy at 43 Regent Street. Mellin's Food was a popular infant food supplement: a 'soluble, dry extract of wheat, malted barley and bicarbonate of soda'. The advert read: 'Mellin's Food for Infants and Invalids: The only perfect substitute for Mother's Milk'.

The year 1908 saw the installation of the first electric illuminated advertising billboards on the frontage of the Monico tea rooms. Illuminated advertisements for Perrier water and Bovril were quick to follow. A popular brand of beef tea, Bovril became the first product to be advertised by neon light in 1910. At a time when most domestic houses were lit by gas, electric and neon illuminations were a novelty that added to the area's brash appeal.

The electric billboard was the latest manifestation of London's confident and assertive advertising industry. Since the early nineteenth century, commercial enterprise and advances in printing resulted in unregulated billboards springing up on every vacant plot of land. Every empty wall was plastered with ephemeral printed notices and signage advertising shops, music-hall attractions, funfairs, property auctions and patent medicines. And since the development of industrial enamelling processes, railway stations and grocery shops were covered in colourful and virtually indestructible signage advertising everything from cigarettes to tea and soap powder.

Nevertheless, the London County Council disapproved of this buccaneering example of private enterprise. It used lamp and signage by-laws within the London Building Act of 1894 in order to prevent 'the exhibition of flash lights so as to be visible from any street and cause a danger to traffic therein'. The vaguely worded by-law was impossible to enforce. A scheme to redevelop the north and east of Piccadilly Circus and to rid the Circus of a 'disorderly rabble of buildings' also ran into the sand owing to numerous objections. Besides, the owners of buildings fronting onto the Circus – the Monico and the London Pavilion – regarded advertising signage as a valuable supplementary income.

With its fast-growing passenger numbers, the Underground also regarded selling advertising space at its stations and access tunnels as a major source of revenue. Advertising on the Tube not only had the advantage of being highly visible but also offered an opportunity for the railway companies to reinforce the message that the Underground offered opportunities for leisure. Day trips to places like London Zoo or the Thames at Chiswick were now possible.

The small horse-drawn buses were covered in enamel adverts for Hudson's Soap, Nestlé's Milk and Oakey's Knife Polish. In the never-ending battle for consumers' attention, Piccadilly Circus's illuminations would very soon be put to the service of Gordon's Gin, Guinness, Black and White Whisky and Sandeman's Port.

PICCADILLY AT NIGHT

By day, London has many focal points such as Trafalgar Square, Oxford Street's department stores, Parliament Square and the Tower of London. But by night, the centre of London is Piccadilly Circus with its illuminated advertising signs and its crowds of pleasure seekers.

This was especially true during the 1890s and 1900s, at a time when Shaftesbury Avenue could boast no fewer than five well-appointed modern theatres between Piccadilly Circus and New Oxford Street. The largest of them all was the London Pavilion, a palace of varieties and music hall.

Theatreland itself stretched as far south as Aldwych and the Strand and as far north as Oxford Circus. Piccadilly was the centre of a vast entertainment hub. Edwardian author Robert Machray provides us with a vivid account of the late-night crowds that thronged Piccadilly Circus around midnight.

The best vantage point to observe street life, Machray points out, was the pavement between Piccadilly and Regent Street, on the north-west of the Circus, opposite the fountain: 'On its steps sit strange female shapes, offering penny flowers ... "Only a penny, sir, only a penny for a bokay!"' The women, mostly old, appear to have fallen on hard times. A blind beggar makes his appearance soliciting small change from the passers-by, a tramp scans the pavement for cigarette ends or small items dropped from pockets or handbags. The author notes a 'squalid, wretched woman selling matches'.

The music halls are now closing and audiences rush onto the pavement to catch buses or hail horse-drawn hansom cabs. Restaurants and public houses will turn customers out at 12.30 a.m., as licensing laws demand, and couples mostly in evening dress spill out onto the streets. 'You catch charming glimpses in the softening electric lights of sylph-like forms, pink-flushed happy faces, snowy shoulders half-hidden in lace or chiffon, or cloaks of silk and satin.'[2]

Open-topped buses with people crowded on the upper deck rumble past, and gaudily dressed young women begin to gather near the fountain. Machray describes a shadowy half world that has suddenly come to life. He continues:

> A girl of the night, on her prowl for prey, casts a keen glance over you and flits silently past like a bat. Behind you – you can see her with the tail of your eye – pauses a Painted Lady, picture-hatted, black-haired, belladonna'd, rouged, over-dressed ... the Circus suddenly buzzes with life; it hums like a giant hive. Here are movement, colour and a babel of sounds.[3]

The colonnade where Regent Street meets Piccadilly was home to a 'peripatetic foreign colony of ladies who make this their rendezvous and turn it into ... a "sordid boulevard"'. Machray continues to describe the women that crowded the streets: 'But what a number of them! And all sorts and sizes, so to say; young and middle-aged; thin and stout, short and tall; Jenny fond of a kiss and fond of a guinea.'[4]

French was the language of choice and the prices were high. This end of Regent Street had been the haunt of ladies of the night since the days of the Regency.

Prostitution was always rife in London's West End. In 1900 there was no attempt on the part of the authorities to curb it. If anything, the police were sympathetic and took pity on some of the women who they knew as 'regulars'. A large part of the job of the police was to keep order, control the traffic and ensure the crowds pouring out of the late-closing music halls could leave safely.

Most of the police were deployed making sure the wealthy diners at the St James's Hall Restaurant, 'Jimmy's', were kept safe from pick pockets and were not jostled as they waited on the pavement for their cabs and carriages.

A FOCUS FOR CELEBRATIONS

The Second Anglo-Boer War had been raging since June 1899, when the President of the South African Republic, a British protectorate, Paul Kruger, issued an ultimatum calling for British forces to be withdrawn from his borders. War was declared and Britain, which governed the neighbouring Cape Colony, responded by sending more troops to re-establish British rule.

The British Army was pitted against a band of Dutch farmers (Boers) who were defending their freedoms. Many young men with no previous experience in fighting enlisted. It was the most serious British involvement in armed conflict since the Crimean War half a century earlier.

But the war had gone badly for Britain. Boer guerrilla fighters knew the land, leading to defeats at the battles of Colenso, Spion Kop and Ladysmith. The fortified township of Mafeking, west of Johannesburg, had been besieged since October 1899 and its 600 defenders led by Colonel Baden-Powell stubbornly held out even as supplies were running dangerously low. Baden-Powell organised raiding parties to seize cattle and herd them back to the township to feed its weary inhabitants.

Meanwhile in Kimberley, General Roberts dispatched a relief column of horsemen under the command of Colonel Mahon to break the siege. Mahon used a code to communicate his position to Baden-Powell: 'Our numbers are the Naval and Military Club multiplied by ten.' The club's address, 94 Piccadilly, was sufficient to alert the defenders of the size of the force coming to their aid.

On the evening of 17 May 1900, news of the relief of the besieged town of Mafeking reached London. The next day was declared a day of national celebration. Bands played the rousing marching song 'We're Soldiers of the Queen, m' Lads', and in Piccadilly Circus itself cheering crowds assembled flourishing banners, young men and women waved Union Jacks from the tops of London buses, and a few patriotic souls carried aloft portraits of Baden-Powell wearing khaki uniform with his trademark wide-brimmed scout hat.

As the day wore on, London, and towns and cities across the United Kingdom, erupted into one almighty outburst of patriotic euphoria. As night fell in Piccadilly Circus people climbed up lamp posts waving the Union Jack; they cheered, got drunk and total strangers embraced each other. The *Oxford English Dictionary* coined a new expression for wild celebrations. The phenomenon was known as 'mafficking'.

Although victory had come at a high cost – 212 defenders and townspeople had been killed and around 600 soldiers wounded in the fierce hand-to-hand fighting – the relief of Mafeking represented the high point of the public support for the British Empire and a genuine outpouring of pride – some might call it jingoism. It banished national humiliation, putting Britain at last on the front foot. A hard-fought guerrilla war ensued, leading two years later to victory over the Boers. Events like this and the contemporary reaction to them underline the differences in accepted norms then and now.

Piccadilly Circus was the focus of those celebrations. Baden-Powell was promoted to major general and returned to England in 1903. He later founded the Boy Scout movement and wrote his classic *Scouting for Boys* in 1908. As a result, thousands of young men joined the Territorial Force eager to share in the British Army's glory.

Virtually as soon as the Anteros statue and its fountain had been erected, it acted as a magnet for nocturnal celebrations – mostly a rite of passage for unruly upper-class youth. There was 'boat race night' when jubilant supporters of Oxford or Cambridge would get up to silly japes such as stealing a police-man's helmet and getting banged up in a cell for the night to appear 'before the beak' at Bow Street Magistrate's Court. Or there was the annual Eton vs Harrow cricket match – which again sparked a West End drinking spree. The young gentlemen used Piccadilly as their playground, with semi-benevolent police officers keeping their outrageous behaviour somewhat in check.

THE CIRCUS GOES UNDERGROUND

In 1900, the average speed of traffic moving through central London was just 5mph. Most of it was horse drawn, but a few exotic motor cars were beginning to make an appearance – coach-built and open-topped, these early cars were a luxury reserved for the upper classes.

But a transport innovation was on its way that would breathe new life into London's increasingly congested hub. In March 1906, a new underground line, the Baker Street and Waterloo Railway, opened a station at Piccadilly Circus. In December of the same year, the Great Northern and Piccadilly Railway was opened, creating an underground interchange. Both of these lines were owned by Underground Electric Railways of London Limited (UERL), better known as the Underground. Formed in 1902, UERL owned central London's three deep-tunnel lines, which formed the nucleus of the present-day Northern, Piccadilly and Bakerloo lines.

London's rapidly expanding underground railway network was enabled by a technique for tunnelling under the soft London clay. The Broadhead Shield was a working platform on which labourers shovelled out the bare clay by hand while being protected from cave-ins by a shield, which was propelled forward inch by inch using hydraulic jacks.

The earliest underground lines from Baker Street to Euston, which opened in 1863, had been dug from the surface in a huge cutting which was then covered by a continuous brick arch – a technique known as 'cut and cover'. Steam trains ran just below ground level in tunnels that were ventilated.

But steam trains were unsuited to deep tunnels. The development of electric locomotives in the early 1900s meant the trains serving Piccadilly Circus Station were fast and clean.

Designed by the architect Leslie Green in a standard house style, Piccadilly Circus Station stood out from the surrounding Portland-stone buildings by virtue of its distinctive ox-blood-red tiles and arcade of semi-circular arches. Behind the frontage the station was constructed using a steel-frame technique, which provided cross beams strong enough to support hydraulic lift machinery. The steel frame could also support several storeys above the ticket hall, making economical use of prime London real estate.

Passengers entered a spacious booking hall decorated in salt-glazed art nouveau tiles and signposted with directions to the different platforms. The station occupied a site at the corner of Jermyn Street and Haymarket and was built to a standard design that still survives today at many London Underground stations on the Northern and Bakerloo lines. The original Piccadilly Station building still stands. Refaced in stone, it is now a shopping arcade.

Almost as busy as the bustling streets above, Piccadilly Circus Station was served by eight passenger lifts to take passengers down to platform level. In 1907, its first full year of operation, Piccadilly Circus Station served around 1.5 million passengers. By 1922 the number had risen to 18 million a year. As the Underground's flagship station, Piccadilly Circus was due a makeover.

Frank Pick, the Underground Group's commercial director, had overseen the takeover of the capital's biggest bus operator, the London General Omnibus Company, in 1912. By the 1920s he had welded bus and Tube operations into a co-ordinated transport network for London. Promoted to managing director and second in command to Underground chairman Lord Ashfield, Pick argued strongly for the extension of the Bakerloo, Northern and Piccadilly lines to the outer suburbs, fighting hard for planning permission against the vested interests of the overground railways.

The jewel in the crown was to be a new underground interchange at Piccadilly Circus. Pick worked closely with the architect Charles Holden to give the station a cutting-edge design.

Holden conceived a massive circular concourse below street level that included a small shopping mall around the perimeter. Construction began in 1922 when permission was obtained to remove the statue of Anteros and its fountain to allow a 5.5m-wide shaft to be dug to remove the spoil from the excavations. The roof of the new concourse was reinforced with a complex lattice of steel girders designed to support 400 tonnes – enough to carry the weight of Piccadilly Circus above ground. The Shaftesbury Memorial Fountain was moved to a temporary site in Victoria Embankment Gardens while construction work was in progress.

Accessed by staircase entrances at all of the major road junctions on Piccadilly Circus, the spacious booking hall was lined with travertine marble, and its octagonal roof pillars were topped by art deco lanterns. Innovations included automatic ticket machines and four escalators to convey passengers to platform level. Above the escalator roof was a massive mural titled 'Hub of Empire' by artist Stephen Bone. There was even a linear clock showing the time in different time zones across the world. The new station opened on Monday, 10 December 1928. The old red-tiled station at the corner of Jermyn Street and Haymarket continued in use until 1974.

THE INTERWAR YEARS

The interwar years saw the demolition of several of the stately palaces to the north side of Piccadilly as aristocratic families, their fortunes, power and sons depleted by the First World War, decided they could no longer afford their upkeep. Devonshire House was demolished in 1923 to create shops, a car show-room, offices and a luxury hotel, the Mayfair, on the corner of Stratton Street.

Following the redevelopment of the site of the Old White Horse Cellar to build the Ritz Hotel, developers eyed the by now run-down rows of grand houses on the north side of Piccadilly with a view to converting them into grand hotels. A syndicate of Yorkshire businessmen succeeded in assembling a site for a luxury hotel which necessitated the demolition of the Savile Club on the corner of Piccadilly and Park Lane. Construction was delayed following the outbreak of the First World War. Supervised by architect Sir Bracewell Smith, the work on site recommenced in 1924 when the building's steel frame blossomed into an imposing hotel.

When it opened in 1927, the Park Lane Hotel was considered to have some of the finest examples of art deco in London, including a ballroom that attracted high society. These interiors suffered neglect over the years, but the magnificent ballroom and all the architectural details have been restored to their former glory. The hotel is now the Sheraton Grand London Park Lane Hotel.

However, the main focus for interwar development was Piccadilly Circus itself. From 1905 onwards, the ninety-nine-year ground leases on Regent Street were due to expire and the landlord, Crown Estates, insisted on the progressive redevelopment of Regent Street and the Quadrant at Piccadilly Circus, supervised by architects Sir Reginald Blomfield and Norman Shaw. The old colonnade and the County Fire Office were demolished and rebuilt further back to allow road widening. The shops and properties along Regent Street were built up to a full seven storeys, adding two more floors to the smaller regency predecessors. The redesign of the Quadrant forced the closure of St James's Hall and its restaurant, while the rebuilding of Swan and Edgar's department store created a site on which the Piccadilly Hotel now stands.

Regency stucco was substituted for Portland stone with frontages executed in the neoclassical style. The redevelopment greatly benefited the many stores and restaurants along Regent Street as designs incorporated plate-glass windows, spacious interiors and, in some cases, escalators to upper floors. Put on hold during the First World War, the scheme was not fully completed until 1928.

WAR LOOMS

With its luxury hotels and shops, Piccadilly appeared peaceful in the late 1930s. But below ground, preparations were being made for a European war that threatened the mass bombing of cities. Alive to the threat posed by Adolf Hitler, the British Government had enlisted the support of London Underground Railways to create civilian shelters and deep bunkers where emergency services could be co-ordinated. Redundant Tube stations or unused parts of the tunnel network could be repurposed for the coming war and managing director Frank Pick was eager to help out.

The German Zeppelin raids of the First World War had caused mass panic and led to Tube stations being used as shelters. A future war would be far more devastating, War Office planners argued, and it would be prudent to plan for a worst-case scenario. As early as 1929, a little-used branch station, Aldwych, was identified as a station that could be completely closed and converted to a shelter for up to 7,000 civilians.

Just off Piccadilly, Down Street Station had been closed in May 1932 and converted to a ventilation shaft as passengers were better served by Hyde Park Corner Station just a few minutes' walk away. In April 1939, even before war was declared, work began at Down Street to convert disused tunnels into a deep shelter for the Railway Executive Committee, the body tasked with keeping Britain's railways running. In 1940, this deep shelter would be used by Winston Churchill to hold important meetings as a stopgap while the cellars beneath the Treasury were reinforced and converted into the Cabinet War Rooms. The disused tunnels of Piccadilly Circus Station became a temporary store for priceless paintings and works of art from national collections.

Above ground, the famous statue of Anteros was removed from its plinth, crated up and sent to the Royal Engineering College at Cooper's Hill, Egham, Surrey, where it peacefully waited out the duration of the war. It did not return to Piccadilly Circus until 1948. The statueless fountain was covered in sandbags and boarded over. Large hoardings screwed in place around the base advertised National Savings' War Bonds.

WAR COMES TO PICCADILLY

The blackout was introduced to London on 1 September 1939, meaning all windows had to be heavily curtained and cars had to be fitted with louvred headlamps, which would be invisible to a bomber circling in the sky above. The stringent regulations had been trialed in a series of major publicity campaigns under the banner Air Raid Precautions (ARP). The blackout was enforced by air-raid wardens empowered to fine anyone caught breaking the law.

Advertising signs and the illuminations of Oxford Street and Regent Street were switched off. On 7 September 1939, the government announced all theatres and cinemas were to close; shows were cancelled and confusion ensued. But a week later this draconian decision was reversed. Theatres, cinemas and places of public entertainment would be allowed to stay open on condition they observe a 10.00 p.m. curfew. It was realised that West End entertainment provided an important morale boost.

Restaurants stayed open, switching custom from civilian to military use and, while the Italian waiters, nightclub owners and restaurant proprietors were all interned for the duration, they were replaced with Soho's cosmopolitan denizens whose countries were fighting on the side of the Allies.

The Blitz, which began exactly one year later, on 7 September 1940, shut most West End theatres as audiences stayed away and theatre managers closed their doors to save lives. On the first day of the Blitz, twenty-four shows had been running in the West End; a week later this had been reduced to just two. Famously, the Windmill Theatre, whose motto was 'We Never Closed', stuck to its mission statement. Girls continued to dance on stage throughout the Blitz, acting as a morale booster and a rallying cry for freedom.

More cinemas and theatres cautiously reopened as a system of air-raid warnings was put in place to act as a measure of protection. At the first sign of an incoming air raid, the theatre manager would stop the show, giving the audience time to find their way to a public shelter. There was a widespread belief that life should carry on as normal.

The Blitz began with the bombing of the City, London's East End and its vast network of docks. The West End was subject to sporadic attack. On 13 September 1940, a German bomber dropped five high-explosive bombs near Buckingham Palace.

Four days later, Marble Arch Underground Station was hit, killing more than twenty civilians. And on the night of 14 October St James's Church in Piccadilly was badly damaged by incendiary and conventional bombs, leaving the roof and nave a charred shell. But firefighters had saved most of the building including its organ, whose case was covered in exuberant carved swags, and the marble font, both the work of the celebrated seventeenth-century master craftsman Grinling Gibbons.

A short Christmas truce observed by the RAF and Luftwaffe, which lasted until 27 December, allowed some West End shows and pantomimes to open to packed houses. The pantomime *Babes in the Wood* put on at the Stoll Theatre, Kingsway, took £50,000 in advance bookings.

Considered safe from bombing, basement nightclubs continued to attract young couples intent on partying. But on the night of 8 March 1941 the Café de Paris in Coventry Street took a direct hit as a German bomb dropped down the club's ventilator shaft in a freak event.

West Indian bandleader Ken 'Snakehips' Johnson was on stage in full swing playing the Andrews Sisters' hit 'Oh Johnny Oh' when the bomb exploded, decapitating him and killing thirty-three people, including band members, partygoers and diners. The devastation led to a momentary pause in the West End's nightlife.

Life continued as near normal as possible. Writing in her account of wartime London, *A Village in Piccadilly*, Madeleine Henrey describes how on a foggy day in November 1941 she dodged the traffic to reach the boarded-up fountain in the centre of the Circus and:

> landed beside the black-shawled (octogenarian) flower seller at the foot of the boxed-up plinth … last survivor of a band of ten who, in the bloom of youth, surveyed the Heart of Empire in its horse-drawn day, tubeless days. This old harpy's wrinkled face lost its smile when, stopping to glance at her pink roses and violets on the wicker basket, I called out: 'How's business?'[5]

Henrey surveys the garish War Bonds posters:

> Why all this on a yellow background? Scott's the fish shop had a better sense of colouring. It's boarded up exterior was pleasantly decorated with murals – two chefs head-to-head, with their tall white caps forming the V sign; a pink lobster on a plate and a reconstruction of Piccadilly and the windmill in 1685.

Although many shops were closed, pubs, cinemas, nightclubs and some theatres stayed open. Showing non-stop Pathé newsreels and features, the Eros News Cinema on the corner of Piccadilly and Shaftesbury Avenue was always full as the public anxiously awaited news from the various theatres of war. The upbeat voice-overs provided by journalists like Bob Danvers-Walker veered towards propaganda – a forgivable sin in the light of the need to raise morale. Further along Piccadilly, the Gaumont News Theatre opened in 1939 also showing news clips interspersed with serials. Formerly the Movietone Theatre, the Gaumont was bombed out in November 1941. On its site stands the present-day Curzon, Soho.

Towards the end of the war Piccadilly Circus at night was, as ever, a haunt of prostitutes. During the blackout, an assortment of women of all ages lined up in the street advertising their charms by the feeble light of small electric torches. Widespread poverty had forced many single women and housewives struggling to make ends meet to offer their bodies in exchange for hard cash. The influx of American GIs supplied a ready market for casual sexual relations.

SURVIVING THE BLITZ

While Aldwych opened as an official air-raid shelter, both London Transport and the government initially resisted the idea of allowing people to go down into Underground stations to spend the night sleeping on platforms. According to Churchill, this would create a shelter mentality and might lead to civil unrest.

They need not have worried. When the Blitz started in September 1940, civilians simply turned up, bedded down on platforms and stairwells and refused to leave. As there was nothing that the authorities could do about it, measures were taken to ease crowding and provide basic sanitation like chemical toilets.

Piccadilly Circus Station had its entrance stairways at street level roofed over with steel girders supporting thick planking and the entire encased in sandbags as a protection against bomb blast. People sheltered with whole families including grandparents and children. Shelterers would arrive early to bag the best places, but as the station became ever more crowded, people slept on escalators or in any available space. To feed people, trains were organised to deliver food and basic provisions, staffed by the Women's Royal Voluntary Society (WRVS).

Each night people kept their spirits up by holding a sing-song as there were usually one or two musicians among the crowd able to entertain with an accordion or banjo.

Piccadilly Circus also had a luxury few other stations possessed. This was a compressed-air waste-disposal system installed to force human waste up to ground level where it could connect with sewers. Early each morning station staff emptied slop buckets from the previous night into the compressed-air system for removal. Evidence of life during the Blitz can be seen in long-disused tunnels, which can be viewed on Transport for London's 'Hidden London' Underground walking tours. As always, bodily waste and its safe and (if at all possible) profitable disposal has been a key feature of Piccadilly, like all town centres.

A TIME TO CELEBRATE

Victory in Europe Day (VE Day) came on Tuesday, 8 May 1945, the same day that Field Marshal Wilhelm Keitel, German High Command, signed the document of unconditional surrender in Berlin.

Crowds gathered across the West End before converging on Buckingham Palace where King George VI, Queen Elizabeth and their two daughters Elizabeth and Margaret, together with Prime Minister Winston Churchill, stepped out onto the balcony.

Just as in a circus 'big top', Piccadilly Circus acted as an arena for moments of national crisis or celebration. None were more dramatic than the celebrations on VE night, when the pent-up anxieties and fears of five years of war were suddenly released in a raucous wave of euphoria.

2

ARISTOCRATIC
PLEASURES

So rais'd above the tumult and the crowd
I see the city in a thicker cloud
Of business; then of smoake; where men like Ants
Toyle to prevent imaginary wants;
Yet all in vaine, increasing with their store
Their vast desires, but make their wants the more.

> Sir John Denham, poem inspired by Burlington House, Piccadilly

A LOCAL ECONOMY

From the Restoration of the monarchy in 1660 and throughout the eighteenth century, the north side of Piccadilly was a prime location for private palaces. With the court residing at St James's Palace when Parliament was in session, the aristocracy needed to be in London for a longer period. The power and wealth of the country were concentrated on this one street.

Standing well back from the busy road, these mansions were hidden from public gaze behind tall walls and protected by massive gates. Their owners pursued private pleasures, enjoying spacious rear gardens and orchards in which they could stroll and gaze on uninterrupted views of distant hills.

As the capital spread westwards, Piccadilly and its environs were the focus of a frenzy of construction work. Workmen gradually transformed the surrounding green fields and country lanes into secluded squares and palatial mansions where society hostesses like the Duchess of Devonshire held sway.

Devonshire House, a nine-bay brick mansion flanked by service wings, had originally been built for Lord Berkeley, a soldier who had served with distinction in the English Civil War. Appointed Lord Lieutenant of Ireland, Berkeley did not live long enough to enjoy his new home. He died in 1678, at which point his widow let the house to Princess Anne and her husband Prince George of Denmark. Anne was to accede to the throne of England in 1702, reigning until her death in 1707. Finally, as home to the Cavendish family, Dukes of Devonshire, the house had an illustrious history before being demolished in 1930.

Following the Restoration of the monarchy, the Reading Road into London was renamed Portugal Street in honour of Charles II's marriage to Catherine of Braganza in 1662. The street took on new significance four years later as the principal western approach to a city that had been extensively destroyed in the Great Fire of London.

The West End, which had escaped the fire's ravages unscathed, grew in importance as a resort for the leisured upper classes. It was both a political power base and a high-status residential district, packed with the leisured rich as residents and visitors.

A GREEN PARK

On the outskirts of London, Green Park was unspoilt countryside well into the eighteenth century when it was tamed and landscaped as a public park. In its early days, this isolated spot was a well-known haunt of highwaymen and thieves. It was also a notorious duelling ground where gentlemen would seek satisfaction by firing pistols from a paced distance. One particularly notorious duel took place there in 1730 between William Pulteney, 1st Earl of Bath, and John Hervey, 1st Earl of Bristol. These former friends fell out because Pulteney indirectly accused Hervey, a well-known court wit, of being gay.

As Piccadilly's mile of mansions spread westwards from the late eighteenth century, the Green Park became a public resort. This wooded parkland linked up with Buckingham House and St James's Park. The open space was used for fairs, public gatherings, military manoeuvres and encampments.

But one particular event cast a cloud over public gatherings. On 27 April 1749, public celebrations were held to celebrate the Treaty of Aix-la-Chapelle and the end of the War of the Austrian Succession. In Green Park there was to be a grand festival of military bands with 101 cannon and public fireworks centred around the specially built 'Temple of Concord', a hastily constructed bandstand made of wood and canvas from which the fireworks would be ignited.

The court composer George Frideric Handel composed *Music for the Royal Fireworks* to accompany the fireworks. Things did not go quite to plan as mixing musicians and fireworks was a bad decision. A rocket misfired and set fire to part of the temple. A woman's dress was set ablaze and a soldier had part of his hand blown off in the cannonade. The event was swiftly cancelled, the public were evacuated and the temple burned to the ground. Handel's music, however, went from strength to strength as it was performed at the Foundling Hospital the following month without mishap.

THE MAY FAIR

Just to the north of Piccadilly lay pastures and a market for agricultural produce. Meat on the hoof, cattle and sheep were slaughtered locally to feed growing demand. Herdsmen driving their cattle would let them graze on fields that are now part of Hyde Park to fatten them up before their final journey to Smithfield Market. During the eighteenth and early nineteenth centuries, herds of cattle and sheep were a common sight along the Oxford Road as they were driven through the streets to the inconvenience of, and danger to, terrified pedestrians. Injuries were not infrequent: one man was gored, others were trampled. It was not unknown for a runaway bull to enter a shop, and the expression 'bull in a china shop' is a literal description of what could occur.

This semi-rural area on the outskirts of London was the scene of the famous annual May Fair, which gave its name to what is now a high-status urban enclave. The fair took place on 1 May on a site to the north and east of Shepherd's Market, which in those early days served as a market for meat, fish and vegetables. It was an event that attracted both rich and poor.

Originally, the May Fair had been held outside St James's Palace. But it was moved from its location outside the palace gates once this building became the principal royal palace in 1698. The last May Fair was probably held around 1840, by which time the area had been completely gentrified. William Hone, writing in his *Everyday Book*, describes the fair in the 1820s thus:

In the areas encompassing the market building were booths for jugglers, prize-fighters, both at cudgels and back-sword, boxing matches, and wild beasts. The sports not under cover were mountebanks, fire-eaters, ass-racing, sausage tables, dice tables, up-and-downs, merry-go-rounds, bull baiting, grinning for a hat, running for a shift, hasty pudding eaters, eel divers, and an infinite variety of other similar pastimes.[1]

The activities listed indicate a riot of fairground entertainments, dangerous sports and eating contests. Eel diving would have involved someone putting their hand into a tank full of wriggling eels. If they managed to catch one in their bare hand, it was theirs to take away. Eels, like oysters, were a common staple of working-class diets at this time.

A MAGNIFICENT PALACE

Edward Hyde, Earl of Clarendon, Keeper of the Great Seal of England and Keeper of the King's Conscience – a post equivalent to today's prime minister – was briefly the most powerful man in England. If the king had a conscience then its 'keeper', Lord Clarendon, certainly did not. He was soon facing accusations of corruption and graft. His critics seized on the fact that a large part of his personal fortune stemmed from a shady and unpatriotic property deal in which he sold the port of Dunkirk to the French.

Granted a large tract of Piccadilly in 1664, Clarendon augmented his wealth by selling off some of this land at a profit. He commissioned the architect Roger Pratt to design a grand mansion, which he felt reflected his status as England's most powerful man. The site chosen was opposite St James's Street so that Clarendon could look down the street towards the king's palace, a building which he considered inferior to his own stately pile. No expense was spared and estimates put the building costs at £40,000.

Clarendon House was completed to great fanfare, the first of the great Piccadilly palaces. Its walls were lined with the finest paintings by great artists like Van Dyke, Titian and Vermeer. Clarendon was rumoured to have diverted building materials from St Paul's Cathedral to create a private chapel.

In spite of its ostentatious magnificence, the house drew praise from the diarist John Evelyn who described it as 'the best contriv'd, the most useful and magnificent house in England'. Architectural historians now regard Clarendon House as the first great classical mansion to be built and a model for future stately homes. But detractors could not forget or forgive its owner's dishonesty and dubbed the mansion Dunkirk House or Clarendon's Folly.

Andrew Marvell wrote a satirical verse summing up Clarendon's over-weening arrogance:

Behold, in the depth of our Plague and our Wars
He built himself a Palace which outbraves the stars
Which house (we Dunkirk, he Clarendon names)
It looks down with shame upon St James.
But 'tis not his golden globe will save him
Being less than the Custom House farmers gave him
His chapel for consecration calls
Whose sacrilege plundered the stones of St Pauls.

Yet Clarendon House was to be as short-lived as the Earl of Clarendon's political career. In 1667, the year the house was completed, the Dutch fleet sailed up the River Medway, scattering the poorly equipped and ill-prepared British fleet and threatening an invasion of London. Clarendon took the blame as a mob of angry Londoners besieged his house, smashing its windows and cutting down the trees outside his property. That same year he fell from power and fled to exile in France.

The house was sold by his family in 1675 to the 2nd Duke of Albemarle at a huge loss for just £26,000. The fate of Clarendon House was sealed. In 1683, Albemarle sold the property to a consortium of investors led by Sir Thomas Bond. A canny speculator, Bond demolished the house to build Dover Street, Albemarle Street and Bond Street.

NOBLE DEVELOPERS

On his accession, King Charles II decided in 1664 to reward Lord Clarendon and Lord Berkeley of Stratton with freehold sizable estates on the north side of Portugal Street. To the east, an adjoining site of 10 acres was to be divided between Sir John Denham and Sir William Pulteney. On the south side of Portugal Street, Henry Jermyn, the Earl of St Albans, was granted land on a long leasehold to build St James's Square.

As Surveyor General of the King's Works, Sir John Denham was well placed to acquire a prime site. Sir John had been tasked with overseeing the rebuilding of Whitehall Palace. He gave contracts to builders and architects and, although not of noble birth, was one of the king's most powerful servants. Denham and Pulteney were granted leases on the vague promise that they would build a number of large houses for sale or rent.

Sir John Denham, however, had no intention of becoming a developer. His aim was to build an imposing home for himself and his new bride, Margaret, a notable beauty and thirty years his junior. Best known as a poet, Sir John believed nothing less than a mansion would secure his wife's affection and loyalty. Sadly, the marriage was a troubled one, as not long after the wedding, Margaret was boasting about being the acknowledged mistress of the king's brother, the future James II.

An amateur architect, Sir John drew up plans for a seven-bay, three-storey house with two side wings and a dormer-windowed garret flanked by stables and servants' quarters. Fronted by a large courtyard, Denham's house was well set back from the road behind a high brick wall with a central gateway onto Portugal Street. Peaceful gardens to the rear provided vistas of open countryside.

Denham was soon hopelessly in debt as he struggled to pay for his luxurious love-nest. In April 1666 he suffered a nervous breakdown. Some attribute this to money worries, others to the pressure of work. Then, in 1667, tragedy struck the Denham family. His young wife Margaret died – some say poisoned by her husband. His mental health in sharp decline, Denham's career as Surveyor General lasted barely two years before he was replaced by his deputy, Sir Christopher Wren. Desperate for funds, Denham sold the unfinished house to Richard Boyle, 1st Earl of Burlington.

ST JAMES'S CHURCH, PICCADILLY

On the south side of Portugal Street, Henry Jermyn, the Earl of St Albans, was granted land on a long leasehold to build St James's Square in 1664. A network of streets followed in the wake of this successful venture including Jermyn Street, King Street and Charles II Street. To set the seal on this aristocratic enclave, a church was needed to provide a place of worship and attract further settlement.

Designed by architect Sir Christopher Wren in 1672, St James's Church, Piccadilly, served the fast-growing and diverse local community that lived in St James's Square and surrounding streets.

The parish of St James's included parts of Soho and Mayfair. Wealthy patrons endowed monuments, works of art and a magnificent organ whose wooden case was carved by Grinling Gibbons. The appointment of clergymen was in the gift of the Earl of St Albans. The congregation included many poor people, as well as the rich and aristocratic, who were segregated in terms of pew seating or stone bench seats.

High-status marriages, christenings and funerals were conducted at this church. The visionary artist William Blake and the Prime Minister William

Pitt were baptised in a marble font that stands in the church to this day. Blake, who lived for a time in Broadwick Street, Soho, has a memorial in the church. The artist Angelica Kauffman was married here.

By 1788, the small graveyard surrounding the church had already become too crowded to accept any more burials. The parish bought a plot of land for a chapel and burying ground adjoining what later became Euston Station. St James's Gardens had many famous burials, including George Morland the artist, Bill Richmond the boxer, known at the time as 'the Black Terror', Captain Matthew Flinders, who mapped the south and east coasts of Australia, and the Christie family vault.

BURLINGTON HOUSE – A GRANDER VISION

Burlington stuck to Denham's plans, requiring only £1,700 to complete the build. The house was to remain in Burlington's family, passing down the generations until its purchase by the government in 1868.

The glory days of Burlington House were just beginning. The 1st Earl was succeeded briefly by his son who died shortly after inheriting. In 1704, the house passed to the 3rd Earl of Burlington, then aged just 10 years old. The house was expertly managed by his mother, the resourceful and energetic Juliana, Countess of Burlington.

Juliana set about restoring, embellishing and extending the house, inspired by the art and architecture of ancient Rome witnessed at first hand by young men who had been on the Grand Tour. Burlington House attracted a rising generation of artists and craftsmen. James Gibbs was involved in drawing up a design to unify the outhouses to the front of Burlington House with a circular colonnade.

Gibbs was succeeded by architect Colen Campbell, who was commissioned from 1710 to 1715 to remodel the interior and to build a grand gateway fronting onto Piccadilly. Campbell's involvement can be charted by the drawings he published for his architectural guide *Vitruvius Britannicus*, a work which drew inspiration from the work of the Italian Renaissance architect Andrea Palladio as well as from Inigo Jones, architect of the Whitehall Banqueting House.

While this work was being carried out, Juliana commissioned the Italian artist Sebastiano Ricci to decorate the walls and ceilings with a series of classical murals based on stories such as 'The Marriage of Bacchus and Ariadne' and 'The Triumph of Galatea'.

45

When the 4th Earl died without issue in 1758, ownership passed to his widow Dorothy, formerly Lady Cavendish. Burlington House was now added to the impressive Cavendish family portfolio, which already included Devonshire House, Chiswick House, Campden House and Chatsworth. Dorothy's grandson, William Cavendish, 5th Duke of Devonshire, was 9 years old when he inherited the property.

After a period when the house was mothballed, its future was finally settled on the young duke's coming of age. Burlington House was gifted to his brother-in-law William Cavendish Bentinck, Duke of Portland. Rising to become a prominent Whig politician, Portland served as Home Secretary in William Pitt's coalition government and later from 1807 to 1809 as prime minister. The fortunes of Burlington House and Devonshire House were now intertwined as these two neighbouring Piccadilly mansions and one extended family became the nexus of Whig political power.

THE ELGIN MARBLES

There was a time when the future of Burlington House looked uncertain. In July 1807, the Duke of Devonshire announced that he was considering selling. Running a vast stately home in the centre of London's West End was a constant financial headache. But finding a buyer willing to take over such a building would prove almost impossible.

With the Napoleonic Wars in full swing, building plans were put on hold and the house was left empty, awaiting a new buyer. The duke put the building to good use in the meantime. He staged the first London exhibition of the Elgin Marbles, newly arrived from the Parthenon in Athens.

To show off the marbles, the duke had a large wooden shed put up in his grounds. Admission was restricted to students of the Royal Academy Schools applying to draw the marbles from life. The exhibition lasted from 1811 to 1816, when their sale to the government was finally agreed.

THE BALLOONIST OF BURLINGTON HOUSE

Following Napoleon's defeat and short-lived exile to the island of Elba in 1814, London was ablaze with victory celebrations. None was more typical of this age of showmanship and derring-do than the aerial displays performed by the balloonist and pastry chef James Sadler.

On 27 May 1814, the intrepid aeronaut brought Piccadilly to a standstill as crowds of stunned onlookers watched him and his 17-year-old son Windham ascend in a hydrogen-filled balloon from the gardens of Burlington House. The balloon rose vertically ever higher until extreme cold caused equipment and valves to freeze and Sadler managed to release gas to begin his descent. Father and son landed at South Ockendon in Essex several hours later.

Born in 1753, the son of an Oxford pastry chef and confectioner, Sadler started his career working in the family business, the Lemon Hall Refreshment House in Oxford. A self-taught engineer and inventor, he became the first ever Englishman to fly when he ascended in a hot-air balloon from Christchurch Meadows in Oxford on 4 October 1784. He returned to the same site a month later and carried out the first ever flight in a hydrogen-filled balloon.

Sadler worked for a time as a technician at the chemical laboratories of Oxford University where he developed testing apparatus and experimented on producing hydrogen gas. In 1791, he invented a rotary steam engine and was appointed chemist to the Royal Navy in 1796, during which time he built the Admiralty's first steam engine at Portsmouth. In 1799 he was elected a life member of the Royal Institution.

On 29 July 1814, Sadler was back at Burlington House making the final preparations to a hydrogen balloon that would be piloted by his son Windham accompanied by his girlfriend, Miss Mary Thompson, an actress from Dublin. The event was a ticket-only affair and a sizeable crowd paid for admission to the duke's private grounds, where huge fabric screens had been erected along the walls of the property to prevent bystanders from getting a view. Those wanting to get even closer to the action could watch the preparations for the ascent from the roof of Burlington House by paying half a guinea. The Duke of Devonshire invited a group of fifty friends to share a specially constructed rooftop hospitality tent where they could watch the proceedings while being served a cold collation.

The flight passed off without mishap despite high winds. Sadler's balloon got as far as Coggeshall in Essex before it finally crashed to earth with both aeronauts emerging unscathed.

Mary was not the only adventuress to reach for the skies. Mrs Letitia Sage, an actress and formerly Letitia Hoare, became the first Englishwoman to fly when she ascended in a balloon launched by Vincenzo Lunardi, accompanied by Lunardi's financial backer George Biggin, at St George's Fields in Lambeth on 29 June 1785. The pair took with them a hamper of provisions including bottles of champagne, which when empty would be thrown out of the balloon as ballast, enabling it to gain height.

The possibilities for seduction implicit in this escapade did not go unnoticed by the idle clubmen of Piccadilly who sensed scandal in allowing actresses to accompany daredevil aeronauts without a chaperone. Brooks's *Betting Book* records that in 1785, 'Ld Cholmondeley has given two guineas to Ld Derby to receive 500 Gns [guineas] whenever his lordship fucks a woman in a balloon one thousand yards from Earth'. It is not recorded whether Lord Derby took up hot-air ballooning given the inducements on offer.

THE SOCIALITE AND THE STATESMAN

Georgiana Cavendish, Duchess of Devonshire, brought celebrity and scandal to Piccadilly in equal measure. On 7 June 1774, the day of her seventeenth birthday, Lady Georgiana Spencer of Althorp was wed to William Cavendish, 5th Duke of Devonshire, at Wimbledon Parish Church. The couple set off to honeymoon at the duke's ancestral estate, Chatsworth House, Derbyshire. In autumn, they arrived at the Duke's London residence, Devonshire House. The grand house had been built by the architect William Kent in 1733 on the site of a house once owned by Lady Berkeley, whose ancestral lands had been sold off to the developers who later built Berkeley Square and Bruton Street.

The marriage symbolised an alliance of Britain's two foremost Whig families and it would bring the world of politics and high society to Piccadilly. The duke, however, showed scant interest in his young bride: he had already made her older sister pregnant and, as was the custom of the times, he kept several mistresses, including Georgiana's friend and confidante Lady Elizabeth 'Bess' Foster. He dined every evening at Brooks's, and played whist until the early hours.

Georgiana was expected to act the role of the submissive wife. Yet within a few months, she was seen around town with one of the greatest statesmen of the age, Charles James Fox. A passionate advocate for the universal rights of man, Fox sided with the American colonists rebelling against oppressive British rule.

Treating the duchess as his intellectual equal, Fox succeeded in transforming Georgiana from idle aristocrat to political activist. Now sharing Fox's political creed, Georgiana was a perfect foil for the dissolute politician.

Rockingham's coalition government fell in 1784, and Fox decided to act on his principles by refusing to stand in a 'rotten borough', which would have guaranteed him a seat, choosing instead to stand as a candidate in a free and fair election as MP for Westminster.

Georgiana threw caution to the wind and shared the hustings with him, offering kisses to local tradesmen in return for votes. The high point in the campaign came as Georgiana, the Duchess of Portland, Lady Jersey and Lady Waldegrave, all wearing the Whig colours of buff and blue and with hats decorated with fox tails, paraded Fox through the streets from St Paul's to Piccadilly to roaring crowds. Georgiana and the Prince of Wales ran ahead of the crowd to welcome Fox to Devonshire House waving laurel branches. Fox scraped a narrow victory.

The Tories under William Pitt swept to power and affairs at Devonshire House continued although Georgiana never again reprised her role as a political activist. She did, however, commence an affair with another Whig politician, a young rising star, Charles Grey. The following year saw matters come to a head. The free-spending duchess, now deeply in debt and pregnant by Grey, confessed the affair. The Duke of Devonshire disowned her, and Georgiana, to avoid further scandal, left with her lover for France. In Montpellier on 20 February 1791, Georgiana gave birth to a daughter, Eliza Courtney.

Georgiana had two legitimate children, a daughter and a son who was to inherit the Devonshire title. Eliza Courtney was adopted by the Grey family. As Earl Grey, Charles would go on to become prime minister of Britain from 1830 to 1834 and give his name to a famous blend of tea.

GRAFTON STREET AND THE AMERICAN WAR OF INDEPENDENCE

Developed between 1770 to 1790, Grafton Street is a secluded enclave forming an L shape that runs between Dover Street and Bond Street. Designed by architect Sir Robert Taylor, the street's terraces of four- and five-storey brick-fronted houses were one of the area's most prestigious addresses and home to two dukes, three lords, two earls and three Members of Parliament.

Grafton Street was developed by Augustus FitzRoy, 3rd Duke of Grafton, who was Whig prime minister from 1768 until 1770, and subsequently Lord Privy Seal under Lord North's government. He had close connections to the American colonies, the Bank of England and the East India Company. One of the first houses to be completed, number three, was rented by Admiral Earl Howe, First Lord of the Admiralty. His sister, the Honourable Mrs Howe, lived at number twelve.

A study of Caroline Howe's long and distinguished life reveals an amazing and little-known story that sheds light on an important period in Anglo-American relations. Caroline played a key role in brokering the frantic diplomatic negotiations between the American colonists and the British Government. The fact that she was treated as family by King George III and Queen Charlotte added to her credentials as a trusted third party.

Between December 1774 and March 1775, Mrs Howe hosted a series of meetings at her house between the ambassador of the American colonies, Dr Benjamin Franklin, and her brother Admiral Earl Howe, acting in an official capacity as a trusted negotiator on behalf of Prime Minister Lord North and Secretary of State for the Colonies, Lord Dartmouth.

Back-door negotiations began in a low-key way when Caroline Howe tentatively invited Franklin to her house to play chess. The location was chosen so as not to attract attention. At their second meeting, Mrs Howe is reported to have remarked, 'And what is to be done with this Dispute between Britain and the Colonies? I hope it cannot end in a Civil War!' The ensuing conversation clearly led to serious peace talks aimed at offering major concessions to the colonists.

This proved to be a catalyst. Admiral Howe and two highly placed British sympathisers for the colonists' cause attended the next meeting arranged by Caroline. Eventually, a list of demands was drawn up, revised and then debated. Dr Franklin immediately set sail for America in hope of a last-minute peace deal. But events were unfolding rapidly, and even as he crossed the Atlantic the battles of Lexington and Concord were being fought and the American War of Independence had broken out. Britain's resolve hardened but the momentum was with the rebels. The US Declaration of Independence became official at the Second Congress at Philadelphia, Pennsylvania, on 4 July 1776. On 3 September 1783, American independence was formally recognised by the Treaty of Paris.

An obituary appeared in *The Lady's Magazine* which praised the old lady in powdered wig and antiquated court costume:

Mrs Howe was distinguished in her outward appearance by a neat scrupulous adherence to the dress which prevailed in the court of George II … She was still more distinguished amongst those who had the pleasure of her acquaintance by the vigour and acquirements of her mind.[2]

FOX AND HIS COURTESAN

Piccadilly may have been awash with rumours that Charles Fox was having an affair with Georgiana, Duchess of Devonshire, but in truth, their relationship was platonic. The courtesan Elizabeth Armitstead was Fox's chosen partner and he remained loyal to her from their first meeting in around 1782 until his death in 1806, aged 57.

Born Elizabeth Bridget Cane in Greenwich, south London, on 11 July 1750, Elizabeth is thought to have been the daughter of a market porter. Details of her early years are sparse but by her mid teens, Elizabeth was a kept woman, an arrangement by which she exchanged sex for the security of a protector – possibly the original 'Mr Armitstead'.

By the early 1770s Elizabeth had turned professional, joining a West End 'nunnery' or brothel catering for the nobility and gentry like that of Mrs Goadby, the celebrated 'Lady Abbess' of Marlborough Street.

Within a few short years the attractive and well-formed Mrs Armitstead had joined the top ranks of the demi-monde where she was written about in newspapers and gossip sheets as rivalling the great courtesans of the day: Mary Robinson, known as 'Perdita' from a role she had acted in *A Winter's Tale* at the Drury Lane Theatre, Grace Dalrymple Elliott, Nancy Parsons and Sophia Baddeley.

Wealthy aristocrats sometimes adopted their favourite courtesans, taking them out of the brothel, giving them a generous income and showering them with gifts in exchange for sex. A leading 'Thaïs' like Mrs Armitstead could become financially independent.[3] By 1776, *Town and Country* reported that she could 'claim the conquest of two ducal coronets, a marquis, four earls and a viscount'. Lord Bolingbroke, the Duke of Dorset, Lord Spencer and the Prince of Wales were at various times her lovers. Elizabeth was able to afford a retinue of household servants and took the lease on a country property at St Anne's Hill in Chertsey, Surrey, and was able to buy a town house in Clarges Street, Piccadilly, where Fox came to live with her.

Charles Fox may have initially paid for Elizabeth's services when he was enjoying a winning streak at cards or at the horse races at Newmarket. But once he had run through his inheritance, the nature of their relationship changed. Fox needed the comfort and stability Elizabeth offered, while the beautiful courtesan found in Fox an unlikely soulmate. Their relationship blossomed into love. It was just as well that neither cared much for society and were prepared to defy convention.

On Monday, 28 September 1795, Fox and Elizabeth married in secret. Elizabeth sold her house in Clarges Street to help pay Fox's gambling debts and the couple moved to Chertsey. Now a contented married man, Fox gradually introduced Elizabeth to his close friends including her former lover, the Prince of Wales.

In January 1806, Pitt died and Fox was offered the post of Secretary of State for Foreign Affairs in William Grenville's 'Ministry of All Talents'. Fox died of liver failure and multiple complications on 13 September 1806 at Chiswick House. His libidinous life of excess had finally caught up with him. Among his lasting achievements was the resolution he moved shortly before his death for the abolition of the slave trade, which was carried by 114 votes to 15. The bill became law as the Slave Trade Act of 1807.

Elizabeth Armitstead returned to St Anne's Hill, where she lived out the remaining thirty-six years of her life in country pursuits.

ALBANY

Home to generations of eligible bachelors, the upmarket gated community known as Albany was designed by architect Sir William Chambers and completed in 1776. Built as a family home, the three-storey, seven-bay brick mansion was originally named Melbourne House after its owner, the newly ennobled Member of Parliament and Irish landowner Sir Penistone Lamb, 1st Viscount Melbourne.

Melbourne spared no expense in indulging his wife's fancy for elegant painted ceilings and frescoes by Italian artists of the day. But he preferred spending his time shooting at his Hertford estate, Brocket Hall, or spending time with his mistress.

Finally, after years of living beyond his means, Melbourne came up with a drastic solution. He arranged a house swap with the Duke of York and Albany, the soldier brother of the Prince of Wales who suggested that the Melbournes might prefer his smaller house in Whitehall. So, in November 1792 the Duke of York moved in, renaming his new home York House.

The extravagant duke was no better at managing his finances than the house's previous owners. York House was an asset that could be disposed of to offset his ballooning debts. On 22 January 1802, the duke agreed to sell York House and all of its furnishings, fixtures and fittings to a builder, Alexander

Copland, for the sum of £37,000, for which he was granted a mortgage by Thomas Coutts and Farrer Brothers. Once Copland had paid a hefty deposit and agreed a schedule of repayments on the loan, he began marketing the scheme to prospective buyers. He issued a prospectus proclaiming, 'Proposals for Dividing and Disposing of the Mansion House and Premises lately occupied by His Royal Highness, The Duke of York in Piccadilly'. The scheme was christened Albany in recognition of the duke's full title, the Duke of York and Albany.

Mr Copland hired the celebrated architect Henry Holland to draw up plans for the conversion of York House. Holland had designed Brooks's and Boodle's clubhouses and was the architect of Carlton House. As part of a plan to maximise rental income, Holland created sixty-nine bachelor apartments known as 'sets' by subdividing the main house and two service wings. He lined the spacious front courtyard with rows of small shops facing one another. And he opened up an underground passage beneath the house to create the Rope Walk, a covered walkway with a continuous roof supported on cast-iron columns. This accessed two parallel long buildings running the length of the garden. The Rope Walk ended with a set of iron railings and a gate onto Vigo Street. Two small shops stood on either side of the gate.

As any speculative builder, Copland used the income generated from the progressive sale of the sets of apartments on ninety-nine-year leases to fund the next stage in the conversion. Money flowed into Coutts Bank and was paid over to the Duke of York in stages.

When all of the initial twenty sets were sold the residents formed a committee to appoint a board of trustees to safeguard their collective interests. Rules were drafted governing the leaseholds and a ground rent agreed that would cover common services. Finally, and importantly, residents were forbidden to make any alterations to the building without the written approval of the trustees – a condition which has ensured the preservation of intact Georgian interiors.

Among the first buyers to move in were the politicians George Canning and Henry Brougham, historian Lord Macaulay, novelist Matthew Lewis, Lord Byron and John Cam Hobhouse. Thomas Austen took a lease on an office premises in the front courtyard, on behalf of his bank Austen, Maunde and Tilson. One of Austen's first visitors was his famous younger sister, the novelist Jane Austen, on one of her rare trips to the capital.

ALBANY'S LITERARY SENSATION

In 1796, a publishing sensation took the reading public by storm. Matthew Lewis's *The Monk*, a Gothic tale of passion and seduction set in a Madrid convent in the time of the Inquisition, sparked moral outrage for its thinly disguised sexuality. Published anonymously, it was not long before the Attorney General sought to ban its sale but to little avail. The book was a bestseller. In a few short years its author was set to become one of Piccadilly's most celebrated literary residents, taking a set of bachelor chambers at Albany, London's exclusive residential enclave.

Lewis's racy plot is laced with illicit love affairs and even incest. The novel's central character Ambrosio, the handsome young abbot of a monastery and widely regarded as a model of virtue and chastity, is tormented by a temptress, Matilda. This impudent girl has entered the monastery in the guise of Rosario, a novitiate monk. Bent on seduction, Matilda throws off her habit to reveal long golden tresses and voluptuous charms, causing the monk to renounce his vows of chastity on the spot. Transformed into an insatiable womaniser, the monk embarks on a new career as a seducer of innocent virgins fooled by his outward appearance of sanctity, even murdering the mother of one of the victims, Antonia, who has caught him in flagrante.

Following in the footsteps of a Gothic tradition popularised by authors like Horace Walpole and Mrs Radcliffe, whose novels *The Castle of Otranto* and *The Mystery of Udolpho* had created a new market for sensational Gothic tales of fantasy, *The Monk* enjoyed an avid following among fashionable young men and women. What the novel's avid readership did not know was that its author, the 20-year-old Matthew Lewis, had just returned from The Hague where he was an attaché at the British Embassy. He was shortly to be elected a Tory Member of Parliament for Hindon in Wiltshire. When a second edition was printed, Lewis made some minor cuts and proudly acknowledged his authorship on the title page. From then on, he acquired the soubriquet 'Monk' Lewis.

By 1802, Lewis had sufficient income to rent apartment K1 at Albany, while keeping his cottage in Barnes as a country retreat. In 1812, Lewis's father died having reconciled himself with his son and leaving him a vast fortune together with his sugar-cane plantations in Jamaica.

This was the year that Monk Lewis formed a close friendship with Lord George Gordon Byron, the romantic poet who had scandalised society. The two were friends of Lady Melbourne whose daughter-in-law, Lady Caroline Lamb, was at the time enjoying a well-publicised affair with Byron.

Two years later, in 1814, Byron was able to secure a large set of apartments in Albany sublet by its owner who was leaving to get married. Owing to the building's strict covenant, any new tenant had to be vetted and approved by a committee, which was in practice an even stricter entry requirement than that of many a St James's gentlemen's club. Byron had impeccable aristocratic connections so the whiff of an affair was no impediment. On the day he moved in Byron wrote, '… got into my new apartments rented of Lord Althorpe, on a lease of seven years. Spacious, and room for my books and sabres.'[4]

Besides convivial evenings with Monk Lewis, Byron took lessons with the celebrated pugilist 'Gentleman' John Jackson and swordsman Henry Angelo, the proprietor of Angelo's Fencing Academy, which occupied a discreet Albany apartment.

Byron's tenancy was short-lived. A year later, he left Albany as he was due to get married and was therefore no longer eligible to occupy a bachelor apartment. He and his new wife, Annabella Milbanke, moved to a grand mansion at 139 Piccadilly. They married in January 1815 and in December of that year his wife gave birth to a daughter, Ada. The marriage between Byron and Annabella lasted barely a year as his wife left him amid rumours of her husband's scandalous love life. Byron left the country for exile abroad. He died of fever at Missolonghi in Greece in 1824 where a romantic impulse led him to rally support for the Greek War of Independence.

Monk Lewis also came to a tragic end. A conscientious landlord, he set out to inspect his Jamaica plantations and to help the transition of his slaves to freedom. But in May 1818 he died of yellow fever on the voyage back to England and was buried at sea.

Byron's daughter grew up to become a mathematical genius. She is better known under her married name of Ada, Countess of Lovelace, the mother of British computing.

NUMBER ONE LONDON

Piccadilly's mansions are indelibly linked with some of the leading players in British history. None is more famous than Arthur Wellesley, Duke of Wellington, whose residence Apsley House was popularly named 'Number One London' because it was the first house anyone encountered approaching London from the west.

Numbered 149 Piccadilly, Apsley House now stands next to the grand entrance arches to Hyde Park looking out over Hyde Park Corner and the

Wellington Arch (also known as Constitution Arch) at the top of Constitution Hill. The house was originally a classical mansion designed by Robert Adam for Lord Apsley, erected and completed in 1778. When built, it stood opposite Tattersall's famous horse auction house and stables. Demolished in 1865, Tattersall's was replaced by St George's Hospital and more recently the Lanesborough Hotel.

How the Duke of Wellington came to own Apsley House appears to have been a fortuitous accident. It had been bought by his brother Richard, Lord Wellesley, Governor of the East India Company in 1807. Unable to afford its upkeep, Richard put it on the market.

In 1818, freshly returned from the Continent where he had led the campaign to defeat Napoleon, the duke offered £42,000 for the freehold, without disclosing he was the bidder. Wellington had received £60,000 in prize money from a grateful nation and in addition was bought a substantial country estate, Stratfield Saye in Hampshire.

The duke commissioned his architect, Benjamin Dean Wyatt, to set about extending Apsley House. Part of the renovations included refacing the exterior brickwork in Portland stone and building the Waterloo Gallery, an impressive art gallery for the many grand-master paintings the duke had been presented with by grateful European monarchs.

Wellington's wife Kitty was a simple soul. No lover of pomp and ceremony, balls or lavish entertaining, she remained at Stratfield Saye in a state of quiet domesticity. The duke, meanwhile, revelled in the bachelor life at Apsley House, receiving visiting foreign ambassadors, princes and generals as well as arranging assignations with society ladies, including the Russian ambassador's wife, Princess de Lieven and Almack's formidable hostess, Sarah Lady Jersey.

One feature of the duke's calendar was the annual Waterloo Banquet held on the anniversary of the victory on 18 June for his thirty-six surviving staff officers who had served with him at Waterloo. As these officers began to die off and numbers dwindled, in 1828 Wellington threw the invitation open to senior serving officers from the regiments involved in the battle.

Initially lauded as a national hero, Wellington fell from grace when, as prime minister, he enacted repressive legislation curtailing civil liberties. Deposed and in opposition, Wellington spoke out strongly against the Reform Bill proposed by Earl Grey's Whig government in 1831 to extend the franchise and end the scandal of MPs being elected unopposed to 'rotten boroughs'.

On 24 April, Wellington was informed that his wife Kitty was dying. The duke rushed to Stratfield Saye to be by her side. It is said that Kitty ran her fingers up the duke's arm to check if he still wore the armlet she had given him many years earlier as a keepsake. He was still wearing it and the couple were reconciled. Kitty died on 27 April, the same day that a mob stoned and smashed ground-floor windows at Apsley House. Servants chased the crowd away by firing a blunderbuss. On his return, Wellington had steel shutters installed to protect his property from further damage.

Finally appointed Lord Warden of the Cinque Ports, Wellington died at Walmer Castle on 14 September 1852. By this stage his legacy as the architect of Britain's victory over Napoleon at Waterloo had been rehabilitated. Queen Victoria's consort, Prince Albert, arranged for a massive state funeral that would mark the passing of a heroic age.

On 18 November 1852, over 1 million people lined the streets for the funeral of the Duke of Wellington. Starting at Horse Guards and bound for St Paul's Cathedral, the procession was over a mile long and included every regiment in the British Army. Foreign royalty and statesmen in carriages followed the solemn cortège up Constitution Hill, past Apsley House, and along Piccadilly, Pall Mall, the Strand and up Fleet Street. London's population came out to pay their last tribute to the man who, more than anyone, transformed clubland and gave it the reputation it has today.

TRIUMPHAL ARCHES

The former Prince Regent, King George IV, had grandiose plans to commemorate the victory of Waterloo and commissioned Decimus Burton to design a triumphal arch in the style of Imperial Rome to stand at the top of Constitution Hill facing the ceremonial archway to Hyde Park next to Apsley House. Known as the Wellington Arch, and completed in 1828, the arch was clearly visible from Wellington's bedroom window, obscuring an otherwise pleasant view.

Intended as the showpiece of a ceremonial route from Hyde Park to Buckingham Palace, the Wellington Arch was topped by an oversized bronze statue of the duke on horseback. Designed by Matthew Cotes Wyatt, and placed in position in 1846, the equestrian statue, weighing 40 tons, was so huge that the arch on which it stood needed to be reinforced to carry its weight. It was immediately ridiculed by the public as being vulgar and tasteless.

In 1891, the Prince of Wales commissioned sculptor Adrian Jones to replace the unpopular Wellington statue with a classical grouping of the winged goddess Peace driving a quadriga – a chariot drawn by four horses. The quadriga was finally erected on top of the arch in 1912. Meanwhile, the statue of Wellington on horseback that so many people had objected to was moved to a nearby plinth and finally to a site in Aldershot where it stands today, half hidden among trees and bushes behind a disused parade ground.

Associated with the Wellington Arch, another monumental arch had been built in 1825 by John Nash in Carrara marble. Known as the Marble Arch, this originally formed a processional entrance directly in front of Buckingham Palace, facing the Mall. Conceived by George IV, the arch became an inconvenient nuisance that distracted from young Queen Victoria's remodelling of the palace. Marble Arch was dismantled and moved to a new position on a traffic island at the end of Oxford Street in 1851.

PAST GLORY

Many of Piccadilly's historic mansions have been demolished not just because they were too expensive to maintain but because the traditions of the London Season which revolved around the Court of St James's died out. Over nearly three centuries, Clarendon House, Berkeley House, Clarges House, Egremont House and Devonshire House have disappeared. The only reminder of their presence is in the street names that commemorate their sites, like Clarges Street and Berkeley Square.

Of the noble mile, just three great houses survive. Albany remains the most exclusive gated apartment building in the West End. Burlington House was bought by the nation and is the home of the Royal Academy as well as a cluster of academic institutions including the Royal Geographical Society, the Geological Society, the Linnaean Society and the Society of Antiquaries.

Apsley House was presented to the nation in 1947 by Gerald, 7th Duke of Wellington, with the proviso that he and subsequent dukes of Wellington could retain a large apartment for their own occupation on the second floor. The link with aristocratic pleasures remains unbroken.

3

INNS, CLUBS
AND HOTELS

To Noble Gentlemen and Families Visiting London. That delightful situation the Bath Hotel and Old White Horse Cellar, Arlington Street, Piccadilly, having undergone considerable alterations and improvements, L Paine (late Bland) begs most respectfully to invite those who may be visiting London to his Establishment, as being one of the most comfortable situations in the metropolis.

Advertisement, *London Courier and Evening Gazette*, 1831

A TOURIST DESTINATION

Piccadilly was the start and end point for stage coaches to and from the south and west of England, and was well served by inns and hostelries. As a result, a diverse service economy sprang up, which covered stabling and the supply of horses, members' clubs, hotels and tourism, and the supply of travellers' needs including books, newspapers, food hampers and luxury goods.

The coaching inns were a drop-off and pick-up point for goods and produce to and from the south and west of England. Besides the busy goods traffic, unscrupulous criminals preyed on innocents arriving in London for the first time. Pimps and madams recruited gullible young girls who arrived in London unaccompanied and knowing no one in the big city.

The arrival of the railways in the 1840s sounded the death knell for the stage coach and the coaching inns. But this was no overnight revolution. Gradually the old coaching inns gave way to hotels as they adapted to the new circumstances, and owning prime sites, they shifted their business model towards hotel keeping and hospitality. The White Horse Cellar was reborn as Hatchett's Hotel.

The age of the coach was long, as was its association with Piccadilly. It is hard to believe, but the telephone, electric light and the motor car had been invented by the time the last stage coach left the New White Horse Cellar.

Coaching inns laid the foundation for Piccadilly's hospitality industry. At first, when the Royal Mail coaches started bringing trade to London, travellers had very limited choice of overnight accommodation. The most basic provision was the lodging house or the tavern. Further up the scale were hotels like the Bath Hotel and Hatchett's. For the wealthy, members' clubs included guest bedrooms on the upper floors and were ideal for short stays as their kitchen served evening meals and breakfast, complemented by bar service. That left a gap in the market ready for exploitation.

Hotels, dining and hospitality have long been a mainstay of Piccadilly's economy. Over three centuries, coaching inns and their lineal descendants, hotels, have occupied prime locations along the mile. The Ritz is a good example. Built on the site of one of England's most famous coaching inns, the White Horse Cellar, the Ritz is just the latest in a long line of hostelries.

When stage coaches were superseded by the railway age, many coaching inns fell on hard times or were repurposed as parcel depots. Piccadilly was different: its central London location meant a steady demand for overnight accommodation and dining. When the White Horse Cellar was demolished in 1815, it was to make way for the Bath Hotel. Another hotel, the Walsingham House Hotel – a massive eight-storey brick and terracotta structure in the Scottish baronial style – opened on the site in 1887. It was built by Lord Walsingham.

EARLY COACHING INNS

The White Bear and the Black Bear stood near one another, on opposite sides of what is now Piccadilly Circus. They marked the point at which Piccadilly ended. Built in the early seventeenth century, they were demolished as part of the gradual development of Piccadilly Circus. Other important inns included the White Swan and the Three Kings at 67 Piccadilly.

Built in around 1635, the White Bear at 221 Piccadilly remained in continuous use as the major coaching inn for the Dover, Margate, Canterbury and Rochester roads for almost 250 years. A regular coach service departed daily at five o'clock in the morning. This coach started its journey further east at the Bell Savage Inn on Ludgate Hill. At half past six in the evening there was an overnight service to Dover.

A print of the White Bear dating from 1820 shows a slightly ramshackle building of three storeys with a large balustraded loggia on the top floor where guest bedrooms looked out onto a hive of activity below, including a recently arrived stage coach. The tavern was demolished in 1870 to make way for the Criterion Theatre.

London's sole surviving coaching inn, the George Tavern in Borough High Street, gives us a better idea as to what the White Bear would have been like in its heyday. Coaching inns followed a similar design principle. Built back from the road, the inn was fronted by a large courtyard, surrounded on all sides by offices, guest accommodation and stabling for the horses. Coaches entered the courtyard through a large gateway and would park in front of the inn to allow passengers to alight and luggage to be unloaded. The four horses pulling the stage would be untethered by an ostler and led to the stables at the rear of the inn to be fed, watered and rested.

With a similar courtyard layout, the Black Bear, Piccadilly, was a depot for the 'carriage trade' and was a rough-and-ready establishment. A supplement to Kent's trade directory, *The Shopkeepers and Tradesmen's Assistant*, lists the Black Bear among the major coaching inns – the Saracen's Head, Snow Hill, the Bell Savage, Ludgate Hill and the Spread Eagle and Cross Keys, Gracechurch Street – which took parcels and goods.

Piccadilly's carriage trade served the street's many specialist stores, warehouses and shops. The Black Bear lingered on as a coaching inn and tavern until the 1860s, when it was reborn as the London Pavilion Music Hall. It was later demolished to make way for Shaftesbury Avenue in around 1885.

THE ROYAL MAIL

Founded in 1635 by King Charles I, the General Post Office was a national mail service based on the 'penny post' for delivery of mail within London and with distance-based charges for letter carrying to all corners of Great Britain and overseas. Riders carried the mail between 'posts' where the postmaster would take the local letters and then hand the remaining letters and any new ones to the next rider.

In 1797, Bristol businessman and theatre manager John Palmer realised there was demand for a fast, secure and reliable mail service. He lobbied the then Chancellor of the Exchequer, William Pitt, and in 1784 Palmer was given permission to conduct a trial journey of a mail coach from Bristol to London.

Stopping only to change teams of horses every 10 miles or so, Palmer's non-stop overnight mail made it to London in sixteen hours rather than the thirty-eight hours it took to make the journey in a conventional stage coach. Departing at 4 p.m. from Bristol, Palmer's mail coach arrived at the Swan with Two Necks on Lad Lane in the City of London at eight o'clock the next morning. There the mail was hurried in leather satchels to the General Post Office at Lombard Street for sorting and delivery.

In 1785, Palmer was appointed Surveyor General and Comptroller of Royal Mails. Within a few short years, mail-coach routes were established between London and Dover, Portsmouth, Poole, Exeter, Gloucester, Worcester, Holyhead and Carlisle. Over the years, new turnpike roads financed road improvements, more frequent maintenance and in places the creation of smooth 'tarmacadam' roads. The final stage, Knightsbridge to Piccadilly, was the last of a series of road improvements.

Each evening, mail coaches for the west of England would depart from the Gloucester Coffee House, having begun their journey in the City of London at the Swan with Two Necks or the Bull and Mouth, Aldersgate, where the mail was loaded and the horses harnessed.

THE BROADBAND OF THE GEORGIAN ERA

The fastest westbound service was *Quicksilver*, the coach which carried the Devonport Mail. Averaging 10 miles an hour, *Quicksilver* was the most reliable mail-coach service on the road in the early 1800s. Leaving the Gloucester Coffee House at 8.30 p.m., the night mail would cross Salisbury Plain at a cracking pace, before pulling into Exeter for a ten-minute stop around midday.

Mail for towns along the way was sorted into mailbags and, as the coach sped past a series of recognised collection points, the local bag would be thrown off and a postman would hoist the town's mail at the end of a pole for the guard to catch. The letters would then be given to letter carriers who would walk the long rural delivery rounds. The mail coach duly arrived at Devonport at about 5 p.m., having taken twenty-one and a half hours to cover a distance of 215 miles.

To ensure speed, passenger numbers were restricted to four travelling inside the coach with one allowed on the roof with the driver and guard. Dr Trusler's *London Advisor and Guide* for 1790 gives detailed information about fares, mail charges and conditions: 'The fare for each passenger is four pence a mile, including 14 pounds of luggage.' This compares with the standard rate of 3½d a mile for an ordinary stage-coach journey.

The mail coach itself was exempt from toll-road charges. When a mail coach approached a turnpike, the guard sitting next to the driver would sound his horn and the gates would be opened, allowing the mail to pass unhindered.

Mail posted by the War Office, the Admiralty and the Treasury was marked 'Upon His Majesty's Service' and carried free. Letters from or to Members of Parliament at any place were franked exempt for postage in England, while newspapers in an unsealed packet and proceedings of Parliament were also post free.

The importance of Piccadilly's role as the hub of the mail-coach network cannot be overstated. Offering a punctual, non-stop service, mail-coach routes which radiated out from London were the broadband of the Georgian era. Legal documents, financial transactions, military commissions, naval intelligence, as well as the latest news of financial markets and overseas trade, could reach any part of Britain in under two days, and in many cases far sooner.

The flow of information between Britain's naval bases in the west and the Admiralty in London was essential when the country was on high alert. Britain could not have fought and won the Napoleonic Wars without the high-speed and reliable mail-coach links between Piccadilly and the naval ports in the west.

AN INDUSTRY IS BORN

Britain's postal service developed rapidly. From 1794 until 1839, the Piccadilly grocer Fortnum and Mason operated a post office within the store and Charles Fortnum was appointed an official 'receiver of post'. A secure iron post box was positioned at the entrance to the store where members of the public could post unpaid letters. Mail without a stamp was paid by the recipient upon delivery.

But anyone wishing to pay in advance could visit Fortnum's post office where letters and packets would be weighed and payment made according to destination. Once paid, a letter would be marked with an ink stamp. It cost 1d for delivery within central London. A letter carried any distance between 60 and 100 miles incurred a postal charge of 6d, while up to 200 miles the charge rose to 8d. Shorter distances cost 2d. The post box was unlocked at regular times throughout the day, when the mail was collected for sorting and delivery. Fortnum's was one of many post offices. On the north side of Piccadilly, grocers Shaw and Robinson had a similar arrangement, as did many of the coffee houses of St James's, which fed into the Royal Mail.

By 1792, sixteen coaches left Lombard Street in London daily with as many inbound. In addition, there were fifteen cross-country mail coaches delivering post around the country. But by 1811, there were some 211 coaches that were criss-crossing Great Britain, delivering the mail.

The number of licensed mail coaches had shot up to 3,000 by 1835. The postal service employed more than 16,000 coachmen and, alongside the coaches, an entire industry grew up in support, including ostlers, coach and harness makers, farriers and whip makers. These trades made up a significant proportion of Piccadilly's shops and small businesses.

Supplying horses was a valuable concession. One of London's greatest coach masters was William Chaplin, who supplied matched teams of horses for half of all the mail coaches that left London each evening, including the Bristol Mail and the Devonport Mail.

Mail coaches survived to the 1830s when railways began to take over. The very last mail coach, the Norwich Mail, left St Martin's Le Grand Post Office in May 1865.

THE OLD WHITE HORSE CELLAR

By the early eighteenth century the White and Black Bear inns were looking decidedly tired and did not offer the premium accommodation sought by wealthy travellers. The new kid on the block was the Old White Horse Cellar located on the corner of Arlington Street, Piccadilly, on the site of the present-day Ritz Hotel.

Built in 1720, the coaching inn was named in honour of King George I's royal coat of arms, which featured the white horse of Hanover. The coaching inn became the terminus for west-bound stage coaches for Bath and Bristol. Business was brisk and, in 1798, the Bath Hotel was built on an adjoining site as an annexe to the coaching inn to provide additional accommodation. There was no courtyard leading off the main street. Coaches drew up outside, having been prepared at one of the coaching inns in the City where there was room for stables.

Besides being a convenient stopping point for coaches, the Old White Horse Cellar was handily situated for tourists keen to experience first-hand the daily royal 'Drawing Rooms', for which members of the public could apply to the Lord Chamberlain to be admitted to St James's Palace to see the royal family in residence during the London Season. An advertisement appearing in the *London Courier and Evening Gazette* in 1831 read as follows:

> To Noble Gentlemen and Families Visiting London. That delightful situation the Bath Hotel and Old White Horse Cellar, Arlington Street, Piccadilly, having undergone considerable alterations and improvements, L. Paine (late Bland) begs most respectfully to invite those who may be visiting London to his Establishment, as being one of the most comfortable situations in the metropolis. The apartments are so arranged that the Court and Drawing Room processions now so frequently occurring at St James's Palace, may be seen to great advantage … Joints from Five o'Clock till Seven.[1]

THE GLOUCESTER COFFEE HOUSE

Almost opposite the Old White Horse Cellar, the Gloucester Coffee House stood on the north side at the junction of Berkeley Street, numbered 76–79 Piccadilly. The only Piccadilly coaching inn licensed by the General Post Office, the Gloucester was the terminus for mail coaches serving the west and south of England.

Famed for his coaching scenes, James Pollard produced a series of paintings of London inns. Incredibly detailed, his bustling scenes meticulously recorded every detail of the inns themselves, the coaches and the travellers boarding. Engraved in 1829, Pollard's painting entitled 'West Country Mails outside the Gloucester Coffee House' shows four Royal Mail coaches drawn up outside the inn almost blocking Piccadilly. They are being loaded ready to start their westbound journey and the red-liveried guards take up their positions as luggage is loaded by hotel servants.

From Pollard's engraving we see that the Gloucester Coffee House is a compact four-bay, four-storey hotel whose first-floor balcony, shaded by a red- and white-striped, painted, metal canopy, is supported on pierced cast-iron columns. The name of the proprietor inscribed above the door is T. Dale, indicating that he was licensed to serve liquor.

The building dates from the early 1780s and may have been purpose built as a hotel and coffee house. The first traceable reference to the Gloucester Coffee House is contained in a notice issued by the General Post Office on 5 November 1785, just over a year after John Palmer ran his first mail coach from Bristol to London. The notice contained a list of coaching inns and the mail routes they served. The list included the 'Gloucester in Piccadilly, from whence coaches set out for Bath and Bristol, Southampton and Poole, Gloucester. Swansea and Carmarthen, Worcester and Ludlow, Windsor, Dover and Exeter.' This represented a massive expansion in mail routes over a short period and a serious commitment to Britain's new mail network.

The proprietor of the Gloucester Coffee House was listed in a trade directory for 1790 enigmatically as 'Slark'. Whoever he was, Mr Slark had landed a lucrative contract with the General Post Office that was to last almost fifty years. In 1805, H. Pulsford was the proprietor. In that year, the Gloucester Coffee House advertised 'good soups, dinners, wines and beds'.

The coaching inn plays a small part in William Makepeace Thackeray's novel *Vanity Fair*. Mrs Bute Crawley, having travelled overnight on the 'Portsmouth mail' from Hampshire, arrives at 'The Gloster' (*sic*). Mrs Crawley, 'numbed with midnight travelling and warming herself at the newly crackling parlour fire', is enjoying 'a comfortable hot toast and tea' when she receives a note from Miss Briggs informing her of Becky Sharp's elopement with Captain Rawdon Crawley. The drama unfolds rapidly.

By the time Thomas Dale took over as proprietor of the Gloucester Coffee House in 1827, the inn's reputation and profitability was at its peak. But the good times would be short-lived. As mail coaches were superseded by the railways from the late 1830s, numbers of travellers passing through or staying overnight at Piccadilly's coaching inns dwindled. The Great Western Railway's line from Bristol to London was opened on 4 June 1838, with passengers alighting at a temporary terminus on Bishop's Bridge Road, now the site of a goods depot. In 1854, Paddington Station was completed. Rail travel became the mode of choice for the middle and upper classes.

The Gloucester's fortunes declined rapidly. In April 1840, an entry in *The London Gazette* makes dismal reading:

> Pursuant to a Decree in the High Court of Chancery ... the creditors of Thomas Dale late of the Gloucester Coffee-House, Piccadilly and of Hendon in the county of Middlesex, Hotelier and Farmer (who died in the month of February 1840) are invited to come forward and prove their debts.

Somehow, Thomas Dale's two sons Thomas and Frederick were able to clear their father's debts and relaunch the business. The Gloucester was no longer a Royal Mail coaching inn but a common or garden family hotel.

In 1842, *Robson's London Directory Street Key and Classification of Trade, Royal Court Guide and Peerage* lists Thomas Dale of the Gloucester Coffee House, 77 Piccadilly, as 'a wine merchant'. The *Visitor's Pocket Companion* for 1851 states, 'Thomas and Frederick Dale: proprietors of the Gloucester Hotel'. The hotel was by then one of hundreds of family hotels and enterprises hoping to attract well-heeled tourists flocking to London to visit the Great Exhibition.

That same year, a small printed notice appeared in the *Cheltenham Journal and Gloucestershire Fashionable Weekly Gazette*: 'Gloucester Coffee House Good Beds Well Aired. NB Close at Twelve and Open at Five in the Morning for the Accommodation of Railway Passengers.' The advertisement was so small, it may have escaped readers' attention. After 1851, nothing more is heard of the once beating heart of the western mails. The Gloucester Coffee House had closed its doors forever.

NEW WHITE HORSE CELLAR AND HATCHETT'S HOTEL

The year 1798 marked a turning point for Piccadilly when the proprietor of the White Horse Cellar, Abraham Hatchett, decided to sell his interest in the inn and build a new establishment directly opposite, on the corner of Albemarle Street. Hatchett would have been seriously concerned at the competition from the Gloucester Coffee House, which only a few years earlier had cornered the lucrative mail-coach franchise. Hatchett intended his new coaching inn as a starting point for stage coaches bound for the north and east. Confusingly, he called his inn the New White Horse Cellar and Hatchett's Hotel.

In 1814, Hatchett placed the following advertisement. It is a detailed but thorough statement of obligations of the stage-coach operator and seeks to allay passengers' fears about their safety and comfort en route:

HATCHETT's NEW WHITE HORSE CELLAR, Piccadilly.—Cheap and Expeditious Travelling to York, Leeds, Hull, Newcastle. Edinburgh, and parts of the North, by the HIGHFLYER POSTCOACH, which sets out every Morning at Six o'clock, with Guard, who goes the whole journey through, and Lamp. The utmost care and attention will be paid to all Passengers travelling by this Coach, and all Parcels sent in it will charged as reasonable as by any other Coach on the North road.[2]

By 1848, in the face of the dwindling stage-coach trade, Hatchett relaunched his New White Horse Cellar as Hatchett's Hotel and Coffee House and moved to 66–68 Piccadilly, the site of the old Three Kings Tavern. The name White Horse Cellar was kept for the sake of tradition.

The story does not end there. Where the Gloucester Coffee House failed, the New White Horse Cellar/Hatchett's Hotel went from strength to strength. Twenty years after railways first appeared, there was a movement to revive the romance of a bygone age. A group of wealthy enthusiasts, including the 8th Duke of Beaufort, bought the last surviving stage coach on the Brighton Road and ran it as a hobby. They chose the New White Horse Cellar as their starting point. These gentlemen were members of the 'four-in-hand club', a loose association of gentlemen for whom the art of driving four horses was a sport.

In 1866 the Brighton stage coach service was further enhanced by a group of investors who each paid £10 for a share in the business. That year, a new stage coach named *Old Times* took to the road, resplendent in its distinctive canary yellow livery. The service prospered and another coach was added. While one coach travelled up from Brighton, the other travelled down, meeting up at the Chequers at Horley where passengers could alight for lunch. These coaches regularly plied the Brighton Road until the late 1880s.

Two additional horse-drawn stage coach services were scheduled to run from the New White Horse Cellar – one to St Albans and the other to Sevenoaks and Tunbridge Wells. *Bell's Sporting Life* of 21 July 1882 ran an advertisement for the summer stage coach service between the New White Horse Cellar and Brighton that ran from June to September. It reads like a railway timetable:

> Departing White Horse Cellar, Hatchett's Hotel daily at 12.30 pm, via Tooting, Mitcham, Sutton, Walton Heath and Reigate (30 minutes allowed here for lunch) Crawley, Hand Cross, Bolney, Hickstead, Albourne arriving at the Old Ship Hotel Brighton at 6.30 pm.

The service from Brighton to London would start at 11.20 a.m. and arrive at Piccadilly at 5.30 p.m.

Passengers paid a premium of 15s to sit on the roof and 10s inside. An extra 2s 6d secured a box seat with 'parcels carried and punctually delivered'. Anyone wanting to return the same day would have to catch a train, but equally an overnight stay in London or Brighton would have been part of the pleasurable experience.

Then on Friday, 13 July 1888, an extraordinary feat of driving made the headlines. Jim Selby, the most celebrated coach driver on the Brighton

Road, accepted a wager of £1,000 that he couldn't drive the *Old Times* to Brighton and back in under eight hours. Selby was aged 44, robust and white haired with a ruddy weather-beaten complexion. He had worked all his life in a livery stables and was regarded as 'the best whip' on the Brighton Road.

A top-hatted Selby set off at 10 a.m. prompt from the New White Horse Cellar with a coach carrying six passengers. Driving at a cracking pace and with sixteen changes of horse – the fastest achieved in forty-seven seconds at the Horse and Groom in Streatham – the coach reached a top speed of 20mph. There was a nail-biting delay at Crawley where *Old Times* was forced to make an unscheduled stop as the railway level-crossing gates were closed.

The coach arrived at the Old Ship Inn at Brighton seafront just after 1 p.m. A rapid turnaround was made and then *Old Times* and Selby were on their way. Along the route bystanders looked on in awe while some people even threw bouquets of flowers at the coach.

Just ten minutes ahead of the 6 p.m. deadline, *Old Times* thundered into Piccadilly and pulled up at the White Horse, cheered on by members of the Coaching Club and by the Duke of Beaufort. Selby had won the bet.

Four weeks after the record-breaking London-to-Brighton stage coach run, four bicyclists wearing knickerbocker suits, riding Ormonde safety bicycles fitted with pneumatic tyres, shaved fourteen minutes off the journey time.

In 1892, the era of stage coach tourism came to an end. In a few years the first automobile would make the journey from London to Brighton. But in April 1892, Hatchett's Hotel relaunched itself as a hotel offering fine dining. The celebrated White Horse Cellar, underneath Hatchett's Hotel, had been converted into a restaurant.

The name Hatchett's survived almost to the present day, undergoing many changes in use and shifting the focus of its core business from hotel to restaurant to nightclub.

THE FAMILY HOTEL

Prince Albert's decision to hold the Great Exhibition in the Crystal Palace at Hyde Park in 1851 sparked a huge influx of tourists from across Great Britain and the world wanting to visit this year-long showcase for British arts, crafts and invention. The boom in tourism provided a much-needed shot in the arm for the West End's hotel trade. Over a million people descended on London over the course of the year, many from far-flung corners of the

British Isles and some from abroad. Piccadilly was particularly well placed as it had an established hotel sector as well as coaching inns and lodging houses.

Durrant's Hotel in George Street opened its doors in 1789 and would still be in business over a century later. In Jermyn Street, the Cavendish Hotel on the corner of Duke Street can trace its history back even further. There was a hotel on the site for at least fifty years before it changed hands in 1811 and was renamed after its owner, Mr Miller. Subsequently reinvented as the Cavendish in the early 1880s, this hotel went on to achieve a reputation for gastronomy and debauchery in equal measure following its sale to society cook Rosa Lewis in 1902.

The Regency period from 1801 to 1820 was the heyday of the high-class family hotel according to London historian Edward Walford. The northern tributaries of Piccadilly, Dover Street, Albemarle Street and Bond Street were particularly popular:

> Here in this street [Albemarle Street] are several large hotels such as the Pulteney, the York, the Queen's Head and the Albemarle. In the days of the Regency, when the club system was as yet in its infancy, the hotels of the West-end were much more frequented than now-a-days is the case … There was then a very large class of men, including Wellington, Nelson, Collingwood, Sir John Moore, and some few others who seldom frequented the clubs. The persons to whom we refer … used to congregate at a few hotels of which The Clarendon, Limmer's, Ibbotson's, Fladong's, Stephen's and Grillon's were the most fashionable.[3]

In 1803, Frenchman Alexander Grillon opened Grillon's Hotel at 7 Albemarle Street in 1803.

Mivart's Hotel in Davies Street catered for an exclusive market and went on to become one of the great West End hotels. It was opened in 1812 and sold to Mr and Mrs Claridge in 1854. They already owned a small hotel next door. By the 1860s, Claridge's was attracting royalty. Empress Eugenie of France stayed there in 1860. The Savoy Group bought Claridge's in 1894, demolishing the old buildings and clearing the site in order to build the magnificent seven-storey red-brick and stucco edifice we see today. This exclusive hotel had 203 rooms and employed 400 staff.

The arrival of the railways could have sounded the death knell for Piccadilly's hotels, which had drawn their custom from stage-coach travellers. Seduced by the speed and comfort of railway travel, families from far afield now felt able to visit the capital for the first time. In a bid to secure the loyalty of their customers, the railway companies built huge luxury hotels next to their termini, like Paddington's Great Western Hotel, which opened in 1854. This was quickly followed by the Great Northern Hotel at King's Cross. George Gilbert Scott's magnificent Midland Grand Hotel at St Pancras, built for the Midland Railway in 1876, was the last word in Victorian luxury with 300 rooms, most with bathrooms en suite.

But for the wealthier travellers looking for an old-fashioned personal service, Piccadilly remained the destination of choice. Long-established hotels continued to exercise a cachet to stay in the centre of the West End, where guests could enjoy easy access to the area's many restaurants, theatres and entertainments. In 1888 a guide for American tourists, *London of Today*, offered the following advice:

> Limmer's in Conduit Street, has earned some distinction as an exclusive and somewhat expensive hotel. Long's Hotel in Bond Street has for more than a century been the resort of gentlemen of fashion. Having long ago outlived the requirements of the day, the old hotel is being rebuilt and before this book issues from the press an entirely new hotel will be opened for the reception of visitors.[4]

Established in 1837, Brown's Hotel in Albemarle Street was the latest addition to a street already famous for its hotels; for example, the Pulteney, Grillon's Hotel, Batt's Hotel and McKellar's were nearby.

By the late 1880s, Brown's Hotel and the Pulteney were under the same management (J.J. Ford proprietors) and had been upgraded with electric lights throughout suites of rooms containing baths. There were even passenger and luggage elevators and telephones. It is surprising how these two private hotels were already competing strongly with the Savoy and Claridge's.

At this point in time, overseas tourists were starting to arrive in London in larger numbers. Americans were notably keen to visit. Several guidebooks written by American authors explain the idiosyncrasies of staying in the West End. One such guide enthused:

> Brown's in Dover Street which lies a few yards westward of Bond Street ... is an old hotel, modernised: that is to say, it combines something of the old with something of the new system. It has all the modern conveniences; the rooms are cosy and pleasant; the service is good; the cookery and wines are excellent. The Pulteney in Albemarle Street is under the same management

and may be equally recommended. The reader will bear in mind that these 'private hotels' so-called have nothing in common with the huge joint stock concerns. Having more of a residential character, these hotels are quiet, and less frequented by the busy class of traveller.[5]

MEMBERS' CLUBS

Hospitality and fine dining were key ingredients in both hotels and members' clubs, not to be confused with gentlemen's clubs or nightclubs. From their inception, clubs had offered dining and accommodation to members who lived outside London. With a rapidly expanding number of clubs catering for different interest groups, it is hardly surprising then that hotelkeepers spotted an opportunity to convert their premises into clubhouses.

The network of prestigious streets north of Piccadilly leading towards Mayfair was as ideal a location for London's expanding clubland as it was for small family-run hotels. Where a newly formed club lacked a base to call its own, it was natural that it should partner with a hotel that not only had comfortable reception rooms, but also an appetising *table d'hôte*. On this basis, a number of hotels switched from catering for travellers to becoming members-only establishments.

The Albemarle Club, the Alfred Club (Lord Byron was a member) and Grillon's Club (formed in 1813 from what had once been Grillon's Hotel) are good examples of this trend. The Stafford Street Club was established in 1852 at Crawley's Hotel. Other hotel-cum-clubs of note included the Green Park Club and the Isthmian Club. By the late nineteenth century, London was home to around 400 clubs, the majority of which were in the West End; many were former hotels.

Large mansions were ideally suited for conversion into clubhouses. And Piccadilly had plenty of these. Watiers, a gambling hall presided over by Beau Brummel and the Prince Regent, was located at 81 Piccadilly at the corner of Bolton Street. Nearby, the St James's Club was located on the corner of Piccadilly and Brick Street. The big expansion of clubs following the victory of Waterloo included the Junior Athenaeum, the 'In and Out' Naval and Military Club, the Guards and Cavalry Club, and the Turf. Nearby were Bucks, the Bath Club, the Savile Club, the Bachelors' Club and the Royal Air Force Club. All were based in or around Piccadilly, and in the case of the 'In and Out' in the palatial former London townhouse of Lord Palmerston, at Cambridge House, Piccadilly.

ROSA LEWIS AND THE CAVENDISH HOTEL

Born in Leytonstone, east London, in 1869, Rosa Ovenden, like many young women of her class, had gone into domestic service as a kitchen maid. Unlike others, she rose rapidly and learned the art of cooking in the kitchens of aristocrats like Lady Randolph Churchill. She managed dinner parties and it was at a house party that she came to the attention of Edward, Prince of Wales.

In need of a married couple to manage a house in Eaton Square, a secret rendezvous where he could entertain his many lady friends, the prince arranged for Rosa to marry his senior manservant, Excelsior Lewis. This cosy domestic arrangement lasted until the king's coronation in 1902.

It may have been the prince who arranged the finance that would enable Rosa and her husband to establish a new life as hotel proprietors. The Cavendish Hotel in Jermyn Street was up for sale and conveniently close to the Court and aristocratic members' clubs of St James's, like Brooks's and White's. The Cavendish was soon attracting a wealthy, and mainly male, clientele including many belonging to the prince's louche circle.

Within the first year of operation, it became clear that Excelsior was drinking and gambling heavily, frittering away what profits the hotel made and leaving bills to local suppliers unpaid. Rosa took drastic action. She threatened him with a knife, threw him out on the streets and began divorce proceedings. Rosa was forced to sack most of her staff in order to pay her legal fees. Clearing nearly £5,000 in debts, she used her superb cooking skills and her bulging address book of aristocratic patrons to start a private catering business while running the hotel almost single-handed.

The Cavendish began to prosper again. Recently bereaved, Lord Ribblesdale took a permanent suite of rooms at the hotel and moved in with all of his furniture and household possessions. Sir William Eden and his family were frequent guests. These powerful men had connections to the Court and the Foreign Office. The high point of Rosa's catering career was when she was asked to prepare dinner for the German Kaiser aboard his private yacht at Cowes in 1907.

Rosa had an astute head for business. She acquired two adjoining properties from the local landlord, giving the hotel additional frontage onto Duke Street and a large courtyard and garden. As the rooms were divided into suites with separate bathroom and dining rooms, many Edwardian gentlemen were able to entertain their lovers while being assured of complete discretion.

Rosa was rightly proud of the Cavendish's reputation for gastronomy. Rising at dawn, she would visit Covent Garden market to buy all of her produce fresh. In an age where hotels like the Carlton and the Ritz could boast of world-class chefs like Auguste Escoffier, Rosa's brigade of cooks could compete with the best. Below is a typical menu available for hotel guests:

CAVENDISH HOTEL

Diner du 26 Juin, 1908
Consomme aux Ailerons
Truite froide a la Cavendish
Blanchailles
Souffle de Cailles a la Valencienne
Piece de Boeuf a la gelee en Bellevue
Jambon de Prague aux feves
Salade
Asperges en branches
Peches a la Marron
Bombe glace Dame Blanche
Friandaises
Laitances a la diable

Rosa Lewis will be remembered as a true eccentric. Kippy, her white Aberdeen terrier, occupied a basket next to the hotel reception and took priority over guests, even upsetting several with its constant barking. At a time when hotels were installing all mod cons, Lewis furnished the Cavendish in the style of an eighteenth-century English country house with Chippendale furniture and chintz armchairs, which gave the place a lived-in feel.

THE RITZ AND THE SAVOY

Born in 1850, the son of a Swiss peasant farmer, César Ritz's upbringing was a far cry from the luxury hotels and restaurants with which his name is now synonymous. Starting out as a waiter at a local inn, restless Ritz packed his bags and headed for Paris, arriving at the outbreak of the Franco-Prussian War. With Paris under siege, upheavals across Europe shook up the old order, creating business opportunities for anyone willing to work hard and invest in new ventures.

Hotels and tourism for the European super rich were a growth market, and the hard-working Ritz was lucky enough to be in the right place at the right time. Offered a job as restaurant manager at the Grand Hotel in Nice, Ritz moved into hotel management where his flair for organisation and hospitality quickly got him noticed. Moving up the career ladder, Ritz ran a succession of luxury hotels in Switzerland and the French Riviera, where he married Marie, the niece of a wealthy hotel proprietor, and ended up running the newly opened Grand Hotel in Monte Carlo.

Ritz's reputation spread to London. In 1889, the impresario and theatre manager-turned-property developer Richard D'Oyly Carte was keen to recruit a manager who could cement the reputation of his newly built Savoy Hotel into one of the best and most luxurious in the world. D'Oyly Carte, whose Savoy Opera was the first public building in England to be lit by electric light, had spared no expense in fitting out his hotel with en suite bathrooms, a palm court and magnificent furnishings.

D'Oyly Carte went to Monte Carlo and eventually persuaded Ritz to join him. Rising to the challenge, Ritz agreed on condition that he could bring with him his brigade of chefs and he would be free to develop outside business interests in parallel with his role at the Savoy. In a short time, Ritz swapped the Riviera sunshine for the fogs of London and brought with him a rising star of French haute cuisine, the celebrated Auguste Escoffier. Ritz's careful management and Escoffier's sumptuous dishes quickly secured the patronage of the Prince of Wales and his mistress Lily Langtry, together with a cast of London's literary and artistic world including Oscar Wilde, the actress Sarah Bernhardt and the opera singer Nellie Melba, for whom Escoffier created a special dessert, pêche Melba.

The Savoy was to lay the foundations for Ritz's own business empire. Ritz already owned hotels at Cannes and Baden-Baden, but by the late 1890s, he and Escoffier were working on their most ambitious project ever. The Paris Ritz opened at Place Vendôme in June 1898. Less than a year later, Ritz and D'Oyly Carte parted company, Ritz having by then raised the finance to buy a rival London hotel, the Carlton.

Standing at the corner of Pall Mall and Haymarket, the Carlton opened in 1899 and soon established a reputation for luxury and fine dining that outshone the Savoy. Naming his company Ritz-Carlton, and now in partnership with his head chef Auguste Escoffier, César Ritz envisaged a series of ambitious hotel and catering ventures backed by private finance.

But Ritz would not enjoy the fruits of his success in building an expanding business empire. In 1902, the Carlton Hotel was gearing up to receive a large influx of guests for the coronation of Edward VII when the ceremony was postponed at the last minute as the king needed to receive emergency treatment for appendicitis. Guests cancelled their bookings in droves. Ritz lost a lot of money and, having expended all of his energies in planning for the big day, suffered a nervous breakdown. He never fully recovered his health and died in 1918.

Ritz may have stepped down from the day-to-day running of his company, but his wife Marie Louise took over and the Ritz-Carlton went from strength to strength. The company won a contract to provide fine dining for the transatlantic ships of the Hamburg-Amerika Line, built the London Ritz in Piccadilly in 1906 and the Ritz Carlton in New York, which opened in 1910.

BUILDING THE RITZ

When it was opened in May 1906, the Ritz Hotel was the most luxurious in London. Its architects, Mewes and Davis, designed a palatial eight-storey French Renaissance building whose stone-clad exterior, mansard roof and dormer windows were supported by an internal steel frame similar to the technique used to build New York's skyscrapers. There were 150 rooms.

Fronting onto Piccadilly, the ground floor included an arcade above the pavement, enabling the hotel to be built at full width and giving extra space to bedrooms on the upper floors. The ground floor included a large restaurant overlooking Green Park, while at the rear of the ground floor was a large winter garden. No expense was spared in designing the interior in the style of Louis XVI, with marble statues, painted ceilings, marble fireplaces, gilt mirrors, sumptuous carpets and masses of gilt stucco, all lit by huge electric chandeliers. A sweeping stone staircase with decorative wrought-iron balustrade led to the upper floors, which were also served by electric lifts.

Although the hotel fronted onto a busy thoroughfare, no street noise penetrated the peaceful atmosphere within. While the public rooms and winter garden were tastefully furnished with gilt rococo furniture, the guest bedrooms included bathrooms and many included a telephone. The impression one had was of a palace.

ESCOFFIER

The first chef at the Ritz was M. Malley, who had come direct from the Paris Ritz. As Newnham-Davis reports, Malley had a talent for inventing new dishes such as salmon with a mousse of crayfish, named in honour of the

Marquise de Sevigny, and pêche Belle Dijonnaise, a dessert made with black-currant ice cream and marc de Bourgogne. Menus included *coeurs de Romain* with almonds and ortolans – complete with their tiny organs. Edward VII enjoyed his sweetmeats so much he ordered Malley's fancy cakes to be made and sent to Buckingham Palace.

Escoffier replaced the extravagant and old-fashioned *service à la française* with *service à la russe*. *Service à la française* involved diners helping themselves from a buffet. The overall impression was one of magnificent profusion. That contrasted to *service à la russe*, for which dishes were brought to the table sequentially and served individually, portioned by servants. The advantage of *service à la russe* was that everyone could taste all the dishes offered rather than be limited to the ones nearest their seat. The disadvantages were that many more waiters and much more tableware were needed.

THE HOSPITALITY INDUSTRY

The business opportunities created by Piccadilly's coaching inns and the Gloucester Coffee House's valuable mail-coach franchise laid the foundations for an entire industry, as entrepreneurs opened clubs, hotels and restaurants. These rose and fell in dizzying profusion across the centuries but have in many ways set their stamp upon the West End as the acme of achievement in the pursuit of pleasure.

4

POPULAR ENTERTAINMENTS

Hither came the 'illustrious' Pidcock, with his wild beasts. Hither also came the formerly famous and still well-remembered Astley with his 'equestrian troop', and his learned horse. These feats were the admiration of never-ceasing audiences …

William Hone, *The Everyday Book*

PICCADILLY – THE 'MAGIC MILE'

By the early eighteenth century, Piccadilly had become a resort for thrill seekers. London's fairs and religious festivals were a traditional link between city dwellers and country dwellers. Held at a site near the present-day Shepherd's Market, the annual May Fair featured boisterous entertainments such as rope-walking, acrobats, fire-eaters and displays of horsemanship.

Like St Bartholomew's Fair, its medieval predecessor to the east of the city, the free and easy atmosphere of the May Fair made it a rendezvous for those seeking sexual encounters. The fair also attracted prostitutes and, even after the event was discontinued, this easy-going reputation stuck and Shepherd's Market became a Bohemian enclave and discreet red-light district. This ghostly rural bacchanalia continued to manifest itself into the twentieth century in the form of louche gaming clubs and expensive call girls.

Piccadilly's unique character was forged by the eternal desire for novelty and excitement – a demand that enterprising showmen exploited to the full. Attractions like Winstanley's Water Theatre, Astley's Hippodrome, Bullock's

Museum and the Egyptian Hall may be long gone but their legacy lives on in unexpected ways.

FROM SAWDUST RING TO CIRCUS

Displays of horsemanship or 'trick riding' were a popular entertainment among all classes, who avidly visited travelling shows and fairgrounds to see horses perform. From 1773 until 1780, showman and former cavalryman Philip Astley – the man credited with inventing the modern circus – staged indoor equestrian performances each evening at his Hippodrome, at the assembly rooms, 22 Piccadilly.

Astley was a larger-than-life character. Standing at over 6ft tall, he had served with distinction in the Seven Years War during which he reached the rank of sergeant major. Discharged from the army, he was presented with a strong and intelligent grey charger, and both man and horse used their skills and agility to earn a living performing at fairgrounds.

By 1768, Astley had made enough money to open a riding school near Westminster Bridge where he gave riding lessons in the morning and shows of horsemanship in the afternoon. But in 1773, he took a lease on the ground-floor ballroom of a building in Piccadilly, which he adapted for his displays, stabling his horses at the back of the premises.

Spectators sat around a sawdust ring as Astley directed a series of acts, which included a rider standing on his horse cantering around the ring. The horses were great actors: they could feign death and leap to life at a word of command, prance on their hind legs and dance in time to music. By a strange coincidence, Astley's shows took place near the site of the present-day Piccadilly Circus.

Astley's name is more commonly associated with his famous Amphitheatre at 225 Westminster Bridge Road, Lambeth. Designed more like an opera house than a circus, Astley's Amphitheatre featured a central ring surrounded on all sides by tiered galleries beneath a vast domed roof. Construction of this amazing building took seven years to complete as Astley ploughed his profits into the project. During this time, evening equestrian performances continued in his Piccadilly Hippodrome.

When John Nash, the architect of Regent Street, came to plan his roundabout at Piccadilly in 1826, he is said to have been inspired by the Roman chariot ring, the Circus Maximus. But could Astley's earlier 'circus' with its performing horses and feats of equestrian skill have exerted a subconscious influence? It is interesting to speculate.

Astley's Amphitheatre in Lambeth ran from 1773 until 1863, when the circus ring was replaced by a theatre and music hall. Astley went on to build amphitheatres in nineteen British cities as well as in Dublin and Paris. The original Amphitheatre went through several changes of ownership and was twice burned to the ground, once in 1794 and again in 1803. When Astley died in 1814, the management passed to his brother John. It was latterly owned and run by circus proprietor William Batty.

The most famous of Astley's performers was the legendary black equestrian Pablo Fanque. Brought back to brief fame in the lyrics of the Beatles' song 'Being for the Benefit of Mr Kite' from *Sergeant Pepper's Lonely Hearts' Club Band*, the real-life Pablo Fanque was born William Darby, of African parents in Norwich, on 1 April 1810. Changing his name to the exotic-sounding Pablo Fanque, in 1840 he made his debut at Astley's Amphitheatre as a member of Batty's Circus. Fanque subsequently went on to become one of the great fairground entrepreneurs of the Victorian period.

At Astley's in 1847, Fanque was given solo star billing for his carefully choreographed show of horsemanship and dressage in which he could make his steed walk on tiptoes, rear on its hind legs and move sideways. As the climax of his act, Fanque would jump in and out of the saddle and stand as the horse cantered around the ring. One can imagine 'Henry the horse doing the waltz'.

WINSTANLEY'S WATER THEATRE

Perhaps the strangest Piccadilly entertainment was Winstanley's Water Theatre, sometimes referred to as the 'Mathematical Water Theatre', at Hyde Park Corner. In existence from 1696 to 1720, the Water Theatre was the brainchild of eccentric West Country architect and inventor Henry Winstanley, who wanted to demonstrate science in action.

Winstanley's aim in setting up his attraction was to raise money to enable him to build a lighthouse at the Eddystone, a dangerous rock off Cornwall. Self-financing the construction, the architect clearly believed that his building could survive the dangerous storm surges that had swept away earlier attempts to maintain a lighthouse on the rock.

Like the Eddystone lighthouse it was intended to fund, the Water Theatre was a wooden tower surmounted by a windmill, which pumped water from the Tyburn stream. Hidden pumps produced fountains of claret, pale ale and spa water from a series of unusual receptacles as if by magic. Visitors were amazed at this marvel of hydraulic engineering.

Incredibly, Winstanley managed to raise sufficient funds to build his light-house. The octagonal wooden tower he built on the Eddystone rock lasted a full five years, saving many ships from being wrecked. Tragically, the light-house was smashed to pieces in a terrible storm on the night of 27 November 1703. Winstanley was in the lighthouse at the time making repairs and was swept to his death by the raging seas.

The Water Theatre outlasted its plucky inventor by almost twenty years. A contemporary account of a visit to the 'Mathematical Water Theatre' in June 1710 describes the interior as looking 'very elegant, although only made of painted wood', and the ceiling was 'crisscrossed by pulleys and ropes to which a refreshment tray is fastened, so that it can be pulled hither and thither about the auditorium'.[1] Trays bearing glasses of claret and ale would no doubt have delighted and amazed.

MUSEUMS AND ATTRACTIONS

During the long eighteenth century there was an emerging cultural divide between low entertainments and cultural enrichment provided by, for exam-ple, a visit to a museum or the Italian opera. At the bequest of Sir Hans Sloane, who left his collection of important cultural artefacts to the people, the British Museum had been established at Montagu House in Bloomsbury, close to the site of the present-day museum, which moved to its current location in 1845 to occupy a monumental classical building designed by Robert Smirke. The Zoological Gardens at Regent's Park were established in 1826 by Sir Stamford Raffles and Sir Humphrey Davy as the world's first scientific zoo.

But there was a fine line separating the quest for knowledge from the thirst for entertainment. To succeed, an attraction had to pay its way – and that meant appealing to a mass market. When Marie Tussaud established her waxworks in Baker Street in 1798 with wax dummies of the leading French politicians, a public curious to experience the horror of the French Revolution flocked to the exhibition. The gruesome depiction of Marat with his throat cut in the bath satisfied the public's lust for gore.

Waxworks became a popular attraction in and around Piccadilly. There was a collection of figures shown at the Queen's Bazaar in Oxford Street in 1830. The Oriental and Turkish Museum, which opened at the St George's Gallery, Knightsbridge, contained models of Eastern life with scenes set in Turkish baths, coffee shops and bazaars peopled with realistic wax figures, all for an admission price of 1s.

Another popular attraction, the camera obscura, delighted the public with views of the surrounding urban landscape and the teeming multitudes who thronged its streets. Part scientific and part novelty, the Cosmorama in Regent Street and Burford's Panorama in Leicester Square were briefly famous for their visual sleight of hand.

WILLIAM BULLOCK AND THE LIVERPOOL MUSEUM

A Sheffield jeweller and goldsmith by trade, William Bullock had a passion for travel, exploration and the natural world. A keen collector of rare and unusual artefacts, Bullock opened a museum in Liverpool in which he displayed objects brought back to Britain from Captain Cook's expedition to the South Seas. Ambitious to make his mark, Bullock moved his collection, lock, stock and barrel, to London where he opened the Liverpool Museum at 22 Piccadilly in 1805 in a hall that had previously housed Astley's equestrian shows.

The museum attracted not only the scientific naturalist but large numbers of the general public who were curious to see novelties like the fossilised tooth of a woolly mammoth or the hind leg of a reindeer and were willing to pay the 1s admission charge.

Highly idiosyncratic, Bullock's collection featured not only specimens of stuffed animals but also antique arms and armour, folk art and *objets de vertu*. An engraved print of his museum dated 1810 shows members of the public surveying an artificial jungle. Among the realistically painted model trees are assembled a random collection of stuffed beasts including an elephant, a rhinoceros, a zebra, two ostriches and a zoological anomaly: a polar bear, who appears to have made his way from the Arctic to sub-Saharan Africa. Even stranger than the assembled wildlife, two stuffed pythons appear to be about to start a fight at the top of a large palm tree while a medieval knight in armour on horseback looks on.

Like many self-styled scientific pioneers, Bullock was self-taught. Combining an enthusiasm for natural history, his exhibitions resulted in his being elected to the prestigious Linnaean Society, an organisation based on Swedish biologist Carl Linnaeus' concept of the classification of species. Bullock claimed that his museum stood 'for the advancement of the Science of Natural History'. Bullock added voraciously to his collection of stuffed game animals, exotic birds and monkeys.

One such exhibition staged in 1810, 'The Interior of Africa', featured an African woman brought to England from the Cape of Good Hope. By this time, Bullock was in the process of reorganising the Liverpool Museum at a new location opposite Burlington House. He put his collection in storage while he commissioned a purpose-built museum in a building that would become one of Piccadilly's most celebrated landmarks – the Egyptian Hall.

THE EGYPTIAN HALL

Bullock's 'Egyptian Temple', popularly referred to as the Egyptian Hall, opened at 170–173 Piccadilly in 1812. Designed by architect Peter Frederick Robinson, this strange building was to remain one of Piccadilly's most colourful oddities until its demolition in 1905.

The idea for building an Egyptian temple came about because William's brother, the Regency sculptor and cabinet-maker George Bullock, was a close associate of the designer Thomas Hope, a leading proponent of the Egyptian style. Hope's house in Duchess Street was famed for its Egyptian room, which was open to the public and illustrated in Hope's design manual, *Household Furniture and Interior Decoration*, published in 1807.

Looking like the entrance to a pharaoh's tomb transported from ancient Egypt, visitors entered through a dramatic doorway flanked by two massive columns topped by stylised lotus flower capitols. Sloping window profiles featured scarab and sphinx decoration and recesses contained two monolithic statues of the gods Isis and Osiris, which completed the effect. In contrast to its antique architecture, in later years, as the Egyptian Hall competed with other London attractions, its owner saw fit to mount gigantic billboards around the building's frontage, advertising forthcoming attractions in bold type.

The bizarre architectural statement reflected the craze for all things Egyptian that followed in the wake of the Battle of the Nile, where Napoleon's fleet was defeated by the British under Nelson at Aboukir Bay in August 1798. From then on, Western explorers raided Egypt at will, carting back trophies of their visit and building impressive private collections of mummies, sculptures and other artefacts. A haul of Egyptian statues captured from the French was brought back to London where it was added to the British Museum's growing collection of cultural artefacts – a legacy bequeathed to the nation in 1753 by the collector Sir Hans Sloane.

Egyptomania can still be seen in surviving curiosities like the Egyptian House in Penzance erected in 1839, the entrance to Abney Park Cemetery in Stoke Newington and a host of mausoleums up and down the country for which the monumental and mystical Egyptian architecture was well suited.

The Egyptian Hall opened to a fanfare of publicity. A contemporary cat-alogue 'printed for the proprietor by Whittingham and Rowland' in 1816 opens with the following title page:

A Companion for the LONDON MUSEUM and PANTHERION
containing a brief description of Upwards of Fifteen Thousand
Natural and Foreign Curiosities, Antiquities and Productions of the Fine Arts
now open for public inspection in the EGYPTIAN TEMPLE,
Piccadilly, London

Unconstrained by academic research, Bullock's showmanship came to the fore as he supplemented his natural-history specimens from Africa, the South Seas and Central America with a vast array of militaria. As a celebration of Wellington's victory at Waterloo, in 1816 Bullock included a display of captured French trophies including Napoleon's bulletproof carriage, which he acquired from the Prussian Army who had captured it on the battlefield. The museum's popularity went from strength to strength.

One of the stranger displays was the 'Pantherion', a set of rooms designed to showcase animals in their natural setting. After paying an extra shilling for admission, visitors were guided down a long corridor made to look like a rocky cave, which opened onto a diorama comprising a new and improved version of his tropical rainforest populated with stuffed animals. In the days before the Regent's Park Zoological Gardens opened to the public in 1847, Bullock's taxidermy was the next best thing to a 'wild encounter'.

A contemporary account in *The Picture for London for 1818* states the gallery was 'intended to display quadrupeds in such a manner as to convey a correct notion of their haunts and habits. In one orange-tree were disposed sixty species of the genus *Simia*, or monkeys.' The display included labels detailing the types of animal, their habitat, diet and chief characteristics.

An astute businessman, Bullock knew that novelty was the key to maintaining his audience. In 1819 he auctioned his permanent collection divided into 2,248 lots, raising a total of £9,971 – three times what Bullock had originally paid for the items.

He now decided to host temporary exhibitions instead. Exploiting public curiosity in the recent archaeological discoveries in Egypt, Bullock had constructed a facsimile of the tomb of Psammuthis, King of Thebes, discovered by Belzoni. Great attention was paid to historical accuracy as all of the hieroglyphics were faithfully copied and reconstructions made using plaster taken from wax casts of all the various statues and features of the tomb. The show was a massive commercial success and, on the first day, 1,900 visitors each paid 2*s* 6*d* to see the tomb.

In 1822, Bullock followed this with an exhibition of Lapland in which a family of Laplanders and their reindeer were shown in front of a painted backdrop. Visitors were given short sleigh rides. As an added bonus, visitors could see a convincing-looking stuffed mermaid in a glass case, which was later exhibited by Turf Coffee House, 39 St James's Street, that same year and immediately parodied in a cartoon by George Cruikshank.

Delegating the running of his museum, Bullock took a gap year to explore Mexico – a dangerous undertaking, beginning with a transatlantic sailing to the Americas. Accompanied by his son, Bullock's epic journey began in November 1822 and was completed in December 1823, making him the first Englishman to visit Mexico since the country had gained its independence in 1821. For six months, Bullock father and son travelled the country, buying souvenirs along the way, including native costumes, pottery and tribal masks. The exhibition he staged on his return was a sensation and was accompanied by a book, *Travels in Mexico*. Dioramas included a Mexican village with a Mexican complete with poncho and sombrero. No one would have seen anything like this except possibly in the pages of a travel book.

Bullock's swansong was to exhibit the Rath, or the Burmese Imperial state carriage, captured by the British in 1824. In 1825 Bullock sold his interest in the Egyptian Hall and embarked on more travels to Mexico and America where he founded the town of Ludlow, Kentucky, in 1828. A restless soul, Bullock found peace and happiness in the New World.

'MUMMY' PETTIGREW

No account of Egyptomania would be complete without reference to one very extraordinary denizen of Piccadilly. From the 1820s to the 1840s, surgeon, eccentric and amateur Egyptologist Thomas Pettigrew drew packed audiences at the Royal Institution, Arlington Street, for his 'Mummy Unwrappings'.

The Italian explorer Giovanni Belzoni, Egyptologist and circus strongman, staged a private exhibition of mummies at the Egyptian Hall in the 1820s, and it was at one of these he first encountered Thomas Pettigrew, who he allowed to unwrap one of the exhibits. Pettigrew, who practised at the Charing Cross Hospital in the Strand, was inspired by mummification and was one of the many British surgeons who learned their skill by practising dissection on corpses bought from graverobbers or 'resurrectionists' – a vile practice outlawed in the Anatomy Act of 1832.

Serious science was sometimes hard to distinguish from showmanship as the line between science and sensationalism was frequently blurred. Founded in 1799 by a group of scientists including Henry Cavendish and George Finch, Earl of Winchilsea, the Royal Institution was awarded its charter in 1800. This august institution's aim was the advancement of knowledge, and it fostered talents like Sir Humphrey Davy and the pioneer of electricity Michael Faraday. The Royal Institution's annual Christmas lectures became a permanent fixture among London's academic circles.

An undisputed expert in his field, Pettigrew was among distinguished company. Pettigrew's studies revealed an enormous amount about the science of mummification and ancient funerary practices, and he was the author of several books, including *A History of Egyptian Mummies*, published in 1834.

Contemporary illustrations show that lectures took place in a semicircular theatre with banked tiers of seating looking down on a central platform. Onlookers would have had a ringside view as Pettigrew kept up a running commentary while his surgeon's knife sliced through the mummy's bandages, enabling him to prise apart layers of bitumen-soaked linen to reveal the ancient scarabs and ankh or good-luck charms placed among the bandages to protect the dead. The *pièce de résistance* came when Pettigrew finally revealed with a flourish shrivelled remains and skulls to which wisps of hair were still attached. No dignity or respect was accorded to the long departed. In an age starved of novelty, people wanted drama – and this was definitely out of the ordinary.

There was a degree of showmanship surrounding Pettigrew. His lectures enthralled and horrified in equal measure. The Duke of Hamilton became so obsessed with the idea of Egyptian mummification that he commanded the eminent Egyptologist and surgeon Thomas Pettigrew to mummify his body after his death and have it interred in a granite sarcophagus and placed in the family vault in Hamilton like a pharaoh.

Stoking fears of ancient curses and mummies coming to life and stalking the streets of Piccadilly, 'mummy unwrappings' captured the imagination and sparked an entire genre of horror stories whose attraction remains unabated to this day. It certainly inspired author Elizabeth Loudon Webb, who in 1822 wrote a novel called *The Mummy* in which a mummy comes to life and strangles the young archaeologist who had it brought back from Egypt.

THE 'FREAK SHOW'

Pseudoscientific curiosity aside, the 'freak show' was one of the most popular forms of entertainment in early nineteenth-century Piccadilly. In an age hungry for novelty, the fashionable crowds paid a shilling each to see giants, dwarves and people with physical abnormalities. Standing over 8ft tall, 'The Irish Giant' Patrick Cotter O'Brien (1760–1806), from Kinsale, County Cork, had already reached the heights of stardom and medical record books.

There were plenty of venues in and around Piccadilly where the insatiable public could fulfil their need to stare at fellow human beings suffering from major abnormalities in the shapes of their bodies. The lack of empathy is alien to us and was the product of contemporary mores, totally unacceptable to our current view. So-called 'freaks of nature', people, animals or plants with unusual physical abnormalities, were common in the nineteenth century and continue to attract audiences today – for example, the so-called 'vegetable lamb' at the Garden Museum. 'Cabinets of curiosities' or 'wonder rooms' were small collections of extraordinary objects, which attempted to tell stories and organise the oddities and wonders of the natural world. The 'cabinet' idea was part of the founding concept of the Victoria and Albert Museum.

Next door to Albany lodged Daniel Lambert, billed as 'the heaviest man that ever lived'. Leicestershire-born Lambert took up residence in Piccadilly in 1806 in a house adjoining Albany. His weight, at the age of 36, was upwards of 1,218lb. Although, in most instances, when the body exceeds the usual proportions, the strength correspondingly diminishes, it is stated that this was not the case with Lambert who tested his ability by carrying more than 4½ hundredweight – a feat that many circus strongmen would fail to accomplish.

From 1825, former bookseller George Lackington took over the lease of the Egyptian Hall from William Bullock and set out to plumb new depths in tasteless entertainment. In his first year, Lackington staged a grotesque exhibition under the title, 'Anatomie Vivante or Living Skeleton'. Claude Seurat, an emaciated Frenchman who had appeared for a limited season at the Chinese Saloon, was booked as the chief attraction at the Egyptian Hall. With a height of 5ft 7in, Seurat weighed just 77¾lb, appearing as little more than skin and bone. Such exhibitions began much earlier, playing to the public awareness of the Napoleonic Wars and Francophobe sentiments encouraged by the government and the media.

Seurat was interviewed by a man called William Hone, editor of *The Every-Day Book or An Everlasting Calendar of Popular Amusements, Sports, Pastimes, Ceremonies, Manners, Customs and Events Incident to Each of the Three Hundred and Sixty-Five Days in Past and Present Times*. Satirist and bookseller, Hone got to know Seurat well and his almanack devotes eight closely printed pages and two engraved illustrations to an account of Seurat's life. We learn, for example, that 'Claude Ambroise Seurat was born at Troyes, in the department of Champaigne on the 10th April 1797, and is now therefore twenty-eight years of age'.

In *The Every-Day Book*, Hone describes how 'The Living Skeleton' would make his dramatic appearance as a hush descended on the audience seated around a small stage:

> In front of a large recess, on one side, is a circular gauze canopy over a platform covered with crimson cloth, raised about eighteen inches from the floor, and enclosed by a light brass railing.; the recess is enclosed by a light curtain depending from a cornice to the floor of the platform, and opening in the middle. A slight motion within intimates that the object of the attraction is about to appear; the curtain opens a little on each side and Seurat comes forth … with no other covering than a small piece of fringed purple silk, supported round the middle by a red band, with a slit like pocket holes, to allow the hip bones to pass through on either side.

Hone attempts to get behind the sensationalism attending 'The Living Skeleton's' public appearances. He writes, 'Some would call him [Seurat] an unhappy or a miserable creature; he is neither unhappy nor miserable. "God tempers the wind to the shorn lamb."' With memories of the Napoleonic Wars still fresh in the public's minds, audiences regarded Seurat as exemplifying the physical inferiority of the malnourished French compared with the archetypal Englishman as a hearty beef-eating John Bull.

Seurat's minders subsequently took him back to Europe on tour where the poor man died four years later at the young age of 32. It was subsequently discovered that his body contained a giant tapeworm, which had been living in his gut, depriving its host of any nourishment and ensuring that he would remain in a skeletal state.

Attractions in a similar vein included 'The Siamese Twins' in 1829: two young men from Siam conjoined at birth by a band of flesh just above the abdomen. The twins enjoyed good health and were well looked after, entertaining audiences all over the world for thirty years. The twins died in 1874 but, having been touted around fairgrounds across Britain, Europe and the USA, they were able to buy a plantation in Carolina and marry two sisters. Their marital bed was built for four – brothers Chang and Eng in the middle and their wives on either side. Between them, they conceived some twenty-one children.

In 1837 the Egyptian Hall showcased 'A living male child with four hands, four arms, four feet and two bodies, born at Stalybridge, Manchester'. Clearly this 'living child' was in fact conjoined twins.

Another of Lackington's acts was the so-called 'Missing Link', half man and half monkey, who was exposed as a fraud when one impertinent member of the audience forced his way into the beast's cage, tore off his mask and revealed the diminutive acrobat Henry Leach. The nineteenth-century world of the freak show was a curious mixture of exploitation and money-making, unleavened by empathy or fellow feeling.

THE 'HOTTENTOT VENUS'

In 1810, one of the worst examples of colonial exploitation ever to have been exhibited in Piccadilly was Saartjie Baartman, more commonly referred to as Sarah. Billed as the 'Hottentot Venus', this exhibition exceeded even contemporary insensitivity and led to a lawsuit. It was held to contravene the Slavery Act passed into law a few years earlier in 1807, which ended the slave trade but stopped short at abolishing slavery itself.

Hendrik Cesars, a mixed-race entrepreneur, and Scottish military surgeon William Dunlop bought slave Sarah, a member of the Khoikhoi people referred to by Dutch settlers as 'Hottentots'. Their aim was to take Baartman to England and show her as a fairground attraction. The shabby transaction was yet another hardship for Baartman, who had been enslaved after both her parents died.

Once in England, the trio headed for Piccadilly. As Dunlop had previously supplied William Bullock with a stuffed giraffe, his Liverpool Museum in Piccadilly was their first port of call.

Advertisements were soon being posted around Piccadilly. Sparking curiosity and lurid interest, Baartman wore a tight-fitting costume that showed off her prominent buttocks. A campaign to free her was launched by prominent abolitionists William Wilberforce and Zachary Macaulay. A benevolent society called the African Association wrote letters to the press and petitioned the court to bring charges against the men who were exploiting an innocent woman for financial gain.

On 24 November 1810, the case came up before the Court of the King's Bench. Bullock, Cesars and Dunlop were charged with breaching the Slave Trade Act of 1807. Concerned that his reputation might suffer, Bullock cancelled all Baartman's future appearances. In response, Cesars protested that Baartman was entitled to earn a living, stating, 'Has she not got as good a right to exhibit herself as an Irish Giant or a Dwarf?'

Unabashed, Dunlop and Cesars left London to tout the 'Hottentot Venus' around country fairs, where she played several musical instruments and smoked a pipe. In December 1811, Baartman was baptised at Manchester Cathedral and married on the same day. The ceremony had been a sham, as her new husband, a man called Henry Taylor, promptly sold Baartman to Frenchman Monsieur Reaux, an animal trainer who took her to his native country. Once in France, Baartman was displayed in fairground freak shows, arriving in Paris in 1814 where she was 'introduced into society'.

Baartman died on 29 December 1815 aged 26, possibly from pneumonia. The naturalist Georges Cuvier made a plaster cast of her body before dissecting it. He preserved her skeleton and pickled her brain and genitals, placing them in jars displayed at Paris's Museum of Man. There they remained on public display until 1974.

After he was elected as President of South Africa in 1994, Nelson Mandela requested the repatriation of Baartman's remains and Cuvier's plaster cast. The French Government eventually agreed and, in August 2002, Sarah's remains were buried in Hankey, Eastern Cape province, 192 years after she had left for Europe, righting a 200-year wrong.

HIGH ART AND LOW CULTURE

In 1825, the bookseller George Lackington bought the lease to the Egyptian Hall and embarked on a new career running an arts venue. Lackington's famous bookshop in Finsbury Circus, the Temple of the Muses, had made him a wealthy man and he believed that he could work the same magic by staging exhibitions that would be popular and educational.

A businessman first and foremost, Lackington realised that the venues had to pay their way. Art exhibitions would not generate enough income to cover the running costs and overheads associated with this large building. So, in 1831, the Egyptian Hall was reconfigured and its ground floor was remodelled to include two shops and a bazaar, while on the first floor, a small and a large hall were hired out for exhibitions, concerts or lectures.

Towards the end of the nineteenth century, tea merchant Jacksons of Piccadilly rented the left-hand side of the Egyptian Hall, numbered 170 Piccadilly, while the hall itself was numbered 171. The right-hand shopfront leased by Epps's chemist was numbered 173. The rent they paid helped put the Egyptian Hall's finances on an even keel.

In his two upstairs halls Lackington alternated art exhibitions with popular shows, which would generate higher revenues. The economics inevitably meant compromise between the conflicting demands of high art and low culture. Under his management, cultural events alternated with freak shows. The Egyptian Hall staged entertainments, exhibitions and lectures such as Albert Smith's magic lantern talk about his climb to the summit of Mont Blanc in 1851.

A list of temporary exhibitions staged at the Egyptian Hall, described in Timbs's *Curiosities of London*, reveal just how fickle public taste of the period was. Taken at random: in 1839, exhibitions included the skeleton of a mammoth ox and a pictorial 'Storm at Sea introducing Grace Darling and the Forfarshire Wreck'; in 1840, an exhibition of Aubusson carpets, a Gibbon monkey from Sumatra and a narrative painting by Benjamin Robert Haydon, titled 'Picture of the General Anti-Slavery Convention', were unlikely attractions.

The following year, the Egyptian Hall was devoted to 'Catlin's North American Indian Gallery consisting of 310 portraits of Indian chiefs 200 views of villages, religious ceremonies and buffalo hunts together with costumes and artefacts such as a wigwam. And filling a room one hundred feet long, the giant Missouri Leviathan skeleton.' This was clearly some unidentified whale that had become stranded in the mouth of the Missouri River. Even more bizarre was 'The Eureka, a machine for composing hexameter Latin verses',[2] which was exhibited in 1845.

GENERAL TOM THUMB

Phineas T. Barnum, the US showman, destined in the late nineteenth century to become the driving force behind Barnum and Bailey's Travelling Circus, was no stranger to Piccadilly.

At the age of 25, Barnum had begun his career by hiring a blind and almost paralysed black woman and putting her on public exhibition claiming she was 160 years old. When she eventually died, he staged a public autopsy, charging spectators 50 cents to watch.

Shortly after losing this money-spinner, the shameless Barnum proceeded to work his magic on a young distant relative named Charles Sherwood Stratton who suffered from an unusual form of dwarfism. After teaching the boy the rudiments of song and dance, he established Stratton as a vaudeville act, which he supplemented with jokes and impersonations of Cupid and Napoleon Bonaparte. Dressing Stratton up in a miniature military uniform, Barnum named his star General Tom Thumb.

General Tom Thumb came to London in 1844, establishing what would become one of the Egyptian Hall's most popular stage acts. To a great fanfare, he would appear on stage dressed in military uniform or riding a miniature horse.

General Tom Thumb was elevated from the typical fairground freak show by the careful attention Barnum paid to publicity and his total control over the performances. Such was the attraction of the versatile dwarf that London historian John Timbs reports his show generated box-office sales of around £125 a day, while in an adjoining room two monumental canvases of uplifting themes inspired by the classics, 'Nero' and 'The Banishment of Aristides' painted by Benjamin Robert Haydon, were 'scarcely visited by a dozen persons in a week'.[3]

Haydon, who had self-financed his one-man show, was bitterly disappointed. He returned to his studio in Chelsea where his wife and children noticed that he appeared withdrawn and preoccupied. A week after the disastrous public exhibition and in despair, Haydon bought a pistol and shot himself.

The period saw a popularity for dwarves, including a British challenger 'Field Marshal Tom Thumb', also known as Richard Garnsey. Born in 1831, no details of Garnsey's precise height or weight exist, but a newspaper advertisement dated 1846 dares General Tom Thumb to share the bill at the Egyptian Hall with his rival 'so that their respective admirers may judge their comparative merits'.

The Field Marshal's act included a 'series of Waterloo Tableaux representing the Duke of Wellington awaiting the arrival of the Prussians; the Duke reading the list of the killed and wounded; the Death of Napoleon and Death of Shaw the Life Guardsman etc'. It is not known how the Duke of Wellington reacted to the news that his heroic leadership was being parodied by a dwarf.

For the next eight years, Barnum and his tiny prodigy toured Britain and Europe, playing to packed audiences. A poster for the Egyptian Hall dated 1852 advertised General Tom Thumb's final tour before leaving for

America. In the bill, the star is described as '14 years old, 25 inches high and weighing only 15 pounds'.

Tickets to his thrice-daily performances at the Egyptian Hall were priced at 1s, with children admitted for half the price. In addition to these daily appearances, Barnum boasted that the 'General and his miniature equipage would Promenade the Streets Daily'.

THE GREATEST SHOW ON EARTH

It seemed as if the world could not get enough of Tom Thumb. If Barnum's hyperbole is to be believed, General Tom Thumb had performed before all the crowned heads of Europe on his tour, including 'Queen Victoria, Prince Albert, the King and Queen of the French, the King and Queen of the Belgians and the Emperor of Russia as well as the Royal Families of Spain'. Barnum's handbill threw in all of the nobility of those countries for good measure. Queen Victoria was given a command performance by Barnum and his star at Windsor Castle.

Barnum's visits to Britain were highly profitable. While on tour in 1850, Barnum was introduced to the opera singer Jenny Lind, popularly known as 'The Swedish Nightingale'. He offered her $1,000 a night to sing in America. Lind's ensuing tour of the USA netted Barnum nearly $15 million in today's money.

He went on to assemble an entire cast of dwarves, including an equally little dwarf woman called Lavinia Warren who Stratton fell in love with and married in 1863. Predictably, Barnum billed the wedding as the event of the year. General Tom Thumb lived with his wife in Connecticut. He died of a stroke aged just 45 in 1883 and was buried in his home city of Bridgeport.

By now P.T. Barnum was well on the way to becoming the world's greatest showman. The circus he launched with James Anthony Bailey in 1871, which became known as 'The Greatest Show on Earth', featured a menagerie of exotic animals, magicians, mechanical marvels and 'freaks', reprising a formula that would have been familiar to audiences at the Egyptian Hall.

Nor was this the end of the story. For on Bailey's death in 1906, Ringling Brothers bought the name and, using the familiar formula of a big top and sawdust ring, 'The Greatest Show on Earth' survived and thrived until 2017.

MAGIC, ILLUSION AND AUTOMATA

Magic shows exercised a strong appeal for audiences hungry for novelty. Crude entertainments had always occupied a niche at fairs where fire-eaters, sword-swallowers, jugglers and acrobats were a staple entertainment for the masses.

An indispensable part of the magic show were automata – intricately constructed dummies whose parts and movements were guided by hidden clockwork mechanisms and rods and pulleys. Automata were a well-established Piccadilly attraction that had thrilled the sophisticated audiences for generations. They were like moving waxworks.

One of the earliest and finest examples was John Dubourg's Mechanical Exhibition, also known as Dubourg's Saloon of Arts, in Windmill Street, Piccadilly. Here were exhibited 500 life-sized automaton figures created by Signor Gagliardi. The figures peopled various tableaux including 'The Slave Market at Constantinople', 'The Brigand's Group', 'The Canadian Insurrectionists' and 'The Coronation of the Queen'. 'The group of Androcles and the Lion is one of the most perfect pieces of mechanical skill we ever saw and is alone worth the whole of the admission money,' gushed the *New Monthly Belle Assemblée* in June 1839.

As late as 1846, the Egyptian Hall exhibited what must surely have been one of the most sophisticated efforts at robotics ever attempted. The attraction was billed as 'Professor Faber's Euphonia or speaking automaton, enunciating sounds and word; played by keys', and was as close as it got to artificial intelligence in the early 1800s.[4]

The celebrated French conjuror and illusionist Jean-Eugène Robert-Houdin regularly topped the bill at the St James's Theatre from 1848 to around 1850. Known as 'the father of modern magic', Robert-Houdin had fled Paris, along with the French court of Louis Philippe, in the wake of the 1848 revolution, bringing with him his stage show known as 'Soirées Fantastique'.

A skilled clockmaker, Robert-Houdin constructed automata such as his mechanical nightingale, a delicate butterfly, a miniature trapeze artist and a mysterious clock supported by a column of crystal with a transparent glass on which the hands moved without any clockwork mechanism being visible. He performed card tricks and enlisted his son Eugène Houdin to be blindfolded, hypnotised and made to float in mid-air in a prone position supported by nothing more than a flimsy rod. Robert-Houdin went on to become one of the founders of the celebrated magicians' club, the Magic Circle.

By the late nineteenth century Robert-Houdin's name had passed into legend. Then two American brothers, Ehrich and Theo Weiss, entertained audiences at the Chicago World Fair in 1893 as the Houdini Brothers. The name of their act was a tribute to Robert-Houdin. Their act involved a new version of a much older escapology trick based on the padlocked box devised by the British magician John Nevil Maskelyne. The older of the two built a solo career as Harry Houdini, a daredevil whose public spectacles included being strapped into a strait jacket, handcuffed and shut inside a heavy pad-locked box submerged in a tank of water.

ENGLAND'S HOME OF MYSTERY

In 1873, two enterprising young magicians, John Nevil Maskelyne and George Cooke, booked the smaller of the Egyptian Hall's two public rooms to entertain the public with 'dramatic feats of escapology'. Playing to packed houses, the show was so successful that Maskelyne and Cooke went on to take a lease on the entire building and remained resident until the hall was demolished in 1905. For over thirty years, spellbound audiences were treated to automata that could play musical instruments and paint pic-tures, the greatest illusions of all time, including the famous 'vanishing lady', and some of the very first moving pictures ever shown. Piccadilly's most popular attraction, the Egyptian Hall became known as 'England's Home of Mystery'.

J.N. Maskelyne was born on 22 December 1839 in Cheltenham, the son of a saddler. As a young man he was apprenticed to a watchmaker, a highly skilled trade that led to an interest in automata – making complex clockwork figures that could be designed to perform tricks. His other hobby was play-ing in a band, which is where he met George Cooke, the man who was to become his business partner.

A cabinetmaker by trade, Cooke shared Maskelyne's love of clockwork automata, and the pair enjoyed being amateur magicians. The catalyst that propelled them into show business was one night in March 1865 when they visited a performance at Cheltenham Town Hall by a touring act from the USA: two so-called 'spirit mediums' called the Davenport Brothers. Maskelyne and Cooke saw through the clumsy illusions the perform-ers used to fool the gullible audience. They easily exposed the fraud by hiring the hall later that year and reproducing exactly the same effects to a startled public.

The pair designed their own magic shows and took to the road with a tour of provincial theatres and music halls, eventually appearing at the Crystal

Palace and St James's Hall, Piccadilly. They were even booked to perform for the Prince of Wales at Sandringham in 1875 – an honour that prompted them to advertise themselves as 'The Royal Illusionists'.

Initially booked to appear for three months, Maskelyne and Cooke were so successful, they would stay on for another thirty years. Small by modern standards, the gloomy Egyptian Hall was lit by a domed skylight and could accommodate up to 300 people. There was a gallery with balcony seats, ten rows of stalls and in front two rows of comfortable armchairs and sofas (fauteuils). Affordable ticketing and endless fascination for children gave the shows a strong family appeal. In 1873 stalls cost 3s, the balcony was priced at 1s and 2s, while the fauteuils closest to the stage were 5s each.

A skilled watchmaker, Maskelyne excelled in making the kind of automata that had been an earlier feature of Robert-Houdin's 'Soirées Fantastique'. He created a card-playing Turk named 'Psycho' who could mechanically deal a pack of playing cards and play at whist with three persons chosen at random from the audience. The magician's other showstoppers were a mechanical artist named 'Zoe', who could draw pictures on a glass screen, and two small musicians able to play the cornet and the euphonium, both instruments requiring a considerable amount of puff.

Maskelyne and Cooke's longest-running illusion was a stage play titled *Will, the Witch and the Watchman*. This called upon the skilled carpentry of George Cooke, who was able to make boxes and cabinets with false bottoms, which would appear empty to an audience one minute before suddenly opening to reveal a person or a strange beast who would then leap out onto the stage as if by magic.

The author Walter MacQueen-Pope was a child when he saw an early film version of this act shown shortly before the hall closed in 1905:

The scene was a village green, and in the midst stood, very oddly, a large cabinet ... The Witch was locked in – you saw her – yet a second later, when the doors were thrown open, she was not there but a huge monkey was there instead, and you saw the Witch fly through the air on a broomstick. And that monkey changed into all sorts of people you never suspected were there at all ... Children were pleasantly frightened or filled with amazed delight and grown-ups, who would not have shown their feelings for the world, felt exactly the same as their small charges.[5]

In 1886, Maskelyne and Cooke staged the famous 'vanishing lady' illusion, which had been invented by the French illusionist Buatier de Kolta, an act that was so popular it was referenced by Alfred Hitchcock in his 1939 film *The Lady Vanishes*, starring Margaret Lockwood, Michael Redgrave and Dame May Whitty. The 'illusionist' in this case turned out to be an enemy agent.

In the original version of this illusion, magician Charles Bertram presented the trick aided by Mlle Patrice. A newspaper was spread over the floor and a chair placed on top of the paper to dismiss any suspicion that a trap door would be used. Then the lady sat down. The magician threw a purple cloth over the lady so that she was completely covered before grasping the cloth in both hands and tossing it into the air. At the same moment, the cloth and the lady vanished. To round off the illusion, the magician would pick up the chair, fold up the newspaper and depart the stage.

What had happened? Known only to a few members of the Magic Circle, the trick was accomplished with mirrors. There were two identical newspapers and chairs but only one lady who remained hidden when the mirror image was suddenly switched. Tricks like this mystified Victorian audiences. Actors springing out of securely padlocked boxes or appearing to float in mid-air were illusions based on the cunning use of mirrors and trap doors. Nevil Maskelyne was appointed president of the Magic Circle.

Maskelyne, Cooke and a close-knit circle of friends and family members, including Maskelyne's two sons, Nevil and Edwin, took part in dramatic sketches featuring special effects like 'The Entranced Fakir' and 'The Philosopher's Stone'. Edwin's fiancée Cassie Bruce stood in as the vanishing lady and acted in numerous other magic tricks.

George Cooke died in February 1905, working to the last. J.N. Maskelyne died in May 1917, leaving the business to be run by surviving family members. When Edwin and Cassie married in 1907, the Dundee *Evening Telegraph and Post* headline ran 'Wizard's Wedding Mr Maskelyne to marry Disappearing Lady'!

MOVING PICTURES

In 1893, a conjuror called David Devant joined the company, initially as a supporting act and later as a business partner. Like Maskelyne before him, Devant would also be elected as president of the famous Magic Circle. Under Devant's influence, the Egyptian Hall became one of the pioneers of the cinema, regarded in its early days as a magical illusion.

The first public showing of a motion picture in London was at the Royal Polytechnic Institute, Regent Street, in late February using Lumière's

Cinematograph. Just days later, on 19 March, Devant introduced his 'Animated Photographs' at the Egyptian Hall using a patented film projector, the 'Bioscope'.

Within weeks, Lumière and Devant were locked in fierce competition as the Alhambra Theatre in Leicester Square installed a Bioscope and the nearby Empire Theatre showed Cinematograph moving pictures. A rival invention, the American Biograph, became a regular feature at the Palace Theatre, Cambridge Circus. Devant took to the road and toured provincial venues with his new invention.

The Bioscope rapidly became one of the Egyptian Hall's most popular attractions. For a short time, Maskelyne and Cooke turned their hands to film-making. With images often appearing blurred or flickering, moving pictures were very crude. Storylines had to be kept simple. In one popular film, a fast-approaching express train would appear in the distance and get closer and closer until it took up the entire screen, as if it would burst through and crash into the audience, who by now were on the edge of their seats. Other films showed a horse-drawn fire engine racing to the scene of a fire, Gladstone's funeral, Queen Victoria's Golden Jubilee procession, the Henley Regatta and the Derby.

Groundbreaking though it was, Devant's Bioscope was soon eclipsed by other, more reliable competitors. The final nail in the coffin came in 1905 when highly flammable nitrate film caused a huge fire at a cinema in Paris, leading to an immediate crackdown. Stringent new safety laws forced the closure of many early moving-picture houses, including Devant's.

In 1905, Maskelyne and Cooke moved to St George's Hall in Langham Place, where the business was passed to the founder's eldest son. The Maskelyne family continued to run England's Home of Mystery throughout the interwar years until St George's Hall was destroyed by enemy action in May 1941. David Devant died in October of that same year.

The last of the dynasty, Nevil's son Jasper, joined the army and was promoted to the rank of major in the Royal Engineers. Tasked with concealing British tanks and army equipment from being spotted by enemy aircraft, Major Maskelyne's Camouflage Experimental Section confused the enemy with dummy tanks, aircraft and field guns constructed out of wood and canvas. Using this illusion first in North Africa and then in the run-up to D-Day, Maskelyne's 'ghost army' was said to have played a key part in the success of the D-Day landings, helping to save lives and shorten the war.

The names Maskelyne and Cooke were recently revived in the shape of a magic-themed cocktail bar at Le Méridien Hotel on Piccadilly Circus, which opened in 2018. It is a small tribute to two colossi of the world of magic.

BIRTH OF THE LEISURE AND ENTERTAINMENTS INDUSTRY

Over three centuries, Piccadilly's popular entertainments reveal surprising continuity. Astley's equestrian shows drew their inspiration from fairgrounds, and there was more than a hint of the circus about the freak shows and magical illusions that formed the staple diet of the Egyptian Hall during the nineteenth century. Fascination with illusion is shot right through Piccadilly's history, from Dubourg's museum of automata to Maskelyne and Cooke's card-dealing robot 'Psycho' and Fortnum and Mason's clock.

Despite their supposed sophistication, modern audiences have been held spellbound by the weird and wonderful. From August 2008 until September 2017, the London Pavilion housed 'Ripley's Believe It or Not!', a franchised exhibition based on the unbelievable phenomena that inspired Robert Ripley's long-running US newspaper cartoon strip 'Believe It or Not!', which ran from 1918 and spawned a museum of carefully curated oddities.

If it had been around 200 years ago, 'Ripley's Believe It or Not!' would have struck a chord with Georgian audiences. Its collection of freaks of nature, like a stuffed two-headed calf, a fish with feathers, a mermaid, shrunken heads and waxworks of the world's tallest man and the world's most tattooed woman, capture the true spirit of old London. The more Piccadilly changes, the more it remains the same.

5

THE WEST END SHOPS

If I were on the turf, and had a horse to enter for the Derby, I would call
that horse Fortnum and Mason convinced that by that name he would beat
the field. Public opinion would bring him in somehow.

Charles Dickens, from Household Words

A NATION OF SHOPKEEPERS

The French Emperor Napoleon famously described the English as 'a nation
of shopkeepers'. Far from being the insult he intended, he was describing
an independent and hard-working nation that embraced enterprise and self-
sufficiency and generally took pleasure in acquiring beautiful things.

By the dawn of the nineteenth century, Piccadilly had become noted for its
many shops. Its character, however, was more like a busy high street but one
that included a great many purveyors of luxury goods. In many ways, this is
how it appears today – although most institutions and business models have
changed profoundly. The area is in a constant state of evolution, adapting to
changed circumstances with creativity and flair.

Georgian and early nineteenth-century shops tended to be small
family-run enterprises. These were often highly specialised, selling a single
product often manufactured on site. A hatter, for example, made and sold
hats to order, a cabinet maker would have supervised tradesmen and possibly
apprentices building bespoke furniture, and so on. There were also 'warehouses': large shops that specialised in bulk orders such as brides' trousseaux
or furnishing houses from top to bottom.

Piccadilly was becoming a shopping destination for luxury goods. In Vigo Street and Sackville Street there were four goldsmiths and jewellers. Today, the retail end of this business is still prominent in Burlington Arcade.

The heyday of the department store in the late nineteenth century coincided with the arrival of mass-transit public transport. Easily accessible by the new Underground railway, Regent Street and Oxford Street became a popular shopping destination. Browsing for fashionable clothes or home furnishings was a leisure activity increasingly enjoyed by young women and comfortably off middle-class housewives from the suburbs.

For the locals, there were always markets like Berwick Street in Soho and Shepherd's Market at the western end of Piccadilly to supply their daily needs.

A CORNUCOPIA OF SMALL BUSINESSES

One of a number of trade directories published at the end of the eighteenth and early nineteenth century, *Kent's Directory* provides a snapshot of the small- and large-scale commercial activity taking place across London. It is, as its title page proclaims:

An Alphabetical LIST of the NAMES and PLACES of ABODE of the DIRECTORS of COMPANIES, Persons in Public Business, Merchants, and other eminent TRADERS in the CITIES of London and Westminster and the Borough of Southwark.

Kent's Directory for 1801 lists around 10,300 shops and businesses across London. The area of Piccadilly was served by no fewer than seventy-eight shops and warehouses, mostly small family-run enterprises.

The sheer variety of trades that could be found in Piccadilly in 1801 is staggering. There was an undertaker, a bootmaker, an engraver, an auctioneer, an 'artificial florist', a black lead pencil maker, a paper hanger, a turner and toymaker, a gunmaker, a Tunbridgeware repository selling marquetry boxes, an optician, a wireworker, a cheesemonger and several saddlers. Everyday items such as oil for household lamps, hardware and crockery were supplied by an ironmonger, an 'oilman', a 'hardwareman' and a 'chinaman'. This mix of shops supplied useful everyday household items and luxury or specialised manufactured articles like guns and saddles.

Some businesses stand out, suggesting that Piccadilly itself was becoming a destination for shoppers seeking certain goods and services. *Kent's Directory* lists Charles Fortnum as 'Grocer and Tea Dealer' at 183 Piccadilly. He was one of eight grocers in the locality, many of whom supplied tea, another luxury. Several others differentiated themselves by being 'wax chandlers' – suppliers of candles. From humble beginnings, Charles Fortnum not only survived but thrived. The shop grew into the internationally famous store, Fortnum and Mason.

Many businesses catered for a mainly male clientele. Saddlers, harness makers and leather cutters served a thriving equestrian economy that included coaching inns, riding schools and stables, as well as the nationally important Tattersall's horse repository and auction rooms. A cluster of twelve linen drapers found in the side streets around Piccadilly Circus supplied dandies with fresh linen and neckcloths, then the height of masculine fashion. Thomas Hunter describes his shop at 17 Mary-le-bon Street as a 'Man's Mercer'.

Cabinet-making and upholstery was another growth area with eight firms listed, including Ince and Mayhew of Grafton Street and Thomas Sheraton of Wardour Street. Given the area's associations with the upper classes and gentlemen of 'the middling sort', there were no fewer than five wine merchants, three of whom had premises in Jermyn Street. Berry Bros & Rudd of St James's was at this stage in its history redirecting its efforts from being a coffee importer to dealing in wine and brandy. The commercial scales were also used by the likes of Beau Brummel, Lord Alvanley and the Prince Regent to check their weight. You can still see the ledger recording this upon request.

TEA, COFFEE AND SPICES

In 1660, the East India Company presented Charles II with 2lb 2oz of black tea. The drink was already popular in Portugal and was a favourite of the king's young bride, the Infanta Catherine of Braganza, who introduced tea drinking at court. The ceremony of tea drinking, which involved blending different types of tea leaves and adding milk and sugar, allowed ladies to show off their fine china cups and saucers, silver spoons and tea caddies, as well as their discerning taste in their mixing of the teas. The gentlemen were keen too: Alexander Charles 'Teapot' Crawfurd earned his nickname by always carrying a small Wedgwood basaltware teapot with him on campaign.

Originally named Portugal Street in honour of Catherine of Braganza, Piccadilly owes more than a little to the queen's royal influence. As part of her dowry, Catherine brought with her a gift of the 'island of Bumbye' (Bombay), then a Portuguese trading colony. The addition of Bombay to the East India Company's growing tally of entrepôts would be a significant factor in the company's expansion and its aggressive takeover of the imploding and strife-ridden Mughal Empire.

As the East India Company built its trading influence in Calcutta, Madras, Bombay and Delhi through the deployment of its private army, a steady stream of spices, teas, muslin, calicos and silver bullion flowed into London. This financial empire was built on ruthless exploitation and a firm belief that European interests – British, Dutch, French and Portuguese – were more important than the well-being and rights of local people, from whatever continent.

Besides the teas and spices from India, sugar, raw cotton, indigo, coffee and mahogany flowed in from the West Indies. These commodities were reflected in Piccadilly's shops from the seventeenth century onwards, which included tea dealers, spice merchants and coffee importers. Piccadilly's shops thrived on luxury imports. George Jackson's 'India Muslin Warehouse' at 212 Piccadilly was patronised by ladies of the haut ton.

The high prices commanded by tea, coffee and sugar reflect not only changing social customs but the high cost of sending the navy to defend vital trade routes. Taxes were raised on sugar imports to pay for fighting the American War of Independence, while the high duty on tea was one of the issues that sparked the war itself.

From an early date, Fortnum and Mason advertised themselves as 'Grocers and Tea Dealers'. To lay claim to being a tea dealer set one apart from a run-of-the-mill grocery store. Contemporary sources reveal that tea was six to ten times the cost of coffee.

Now a tourist tea and souvenir shop, John and Richard Twining's Tea Warehouse, established in 1800 at 216 The Strand, is still trading from the same address today. Over the years, Twining's has supplied many of Piccadilly's tea dealers and grocers.

READING FOR PLEASURE

Contemporary trade directories reveal that Piccadilly was associated with bookselling and publishing from the mid-eighteenth century. Historically the trade had been centred around St Paul's near to Stationer's Hall. Now it had started to expand westward. The street's booksellers included John Almon, who set up in Piccadilly in 1763, James Ridgway, John Stockdale,

John White, William Pickering, Thomas Thorpe, John Debrett, John Burke and, of course, John Hatchard. By the early 1800s, their shops clustered on the south side of the street from St James's Church, Piccadilly, all the way to St James's Street.

Many booksellers published books on their own account as they were well placed to spot market opportunities. Religious or political tracts were highly popular. Listed as a bookseller, John Debrett occupied premises at 179 Piccadilly; he had taken over the business from the radical John Almon, who traded at 178 Piccadilly between 1763 and 1781. Today, his name is better known as the originator of *Debrett's Peerage*.

With four major coaching inns, the street was a destination for travellers into and out of London, and Piccadilly was an attractive location for booksellers on account of passing trade. Numerous coffee houses attracted a literate and influential clientele, including Members of Parliament, clergymen and lawyers. The ducal mansions that lined Piccadilly and the gentlemen's clubs of St James's possessed substantial libraries.

POLEMICISTS AND PAMPHLETEERS

Piccadilly booksellers and publishers played a leading role in the fight for American Independence. Their role in exporting books and pamphlets to America and in making the case for independence to the British Parliament played a major role in influencing opinion on both sides of the Atlantic.

Interest in political literature was running high and the Piccadilly bookseller-pamphleteers John Almon, John Stockdale and James Ridgway found their shops had become meeting places for radicals and political activists. Their bookshops stood opposite Burlington House, then at the centre of a powerful Whig coterie. Despite support from high places, anyone publishing or selling a tract deemed by the government to be seditious could find themselves prosecuted, imprisoned and in all probability bankrupted.

In 1763, John Almon opened a bookshop at 178 Piccadilly where he published many books by Americans and selected authors and titles that championed the freedom of colonists rebelling against British interference in their affairs. Almon became a close associate of the American printer, scientist and diplomat Benjamin Franklin who, as a representative of Pennsylvania, lived in England from the mid 1750s until 1775. When in London, Franklin lodged in a house in Craven Street just off the Strand, close enough to Almon's bookshop to make him a regular visitor.

In January 1775, largely as a result of the American connection, Almon published the *Journal of the Proceedings of Congress*, making him one of the very first English publishers to recognise the legitimacy of independence. He also published the work of another influential American statesman, John Quincy Adams, who later became the sixth President of the USA.

In May 1767 Almon, with help from Wilkes, published *The Political Register*, a pamphlet that, among other things, campaigned for the government to repeal the Stamp Act, which imposed duties on many everyday items imported by the American colonists, including newspapers, books and legal documents. The colonists were vocal supporters of Wilkes, enthusiastically joining in the popular cry 'Wilkes and Liberty'. The Stamp Act was finally repealed in March 1766.

Almon handed over the business to his partner John Debrett in 1781.

A 'LITERARY COFFEE HOUSE'

One eighteenth-century bookseller not only survived these turbulent times, but is still trading in the same location having passed through the hands of different owners. When 29-year-old John Hatchard set up as a bookseller at 173 Piccadilly, he took over an existing shop, White's, and agreed to buy the outgoing bookseller's 'goodwill' for £31 10s. Having laid out all of the money at his disposal, Hatchard wrote in his diary, 'This day, by the grace of God, the good will of my friends and £5 in my pocket, I have opened my bookshop in Piccadilly, 30th June, 1797.'

Hatchard had learned his trade thoroughly, first as an apprentice to John Ginger, who had a shop in Great College Street, Westminster, and later as a shopman to Thomas Payne, bookseller of Mews Gate, Castle Street, St Martin's, just to the north of what is now Trafalgar Square. Unusual among booksellers, Payne ran a coffee house alongside his main business, a selling point that attracted customers to stop and browse. The 'literary coffee house' was an idea John Hatchard eagerly embraced.

The highly charged, intellectual nature of the coffee-house debate overflowed into the literary world. Specific coffee houses were closely associated with authors, poets, journalists and wits in what was to be a foretaste of late-Victorian café society. The coffee houses of St James's were attracting authors and men of letters like Alexander Pope, Joseph Addison and Richard Steele.

Although there is no evidence to suggest that Hatchard actually sold coffee, he offered hospitality and an open fire. Intellectual conversation acted as a social lubricant, and favoured customers would sit and take their time reading and discussing the books offered for sale.

Soon Hatchards was attracting not just these luminaries but politicians like George Canning, William Wilberforce and the evangelical preacher and social campaigner Sydney Smith. Writing in the *Edinburgh Review*, a magazine he co-founded in 1802 with Francis Jeffery and Henry Brougham, Smith describes:

> a set of well-dressed prosperous gentlemen who assemble daily at Mr Hatchard's shop, clean, civil personages, well-in with the people in power, delighted with every existing institution and almost with every existing circumstance; and every now and then one of these personages writes a book, and the rest praise that little book, expecting to be praised in turn for their own little books.[1]

Hatchard was a Tory, but above all else, an evangelical Christian. The first title he published was a patriotic pamphlet, *Reform or Ruin? Take Your Choice* by John Bowdler. Shortly after, Hatchard was appointed publisher to *The Christian Observer* and also of the *Reports of the Society for Bettering the Condition and Increasing the Comforts of the Poor*, an anti-slavery organisation founded in 1797 by William Wilberforce, Sir Thomas Bernard and E.J. Eliot. The society held its meetings at Hatchards and went on to form the nucleus of the Clapham Sect, a 'Low Church' reforming body within the Church of England.

Hatchard's 'literary coffee house' did not just attract pious Christian reformers and anti-slavery campaigners; the stock of books was varied enough to appeal to horticulturalists, for at a meeting held at the house of Mr Hatchard the publisher in Piccadilly, the Royal Horticultural Society was founded on 7 March 1804.

By this time, the business had grown so rapidly that it had moved seven doors down to a bigger shop at 187 Piccadilly. Today, Hatchards still occupies the same premises that it acquired in 1801.

BURLINGTON ARCADE

His mansion may have been surrounded by high walls but it was said that 'the great annoyance to which the garden is subject from the inhabitants of a neighbouring street throwing oyster shells &c over the wall' prompted Lord

George Cavendish, the new owner of Burlington House, to build a row of shops along the west wall to act as a screen.[2]

Lord George, 1st Earl of Burlington, had just moved back into his uncle's house, and he needed to incorporate a shopping arcade and a row of shops along the frontage of his house to generate a rental income that would fund an ambitious programme of improvements. These works included a complete remodelling of the interior of Burlington House based around a grand staircase and a series of interconnecting public rooms, which were built between 1815 and 1819.

Redevelopment of the house to provide a rental income was considered. One scheme involved demolishing the boundary wall facing Piccadilly on either side of the great gate to build a parade of shops with apartments above.

In 1818, architect Samuel Ware was tasked with drawing up plans for a covered passageway lined with shops between Piccadilly and Vigo Street. The arcade was top lit with glass roof lights and accommodated seventy-two small two-storey shops 'for the sale of jewellery and fancy articles of fashionable demand, for the gratification of the public'. Each end of the passageway would be closed off by means of iron gates and railings.

The arcade opened on 20 March 1820 as a private shopping mall, built as a place where genteel ladies and gentlemen could shop safely away from the dirty and crime-ridden streets of London. At night the gates would be locked to keep the shopping precinct safe. In order to preserve the exclusivity, entry to the arcade would be restricted to the beau monde and patrolled by beadles recruited from troopers who had served with Lord George's regiment, the 10th Hussars. They were tasked with ensuring that aristocratic shoppers adhered to a strict set of by-laws that forbade running, singing, carrying large parcels and opening umbrellas anywhere in the arcade.

From the outset the arcade was a commercial success and followed in the tradition of covered malls in cities across Europe, including the Palais-Royal in Paris, which opened in 1784, and the Galerie Feydeau, 1791, the Galeries Royales Saint-Hubert in Brussels and the Galleria Umberto I in Naples.

Burlington Arcade was the forerunner of several West End shopping arcades, notably Royal Arcade and Prince's Arcade connecting Piccadilly with Jermyn Street and the Royal Opera Arcade running from Charles Street, Haymarket to Pall Mall. Arcades provided covered shopping and semi-private spaces ideal for small high-value luxury goods and art galleries.

Burlington Arcade was partly destroyed by fire in 1836 and badly damaged in a bombing raid during the Second World War. Today, with rebuilding and consolidation of small boutiques into bigger units, there are forty shops lining the arcade, including luxury brands that include Manolo Blahnik, Penhaligon's, Church's Shoes, Lalique and Crockett & Jones. The arcade is now owned by David and Simon Reuben who bought the lease in 2018.

BY ROYAL APPOINTMENT

The origins of the royal warrant go back a long way – to the Middle Ages, in fact. Royal purchases were made through an institution and an actual place called 'The Great Wardrobe', which was located at Baynard's Castle, close to the Thames at Puddle Wharf, Blackfriars. Keepers of the Wardrobe procured cloths, hangings, beds and carpets for use by the royal household. Built by the Normans, the original castle burnt down in the reign of King John, but its successor was used as a palace by Henry VII and gifted by his son Henry VIII to Catherine of Aragon shortly before their wedding. It was destroyed in the Great Fire of London in 1666.

By the seventeenth century, purchases for Whitehall and St James's Palace were organised through two officials, the Lord Steward and the Lord Chamberlain. Everything above stairs, such as robes, saddlery, furniture, artists and craftsmen, was the former's responsibility. The Lord Chamberlain looked after the kitchen including equipment, the supply of food and produce, wine and everything from coal to lamp oil. Often tradesmen would pay these powerful officials a fee or payment in kind in return for being awarded an exclusive warrant. It was a system that encouraged corruption and graft. By the time the Royal Warrant Holders' Association had been formed in 1840 this abuse had been stamped out.

The merchants of Piccadilly and St James's were uniquely placed to hold royal warrants because of the proximity of the court. Among the early royal warrant holders were Johnson and Justerini, forerunners of the wine merchant Justerini and Brooks, who in 1779 were able to advertise themselves as 'Foreign Cordial Merchants to the Prince of Wales'. The royal warrant of Jermyn Street perfumer, Floris, was first awarded by King George IV in 1820. When a firm or shop added the description 'supplier to His Majesty' it was generally understood to be a mark of quality.

Kent's Directory of 1800 lists a number of firms as having a royal connection. These included William Allnutt, woodturner to His Majesty, 183 Piccadilly;

Cooper D. & P. Silk Mercers to His Majesty, 28 Pall Mall; David Davies, sword-cutter to His Majesty, 10 St James's Street; Gee, chairmaker and turner to His Majesty, 49 Wardour Street, Soho; Perrigall and Duterrau, watchmakers to His Majesty, 57 New Bond Street; and Thomas Taylor, shoemaker to the Royal Family, 9 Old Bond Street.

Swaine and Co., 'Whip-makers to his Majesty' at 238 Piccadilly, antecedent of the luxury leather, umbrella and cane retailer Swaine Adeney Brigg can be found today at 7 Piccadilly Arcade, still the proud owner of a royal warrant.

The system of royal warrants was formalised early in the reign of Queen Victoria when a group of twenty-five warrant holders met on 25 May 1840 at the Freemason's Tavern in Great Queen Street to form a dining club. They proposed holding an annual dinner on the queen's birthday. It was proposed that the club be named 'The Royal Tradesmen's Association for the Annual Celebration of Her Majesty's Birthday'.

The following year's annual dinner attracted eighty guests and was the birth of the Royal Warrant Holders' Association. The Piccadilly grocer Fortnum and Mason was awarded its royal warrant that same year, and still has it to this day.

MR FORTNUM AND MR MASON

When royal footman William Fortnum met shopkeeper Hugh Mason of St James's Market few would have guessed that the friendship would lay the foundations of a Piccadilly grocery store destined to grow into a world-famous luxury brand.

Fortnum lodged at Mr Mason's house, and his work in Queen Anne's St James's Palace came with a valuable perquisite. The queen insisted on having fresh candles every night, allowing Mr Fortnum to dispose of the old ones. These part-used candles were sold in Mason's shop. Trade was so brisk that eventually Fortnum left royal service and the pair were able to set up in a small shop in Duke Street, Piccadilly, selling groceries and candles. The year was 1707.

When Fortnum and Mason started trading, candles were still the only means of domestic lighting. Quality refined wax candles were highly prized as they lasted longer and gave a better light. In those days, poor people, if they had any artificial light at all, used rush lights – dried rush stems dipped in wax held by an iron clip. The majority of candles were made of tallow or pig's fat, which smoked when lit and smelt bad. Only the better off could afford pure beeswax candles and then they were used sparingly, say in a candelabra to light up a dinner table, a wall sconce to reflect light in a dim passageway, or for a single candlestick to provide light for reading, needlework or to light the way to the bedroom.

The shop also stocked other luxury products such as tea imported from India and China, refined sugar processed in London from raw molasses shipped back from plantations in the West Indies and spices imported from India. As the East India Company rose to prominence and overseas trade became more reliable, so West End grocers in particular began to stock foodstuffs seen as essential ingredients of aristocratic fine dining. Fortnum and Mason started advertising itself as 'Tea Dealer and Spice Importer'.

Through the eighteenth and nineteenth centuries, the famous store went through various changes, passing down the generations as family members entered or left the business, but always expanding. William Fortnum and Hugh Mason were succeeded by their sons, but it would appear that the Fortnum family not only inherited a share of the business but took over the day-to-day running. *The London Directory* for 1771 lists 'Charles Fortnum, Grocer' as trading from a shop that stood on part of the site of the present store. Three years later, business was clearly booming as Fortnum took on the lease of the next-door premises, thereby expanding his store. On his death in 1814, Charles Fortnum esquire of Reading made a will leaving his share of the family business to his three children, Charles, Richard and Ann.

In 1817, the Mason family appear once more as John Mason joins Charles Fortnum to become a partner in the business, now listed in *Kent's Directory* as 'Fortnum and Mason, Tea Dealers and Grocers'. A new wave of expansion came in 1834 as the freeholder granted the partners long leases on what were now three adjoining properties, including a warehouse to the rear with an entrance on Duke Street. Fortnum and Mason were therefore able to redevelop the site to create a single block. The new store was opened in 1835.

Continuing to expand, Fortnum and Mason took over the shop adjoining to the west in 1844 and, in 1909, acquired a small shop on the corner of Duke Street, enabling the store to consolidate. Dating from 1926, the present building fronts onto Piccadilly and Duke Street and extends back as far as Jermyn Street.

Becoming a fully integrated department store, Fortnum and Mason's ground floor is given over to tea, confectionery and luxury foodstuffs. With a food hall and wine and spirit department in the basement, the store includes china and fashion departments, a café and a restaurant. Combining tradition with modernity, the store's image is best expressed through the eye-catching turquoise used throughout the store on everything from interior design to publicity and marketing material.

A symbol of Fortnum and Mason, the giant clock on the store front features two carved automata modelled on the firm's founders Mr Fortnum and Mr Mason. They appear from behind closed doors to meet on the hour and bow to each other to the accompaniment of chiming bells playing eighteenth-century tunes. This quirky clock may look ancient but in fact was installed in 1964. Its complex mechanism took three years to make and was the work of Thwaites & Reed of Clerkenwell, clockmakers since 1740.

THE FORTNUM HAMPER

Fortnum's was and still is associated with that great British institution, the food hamper. Specialising in pre-cooked or preserved delicacies and fine wines, a Fortnum hamper was a substantial wickerwork carrying case in which foodstuffs were cushioned against accidental damage by wood shavings.

By the 1730s, Fortnum and Mason were preparing hampers for travellers to sustain themselves on long coach journeys. Their shop was near several busy coaching inns including the White Horse Cellar and the White Bear. Food needed to be pre-cooked and prepared so that it would remain fresh enough on a long and bumpy coach ride. Carved ham, game pie, pickled vegetables and rich fruit cake were a favourite.

In 1738, Fortnum and Mason were credited with inventing the Scotch egg, a hard-boiled egg wrapped in sausage meat and coated with breadcrumbs. It was an instant success and became a staple of the Fortnum hamper.

Over the coming years, the hamper grew more sophisticated to cater for a new luxury market beyond the hard-pressed stage-coach traveller. At the height of its popularity, the hamper became indelibly associated with summer garden parties and outdoor sporting occasions. A hamper might contain a couple of bottles of champagne or fine wine, a tin of pâté de foie gras, bottles of condiments, lobster salad, dressed crab, ham, pickled walnuts and an Indian pickle called piccalilli – providing an al fresco feast for which servants laid out a tablecloth and opened a canteen of cutlery for the diners.

In her 1758 cookery book, Hannah Glasse gives the recipe for piccalillo, or pickle lila, describing it as a spicy mix of preserved vegetables including gherkin, onion and cauliflower cooked with mustard and turmeric. An even earlier recipe exists from 1694. Fortnum's still produce their own brand of piccalilli, the similarity in name between the pickle and the store's London address being purely coincidental.

Hampers were closely associated with social events like tennis at Wimbledon, the Harrow and Eton cricket match, Henley Regatta and, above all, Derby Day, customarily held on the first Saturday in June. On that day, just after dawn, carriages would line up along Piccadilly while liveried servants entered the store to be handed pre-ordered hampers. These would then be loaded onto the carriage, either roped to the roof or slung securely beneath the chassis, before setting off for Epsom Downs. The custom has a certain resonance with today's online 'click and collect' services.

In an article entitled 'Epsom', which Dickens wrote for the magazine *Household Words* published on 7 June 1851 and reprinted in the *Sporting Times*, the author writes:

> Look where I will ... I see Fortnum and Mason. And now, Heavens! all the hampers fly wide open, and the green Downs burst into a blossom of lobster-salad! ... and all around me there are tablecloths, pies, chickens, hams, tongues, rolls, lettuces, radishes, shellfish, broad-bottomed bottles, clinking glasses, and carriages turned inside out.

But it wasn't just picnic hampers. The enterprising company took the idea of hospitality to a new level. By the 1920s, Fortnum's were catering for society sherry and cocktail parties for which they could supply a full service, including a marquee, cutlery and canapes in addition to drinks. By the 1950s, Fortnum began advertising school and university tuck boxes, which could be dispatched by anxious parents to their children's boarding school to eke out less than appetising school dinners, or to provide a treat for homesick students. Tuck boxes could be ordered with a menu of choices including assorted English toffees, English honey and fruit cake, tinned sardines, potted pastes, tinned sausages and strawberry jam.

THE 'EXPEDITIONS DEPARTMENT'

The expansion of Britain's influence overseas, which brought in its wake conquest and exploration of distant shores, was a market Fortnum's rightly claimed as its own. Tinned, potted and preserved foods were a mainstay of the grocery business and their long shelf life and nutritional value meant that they were ideal for provisioning long sea journeys, expeditions and even military campaigns.

The introduction of tinned food as early as the 1840s made it possible to store pre-prepared food for long periods. Galvanised cylindrical metal tins were mass produced and filled with ingredients such as soup or cooked meat before their lids were soldered on to create an airtight seal. Typical tinned foods included grouse and hare soup, sardines preserved in oil, and complete meals such as veal and peas, pheasant, grouse or partridge with vegetables.

Fortnum and Mason eventually set up a dedicated Expeditions Department which supplied many of the major expeditions of the nineteenth and early twentieth century, as well as early military campaigns. Queen Victoria, for example, ordered food hampers to be sent out to British troops fighting in the Crimean War in 1853.

Fortnum's could supply the necessaries for any exotic adventure including little luxuries like cheeses wrapped in muslin, which were packed in wooden crocks, and sugary foods high in calories such as jams, marmalade, honey and bottled fruits. In the Victorian heyday of expeditions, the Piccadilly store stocked a vast range of equipment including mosquito nets, camping equipment and even collapsible canvas boats for fording rivers. The store, for example, supplied Sir John Franklin's 1845 naval mission to discover the North West Passage, Henry Morton Stanley's epic journey to find the missing Scottish missionary David Livingstone near Lake Tanganyika, Howard Carter's excavation of King Tutankhamen's tomb, as well as expeditions led by Scott and Shackleton to reach the South Pole.

In support of Sir John Franklin's 1845 naval mission to discover the North West Passage – the navigable sea route between the Atlantic and Pacific Oceans – Fortnum and Mason provisioned HMS *Erebus* for a lengthy voyage. The store duly delivered 65,000lb of tinned, dried and bottled foods, including desiccated soup, patent meat and game lozenges, sugar, dried fruit, tea, coffee, cocoa paste, chocolate powder and tinned condensed milk, as well as eighteen oxen and one milch goat!

CONQUERING EVEREST ON PÂTÉ DE FOIE GRAS

The prize for the best-kitted-out expedition must surely go to the Alpinist and First World War veteran George Mallory. He led three British expeditions to reach the summit of Mount Everest in 1921, 1922 and 1924.

Buoyed by youthful enthusiasm and a truly prodigious quantity of provender from Fortnum and Mason, the final British Everest expedition took with them a full canteen of Fortnum and Mason cutlery, plates, dishes, cups and saucers, coffee pots and cruet sets, all to be packed into plywood cases. The order included sixty tins of quails stuffed with foie gras, four dozen bottles of vintage Montebello champagne and several bottles of 120-year-old rum. The crated comestibles were transported by seventy porters and 300 pack mules up to the advanced base camp.

Kitted out in tweed jackets, felt hats and layers of woollen underwear, Mallory's team believed that their luxury provisions would sustain their spirits and help keep out the cold. The champagne would be kept on ice to celebrate their successful climb.

At first, all appeared to go well. The weather held out and the technique of carrying bottled oxygen helped at high altitude. Mallory and his climbing partner Sandy Irvine were last seen as tiny dots up in the clouds surrounding the world's highest peak.

But on 8 June 1924 came news of the climbers' untimely deaths when the pair failed to return to base camp. The remaining party were in no mood for celebration as they mourned the loss of their comrades and prepared to head for home. Did Mallory and Irvine ever reach the summit or did they die before reaching their goal?

In 1999, climber Conrad Anker found Mallory's remains in what is known as the 'death zone' of the mountain, where bodies can sometimes be discovered jutting out of the melting snow and ice. The body was found intact. Everything was there, apart from a photograph of Mallory's wife Ruth, which the explorer had vowed to leave at the summit. He had died on his way down from the mountain. But an even greater mystery surrounded the Everest expedition. What happened to the champagne and the quails stuffed with foie gras?

A CONSUMER REVOLUTION

The Great Exhibition of 1851 is popularly credited with awakening the British public to the ever-growing range of consumer goods being produced by Britain's factories. In truth, the artefacts on display tended to be luxury items of the very highest quality, such as Wedgwood or Minton dinner services, Elkington silver plate, Gillow's furniture and expensive silks and cashmeres from India.

It was instead the Grand Exposition in Paris in 1855 that led to the concept of the department store. Described as the *grand magasin*, Bon Marché, a Parisian store founded in 1852, displayed its wares like a public exhibition and put clearly visible price tags on all its merchandise. Visitors were free to browse attractive displays at their leisure and many shoppers bought on impulse, thus increasing the store's turnover.

The West End's quaintly named 'warehouses' started to follow suit. Stock normally kept hidden away on shelves and in cupboards, and fetched for the customer by a shop assistant, was made more accessible on countertops and in glass-fronted cabinets. A recent innovation, plate-glass windows showcased colourful displays, fashionably dressed mannequins and placards advertising special offers.

William Edgar and George Swan's drapery warehouse was founded in 1812. The store specialised in bolts of dress material, bed linen, curtain and upholstery fabrics, linen and rugs. In 1816, the store moved to 49 Regent Street, close to what would eventually become Piccadilly Circus. By 1848, it had expanded to occupy one entire corner of Piccadilly Circus at the Quadrant and had become a department store, adding fashion, jewellery, fragrances and household items to its burgeoning stock. Its large plate-glass windows were full of displays of the season's latest modes.

Swan and Edgar's journey from draper's shop to department store was repeated across the West End. Founded between 1790 and 1840, Dickins and Jones, Marshall and Snelgrove, and Debenham and Freebody all began life as drapers. A relative latecomer, John Lewis founded his drapery business on Oxford Street in 1860 and expanded rapidly to become a full-service department store. His son John Spedan Lewis introduced profit sharing to incentivise staff in 1929 and transferred ownership of the business to its staff in 1950, creating the partnership model that would make the store a formidable brand.

THE DEPARTMENT STORE

The West End department store was a late Victorian phenomenon that made the West End a destination for shoppers. Shopping had become a leisure pursuit that, thanks to the emphasis on drapery and haberdashery, was attracting newly independent middle-class women in search of the latest fashions. In the nineteenth century it was common for women to make their own clothes or buy lengths of material to be made to measure by a dressmaker.

In order to attract and retain their loyal customers, stores had to look after the comfort and convenience of their female shoppers. Once inside, shop-walkers in tail coats would direct customers to the various departments and the store had plenty of seating areas where ladies could relax and inspect the goods for sale.

Most department stores had a café and tearoom, rest rooms and toilets. The store thus became a destination for a day out, and stores began to attract shoppers further down the social scale as it was somewhere safe. It did not cost anything to look at and admire the goods on offer. It was a place to visit with friends as part of a fun day out.

By the 1880s, Swan and Edgar was lit by electricity. A consumer revolution had resulted in a burgeoning fashion industry and a wide range of products for furnishing the home as well as labour-saving products for cleaning it.

Stores differentiated themselves by establishing a strong identity or brand. Among the most powerful was Liberty's, which opened on the corner of Regent Street and Marlborough Street in 1875. Created by Arthur Lasenby Liberty, the store was built in mock Tudor style.

Strongly identified with the aesthetic of the English arts-and-crafts movement and art nouveau, Liberty's imported expensive *objets d'art*, and rugs from Japan and the Far East, and commissioned English designers like Archibald Knox to create decorative items in silver, copper or pewter, including clocks, candlesticks, kettles, coal scuttles and much more.

Stores were strongly associated with particular locations where they built loyal customer bases: Harrods of Knightsbridge, Heal's of Tottenham Court Road, Harvey Nichols of Knightsbridge, Whiteley's (the Universal Provider) of Westbourne Grove, Bayswater, and Barker's of Kensington. Stores specialised in stocking different ranges of products appealing to different markets and tastes, thus enabling shoppers to compare prices and quality.

Piccadilly veered towards fashion and gentlemen's apparel, including Simpson's of Piccadilly, Lillywhite's for cricketing and sportswear, Cording's for hard-wearing country tweeds, Austin Reed for suits and Aquascutum, which, as its Latin-inspired name suggests, originally sold waterproofs.

SELFRIDGES – THE FIRST MODERN DEPARTMENT STORE

It took an American tycoon to transform the West End department store into a sensual delight. Retail magnate Gordon Selfridge opened his famous Oxford Street department store on 23 March 1909. He was on a mission to make department stores welcoming and shopping a memorable experience with ever-changing displays that piqued customer interest. He is believed to have coined the phrase 'the customer is always right', a sentiment that would have appeared to be dangerous heresy in the class-conscious and deferential Edwardian era.

It is difficult to overstate the impact Selfridges had on West End shopping. When opened, his store was the biggest of its kind, with a statement entrance portal flanked by bronze statues and an enormous illuminated clock. The monster store's spacious interiors, sweeping staircases and electric lifts were designed as a temple to shopping and Selfridge abandoned the traditional glass display cases in favour of allowing people to see and touch the merchandise. Moving the colourful and extravagant perfume counters front of house provided a welcoming vista, encouraging women to browse for fragrances.

Selfridge used the power of advertising to the maximum and employed a journalist as well as a full-time publicist to make sure Selfridges would use every opportunity to create news stories. Advertisements appeared in the press illustrating the latest fashions. Selfridges captured the public imagination by exhibiting the monoplane in which Louis Blériot had flown the Channel in 1909.

As historian Erika Diane Rappaport observes, '… journalists figured consumption as a female, public and sensual entertainment … countless writers joined a maverick American entrepreneur to create an international culture of pleasure on the western border of the West End.'[3]

SIMPSON'S OF PICCADILLY

Just as Gordon Selfridge had transformed the department store into an exciting leisure activity aimed at suburban women, so ready-to-wear tailor Alec Simpson was poised to take men's outfitting to the next level. His father Simeon Simpson had founded a mass-market menswear factory, the House of Simpson, in 1894 to supply ready-made suits to provincial stores. In response to growing demand, he opened a modern factory in Stoke Newington in 1929.

Alec set to work modernising the business. In 1934 he designed a new type of casual high-waisted trousers, which he marketed under the trademark DAKS. Costing 30s a pair, DAKS became the height of fashion. They were tailored straight from the hip and secured by two adjustable fastenings, meaning they could be worn without a belt or braces. The idea was hugely popular with young men and women who found slacks offered comfort and freedom of movement, making them ideal wear for sports like golf and tennis.

Not content with selling his clothes through other menswear outlets, Alec Simpson decided to invest in his own London store. On 27 March 1935, he bid for the lease of the recently demolished Geological Museum site in Piccadilly, a plot with a 71ft frontage onto Piccadilly and Jermyn Street. Commissioning the architect Joseph Emberton, the new store, Simpson's of Piccadilly, was a seven-storey steel-framed building in the modernist style, clad in Portland stone and with a generous amount of glazing on each storey surmounted by an open loggia running the length of the top floor. The ground-floor display windows were designed with convex glass, a feature that magnified and enhanced window displays. It was a bold architectural statement.

The store's interiors were designed by Hungarian architect László Moholy-Nagy, finished in travertine marble and a large uncluttered floorplate, with floors linked by a central staircase, lit by a massive art deco stainless tubular-steel chandelier.

Outdoing Gordon Selfridge's publicity stunt, Simpson had three aeroplanes dismantled and re-assembled on the fifth floor as a talking point and as affirmation of the store's modernity. Simpson enthusiastically held launch parties to highlight the season's latest fashions.

Besides advertising the latest DAKS trousers and sports jackets in high-quality cloth, Simpson decided to make a play for the quality market and introduced a bespoke cutting department where clothes could be tailor-made to order. In doing so, he laid down the gauntlet to the West End's exclusive home of gentlemen's tailoring, Savile Row. Men could now expect to be fitted for a quality suit that was, to all intents and purposes, indistinguishable from a premium item and far more stylish than anything that could be bought from mass-market high-street tailors like Montagu Burton.

But this was not all. In 1937 Simpson launched a ladieswear department selling everything from high fashion and millinery to casual dresses, blousons, slacks and trouser suits. For the sporty girl, Simpson's sold beachwear, tennis skirts and skiing outfits. The stylish twinsets and trouser suits found a ready market.

The idea of a department store took hold as Simpson set up a hairdresser, a riding and country shop, a florist's and even a dog shop. Tradition was all important and before he died, at the young age of 34, Alec Simpson launched annual fashion shows and events that tied in with film launches and upmarket nightclubs like Ciro's. International film stars were courted by the company to endorse its products. Prince Philip became a customer and a royal warrant was duly issued in December 1954.

LUXURY BRANDS

The evolution of the West End saw it change from a high street serving local people to a high street serving diverse and international communities. The brands are now international, but the institutions, whilst not unchanged, preserve much of their commitment to service and quality.

One of the earliest known images of Piccadilly, showing the gates of Hyde Park alongside a row of houses and a tavern on the site of what is now Apsley House. (Author's collection)

The Quadrant, Regent Street, designed by John Nash and built between 1813 and 1820. (Wikimedia Commons)

The greatest showman on earth, P.T. Barnum, with his pint-sized prodigy General Tom Thumb.
(Wikimedia Commons)

Freak shows staged at the Egyptian Hall included Claude Seurat, the 'Living Skeleton'. (Author's collection)

The immensely popular Egyptian Hall opened in 1812 and reflected the era's fascination with ancient Egypt. (Wikimedia Commons)

Inside Piccadilly's iconic Criterion Bar. It was immortalised in literature by Arthur Conan Doyle as the place where Dr Watson first met Sherlock Holmes. (Wikimedia Commons)

The leg show was a staple of West End stage shows from the 1840s to the 1970s. Here, Tiller Girls are rehearsing their high-kick routine backstage at the London Palladium. (PA Images/Alamy)

GERTIE MILLAR

Gaiety girl Gertie Millar was the star of the musical comedy *Our Miss Gibbs*. She married the 2nd Earl of Dudley in 1924. (Wikimedia Commons)

A bustling Piccadilly Circus in the late nineteenth century. (Author's collection)

Plans for Piccadilly Circus Underground Station after its modernisation. (Wikimedia Commons)

Kate 'Ma' Meyrick (front, right of centre), the 'Queen of Clubs', most notably the 43 Club. (Author's collection)

Customers enjoying afternoon tea at Lyons Corner House on Coventry Street, 1942. (Author's collection)

The famous Windmill Girls with a sailor on leave in 1943. (Author's collection)

Opposite: Will Bentley (top), the founder of Piccadilly's Bentley's Oyster Bar, was part of Bentley, Russell and Graham, a troupe of comedians. (David and Pauline Bentley)

An 1860s engraving of the oyster bar in Haymarket. (Author's collection)

Evans's Song and Supper Rooms drew rowdy male audiences. (Author's collection)

Known as the 'Queen of Happiness', US entertainer Florence Mills shot to stardom in C.B. Cochran's revue *Blackbirds*. (Wikimedia Commons)

American Jazz musician Dizzy Gillespie topped the bill at Soho's Shim Sham Club, inspiring artists like Ronnie Scott. (Wikimedia Commons)

Crowds gather in Piccadilly Circus to celebrate VE Day. (Pictorial Press Ltd/Alamy)

A 1957 advert for Murray's Cabaret Club. (Author's collection)

Strip-club owner Paul Raymond with his girlfriend, Fiona Richmond. (PA Images/Alamy)

6

EATING OUT

Romano's — Italiano's — Paradise in the Strand.
At Romano's — as Papa knows —
The wine and the women are grand!

The Sisters Leamar music-hall act

A TASTE FOR HIGH LIVING

Traditional English cooking is hard to find in London's West End, a district noted for its cosmopolitan culture and international cuisine. The spirit that animated Romano's in the Strand illustrates just how far Londoners had embraced fine dining by the close of the Victorian age.

The first taste of Continental gastronomy arrived with the Parisian chefs who fled Paris at the end of the Napoleonic Wars and began serving fine French cuisine in the gentlemen's clubs of St James's. Celebrity chefs like Jean-Baptiste Watier, Auguste Labourie, Charles Francatelli and Alexis Soyer made names for themselves educating the palates of the English upper classes.

For the ordinary Londoner, things were different. Up to the 1850s and '60s, grills and supper rooms served traditional English fare like lamb chops and roast beef with seasonal vegetables. But by the 1870s, continental cuisine had made the leap from the tables of St James's members' clubs to a burgeoning restaurant sector, catering for people of the middling sort. Menus started appearing in French and Italian listing a wide range of new and unfamiliar dishes using expressions like *hors d'oeuvres* and *plat du jour*. A treat was in store for the adventurous diner.

The Peninsulaire Restaurant in Glasshouse Street off Regent Street, for example, served English, French and Italian cuisine. It advertised a 'Parisian dinner for 3s and 6d included lobster bisque, whitebait a la diable, pommes nouvelles au beurre followed by poulet au cresson and to conclude Bavarois au Maraschino. Followed by camembert and Turkish coffee.'[1]

In between the food stall and the restaurant stood the dependable tavern or coaching inn serving traditional country fare – pies and baked or roast potatoes.

STREET FOOD

London was a deeply divided society where, living in hopelessly overcrowded conditions with no means of cooking, the poor existed largely on street food. Few besides the rich could afford to dine at home. Writing in 1851, Henry Mayhew in his survey of the capital's underclass, *London Labour and the London Poor*, describes the various tradesmen and women – pie-men, sellers of boiled puddings, muffin-men, sellers of gingerbread-nuts, sellers of ices and ice-creams, sellers of hot-cross and Chelsea buns. Mayhew notes that:

> men and women, most especially boys, purchase their meals day after day in the streets. The coffee stall supplies warm breakfast; shell-fish of many kinds tempt to a luncheon; hot eels and pea soup, flanked by a potato 'all hot' serve for a dinner; and cakes and tarts or nuts and oranges with many varieties of pastry ... woo to indulgence in a dessert.[2]

Refreshment stalls catered for the crowds of people streaming out of the theatres and music halls with tea, coffee, ginger beer and lemonade. The coffee stall at Hyde Park Corner was still doing a roaring trade in the late 1930s – part of an unbroken tradition dating from the Victorian age. But if you could not afford a tea or coffee, there was an increasing number of public fountains set up by charitable subscription to provide fresh drinking water, such as the pump with its iron cup and chain on the wall of St James's Church, Piccadilly, and the Shaftesbury Fountain at Piccadilly Circus.

Late into the night, the West End teemed with hawkers waiting to ambush the torrent of humanity pouring out of taverns, public houses, penny gaffs and music halls. Together with a small army of mendicants, street musicians, industrious beggars and ragged match girls, street-food sellers offered greasy delicacies. The pig's trotter man would bawl, 'Penny a trotter – you won't find 'otter!' Stalls sold hot pies, pickled whelks, hot eels, kidney pudding, pea soup, roast chestnuts and muffins.

The traditional hot chestnuts and whelks were decent enough food. But some of London's poor must have endured virtual starvation. Journalist and London chronicler George Sala describes a sandwich seller whose stock in trade was:

> two slices of pale substance resembling in taste and texture sawdust pressed into a concrete form, between which is spread a veneer of inorganic matter ... While the poorest may seek out an ancient dame bearing a flat basket lined with a fair white cloth. She will administer a brace of bones covered in a soft white integument which she will inform you are 'trotters'.[3]

The Haymarket and Piccadilly were also the chief focus for night-time revelry and their side streets contained numerous brothels. This was a vibrant but infernal world where Darwinian capitalism ruled supreme and none but the hardiest and most unscrupulous survived.

For over half a century, the Royal Albert Potato Can stood as a landmark at the corner of Coventry Street and Haymarket – a portable stove that was carried into position and fired up each evening by its owner. This stall, named in 1840 to honour Queen Victoria's wedding to Prince Albert, was a celebrated part of West End tradition, and remained in business until around 1870 when Piccadilly Circus was widened and the White Bear coaching inn demolished to make way for the Criterion.

The patriotic hot-potato seller sold his popular and cheap treat to the theatre crowds. Baked over a brazier of hot coals, the jacket potatoes were served cut in two, spread with grease and garnished with salt and pepper. Sala described the Potato Can's smart enamelled stove as a 'three-legged emporium of smoking vegetables gleaming with black tin painted red, and brazen ornaments, where the humble pilgrim of the Haymarket may halt and sup for a penny'. By the late 1860s, the Potato Can stood out as a relic of a period when the Haymarket echoed to the cry of itinerant street-food sellers. By then, restaurants and smart hotels were starting to take over and the street was becoming more gentrified.

The Potato Can may have long gone but street food has recently undergone a revival, courtesy of numerous open-air markets and outdoor venues. These pop-up stalls offer a wide range of choice, from traditional snacks to international cuisine, and offer aspiring chefs a chance to try out their skills. The missing staple is oysters. Oysters are now a luxury commodity and no longer a street food. They were the fast food of choice for the London working classes, and had been ever since the times of the Romans. Anyone who has ever dug in the garden of a Georgian house and found piles of empty shells – the remains of the workmen's lunch – will be well aware of this.

THE RISE OF THE WEST END RESTAURANT

When *Kelly's Directory* first began listing restaurants as a separate category in their own right in 1880, there were only twelve such establishments in the whole of the West End. Defined as a place where diners could be seated at a well-laid table with tablecloth and enjoy a varied menu, fine wines and waiter service, restaurants were seen as a foreign import. Prior to their arrival, London's streets boasted countless chop houses, oyster rooms, eel and pie houses, grill rooms, dining rooms, fish bars and various forms of fast food.

Writing in 1859, George Augustus Sala extolled the virtues of basic tavern fare in his famous London guide *Twice Round the Clock*, waxing lyrical on the subject of pork pies, sausage rolls and Banbury cake. In one tavern in the Haymarket he found on the menu 'unpretending chops, steaks, kidneys, or Welsh rabbit, washed down by the homely British brown stout'. If you were a City clerk you might also have been served a lobster and lettuce such as Dickens described in *Bleak House*.

Sala singles out the Haymarket as a centre for eating out and lists many supper houses, including 'a crowd of hotels, restaurants, cigar divans, coffeehouses and establishments for the sale of lobsters, oysters and pickled salmon … according to the seasons in which those dainties are considered most fit to be enjoyed'. The Haymarket was home to a number of restaurants, including the Maison Dorée, the Café Anglaise and Vachettes. Sala describes other 'second class French restaurants … where succulent suppers may be obtained at moderate prices'.[4]

In 1889, the Savoy Hotel Company was founded to operate restaurants at the Savoy, Claridge's and the Berkeley. Hotels offered a fixed-price *table d'hôte*. Multi-course luncheons served at set times encouraged the public to dine at hotels.

Competition was fierce and, to woo customers, enterprising restaurants provided professional entertainment, usually in the form of a small orchestra, which would play on a balcony overlooking the diners. Hotel dining rooms often had sufficient space for a dance floor where guests might enjoy latenight dancing.

The fashion was adopted by the West End's premier restaurants like the Café Royal and Romano's:

> Nearly every big restaurant in London today is compelled to provide some form of amusement for its guests. With the opening of the London Casino, we had for the first time a whole theatre turned into a restaurant offering a full-sized entertainment on the stage and dancing in between, with a regular meal served.[5]

Demand for fine dining was fuelled by theatres, hotels and tourism. By 1900, *Kelly's Directory* listed ninety-two restaurants. The fact that restaurant cleanliness and hygiene were inspected by local authority food standards departments helped reassure an anxious public.

FINE DINING COMES OF AGE

At the heart of London's theatreland, Piccadilly was the undisputed centre of restaurants and fine dining. Known popularly as 'Jimmy's' and built in 1858, St James's Hall Restaurant in Piccadilly was one of the West End's oldest restaurants. The cuisine was cosmopolitan and the service unhurried.

Associated with St James's Hall, where concert goers could enjoy classical music in the large upstairs auditorium or a minstrel show in the basement hall, the restaurant attracted a mix of pre-concert diners and couples wanting a more leisurely experience. Demolished in February 1905, St James's Hall once stood on the Quadrant between Regent Street and Piccadilly with entrances on both streets. The site is now occupied by Le Méridien Hotel.

The dark corners of the restaurant were a favourite haunt of gentlemen wanting an intimate dinner *à deux* with a *demi-mondaine* or mistress. It was said that wives were rarely seen. The censorious Robert Machray observes that, by midnight, the St James's Restaurant would be full of people, mostly women in evening dress:

> presenting a generous display of their charms … Here is the chiefest temple of the demi-monde. So long as a member of the scarlet sisterhood can put in an appearance at 'Jimmy's' she fancies she is not wholly a failure!!![6]

Despite its somewhat shady reputation, St James's Restaurant became a limited company in 1887 – the first West End restaurant to do so. This example was followed by Kettners and the Frascati Restaurant in Soho. By becoming a limited company, a restaurant could attract shareholders and investment to expand. The trade was brisk and solid profits guaranteed with share dividends of around 5 per cent a year.

Linking one's restaurant to a theatre guaranteed trade. In 1873, mass-catering to fine-dining conglomerate Spiers and Pond bought a vacant development site on the south side of Piccadilly Circus to build a theatre and restaurant complex called the Criterion. They had dipped their toes in the water by running a franchised restaurant at George Edwardes' Gaiety Theatre, which had proved a profitable investment.

Within a few years, the bar and restaurant known as 'The Cri' was rivalling Jimmy's in terms of popularity. A publicity flyer for the restaurant proclaimed, 'One can go to dine, go to the play, and sup without having to pass into the street in order to do so.'

Felix William Spiers and Christopher Pond were a couple of Australian entrepreneurs. Spiers had made huge profits in the 1849 Gold Rush and had promptly invested them in catering, where he met his business partner Mr Pond. By the 1860s the pair set sail for Britain in search of their next business venture. While Spiers, the older of the two, excelled at accounts, Pond had a talent for hospitality.

Initially their catering business, like the bookseller and stationer W.H. Smith, was located in busy railway stations. Spiers and Pond were awarded franchises by the London, Chatham and Dover Railway and the Metropolitan Railway to run station buffets. The Criterion represented a step change from mass catering to fine dining, but it worked and the entire operation was run from Spiers and Pond's headquarters at the Silver Grill café in Ludgate Hill.

The Criterion was the first step towards a modern operation in which Spiers and Pond developed a huge catering business running restaurant franchises at the Drury Lane Theatre, the Science Museum in South Kensington and Palgrave's Restaurant in the Strand.

The Criterion has a major claim to literary fame as it features in Arthur Conan Doyle's first Sherlock Holmes adventure, *A Study in Scarlet*, as the place where Dr Watson is told of his prospective room-mate after he meets a friend at the Criterion: 'I was standing at the Criterion Bar, when someone tapped me on the shoulder, and turning round I recognized young Stamford, who had been a dresser under me at Barts.'

THE MONICO

Not to be confused with New York's famous Delmonico restaurant, Piccadilly's Café Monico was established in 1877 when Giacomo and Battista Monico opened their café restaurant at 15 Tichborne Street, a tiny side street just off Piccadilly Circus. An advertisement in 1878 refers to the 'Grand Café Saloon, Grill Room and one of the Best Ventilated Billiard Saloons in London. Supper after the Theatres. Restaurant Open till Half-Past Twelve.'

Monico's fortune was made when the Metropolitan Board of Works, which was overseeing a major redevelopment of Piccadilly Circus in 1885–86, created a new road layout that thrust the café restaurant to centre stage. In order to create a junction with the newly constructed Shaftesbury Avenue, a substantial part of Tichborne Street was demolished. The sole survivor was Monico's, which by a happy accident now faced the corner of Piccadilly Circus and was renumbered 46 Regent Street – a prime site ideal for attracting passing trade.

The Monico brothers invested in enlarging their premises to take advantage of their new position, more than doubling their accommodation. The Shaftesbury Avenue front of the Monico Restaurant incorporated a wide entrance lobby and awning, three arched Italianate windows on the first floor, three pedimented windows above and smaller windows on the floor above. The frontage was faced with polished grey marble and Burmantoft buff-coloured terracotta tiles and enclosed by two classical Corinthian columns. When electric advertising billboards went up around Piccadilly Circus, Monico's decided to put its own name in lights, and the café can be seen tucked away beside its neighbour whose frontage advertised 'Guinness Is Good for You'.

The interior made lavish use of marble columns and arches. With a café salon, grill room and buffet on the ground floor, a grand staircase and passenger lifts connected the entrance with the first-floor dining room and a Masonic suite on the next level. The palatial dining room and winter garden was overlooked by a balcony where a small orchestra might play at certain times such as during Sunday lunch. At the Monico, diners ate to an accompaniment of the Bellini orchestra from Naples whose wide-ranging repertoire included popular marches, waltzes and operatic overtures. On the top floor, a roof courtyard could be enjoyed, weather permitting.

With all its many facilities, the Café Monico was hugely popular for its 1s 6d afternoon teas and for its Italian ices and four-course dinners. Pre-theatre dining formed a large part of the trade, and in 1928 the Monico was advertising 'Four-shilling *table d'hôte* suppers and seven-shilling dinners'. The Monico lacked a drinks licence.

This was a respectable middle-class café where families were as welcome as single men whiling away a solitary hour. As one satisfied customer wrote:

> to have a chop at the Café Monico or to pass an hour with your Henry Clay [cigar] and chocolate, with the eye glancing at the mirrors of the salon with its fernery and fountains, its marble tables and velvet settees, or the beautifully decorated ceiling and walls, is to feel that luxury can be had at small cost.[7]

An 'International Hall' and a winter garden completed the Café Monico's generous accommodation, and its catering facilities led to it being used as a conference hall and a wedding venue. The first World Weightlifting Championships were held at the Monico in 1891 and the hall hosted the London International Chess Championship in 1899. The billiard saloon with its dozen billiard tables gave the Monico a distinct masculine ambience.

The Café Monico survived until 1954, when the site was bought with a view to demolition and replacement with an office block as part of an envisaged comprehensive redevelopment of Piccadilly.

CAFÉ SOCIETY

Berlin, Vienna, Paris, Budapest, Brussels and New York could all lay claim to what in the late nineteenth century became known as 'café society'. Artists, writers and musicians often living in poverty and on the margins sought lodgings in affordable run-down inner-city districts, which then became hubs of creativity. Paris's Les Deux Magots, the Florian in Venice, the Café Central in Vienna and Oscar's on Fourth Avenue, New York, attracted bohemians because they were easy-going places where groups of friends could debate ideas over endless cups of coffee or strong liquor.

London was no exception. Situated on the borders of cosmopolitan Soho and bustling Piccadilly, the Café Royal at 68 Regent Street attracted London's literary and artistic scene of the 1880s and '90s, most famously the playwright Oscar Wilde, the impressionist artist James McNeill Whistler and the illustrator Aubrey Beardsley.

Wilde was in the vanguard of the Aesthetic movement, a group of influential writers and artists that included Algernon Charles Swinburne, James McNeill Whistler and Sir Edward Burne-Jones. Aesthetes led taste by adopting an unconventional and often flamboyant style of dress. The symbols of

Aestheticism were the sunflower and the lily. Wilde himself dressed like a dandy with a gardenia or a green carnation in the buttonhole of his frock coat.

Wilde's writing career was flourishing. In 1893, he tasked his wife with compiling a collection of his epigrams, the witty sayings that were becoming his trademark. The small book was to be published privately by Constance's friend, the young manager of Hatchards bookshop, Arthur Humphreys. Fifty copies of the book called *Oscariana* were printed, appearing in January 1895, coinciding neatly with the premiere of his best-known play, *The Importance of Being Earnest*.

It is no accident that Café Royal came to attract an artistic clientele. Its proprietor Daniel Nicholas Thenevon had fled Paris in 1863, leaving behind a bankrupt wine business and a pile of unpaid debts. Thenevon had just five gold sovereigns with which to begin a new life for himself and his wife in London. Changing his name to a more English-sounding Daniel Nicols, he headed for Soho where he joined a small expatriate French community. Shortly after his arrival he bought a semi-derelict oilcloth store in Glasshouse Street, which through hard work he converted into a small but thriving café restaurant while his wife earned money as a seamstress.

As trade increased the industrious café proprietor bought two adjoining properties when they fell vacant and also a tailor's shop fronting Regent Street, which was added to his expanding list of properties in 1865. Nicols fitted the shop with a plate-glass window and proudly named it the Café-Restaurant Royal, offering French gastronomic cuisine. To accompany the dishes, the finest wine cellar in the whole of London offered champagne and vintage clarets.

The outbreak of the Franco-Prussian War in 1870 brought a string of exiled French royalists together with expatriate artists such as Gustave Doré, Henri de Toulouse-Lautrec and the poets Verlaine and Rimbaud. The Café Royal would soon acquire its reputation as a cultural hub.

The scene was set for a major expansion, and over the coming twenty years Nicols acquired further properties around the corner in Air Street and commissioned major reconstruction work to join the disparate buildings into one huge establishment. His son-in-law joined the business and suggested the now famous Café Royal signature, the letter N surrounded by a laurel wreath. Thinking the letter N stood for the initial of his surname, Nicols readily agreed. In fact, the letter was widely understood to be a tribute to France's last emperor, Napoleon III!

Having the space to expand, Nicols remodelled the interior in the style of Louis Quinze with carved gilt panelling, ornate plasterwork ceilings and tall mirrors. The great and the good flocked to the Café Royal, which now boasted the Restaurant, the Grill Room, a brasserie known as the Domino Room and private dining rooms known as *salons privés*, where celebrities and politicians might dine unobserved or where a man might discreetly entertain his mistress. There was even a Masonic temple.

By the late 1880s, James McNeill Whistler and Oscar Wilde were meeting regularly to enjoy a cheap bottle of claret and a frugal meal in the Grill Room. The pair were sometimes joined by the illustrator Aubrey Beardsley. As Wilde's fame and reputation grew, he upgraded to the Café Royal's restaurant where he could often be found holding forth to a select group of spellbound admirers. Although married to Constance, Wilde began to arrange intimate assignations with his lover Lord Alfred Douglas, or 'Bosie' to his friends, at the Café Royal's most secluded spot.

The Café Royal's bohemian credentials were burnished by a stellar cast list that included virtually all of the nation's literary and artistic talent. On any given day you might find the garrulous playwright George Bernard Shaw, man of letters Max Beerbohm, poets Ernest Dowson and Richard Le Gallienne, and literary tyros W. Somerset Maugham, Arnold Bennet, G.K. Chesterton and even a youthful D.H. Lawrence. The Café Royal inspired artists like Walter Sickert and William Orpen, who sketched and painted its plush interiors.

PARADISE IN THE STRAND

In 1874, an Italian waiter at the Café Royal handed in his notice just as Daniel Nicols was counting up the week's takings. His name was Alfonso Nicolino Romano. He mumbled that he was leaving to set up his own restaurant. Surprised at the request, Nicols inquired, 'How much money have you got?' The reply came easily, 'Just the two sovereigns I earned this week and whatever change I have in my pockets.'

It was an honest answer. Romano, an inveterate gambler, had, in fact, lost all of the money he should have been putting aside to make the down payment on renting a small shop. It did not matter. His bookmaker lent him the deposit as he reckoned one of his best customers would be better able to continue to bet on the horses if he had a job and a regular source of income.

And so Romano opened the Café Vaudeville in the Strand, in those days a down-at-heel distant cousin to bustling Piccadilly and a far cry from the centre of fashion. Serving plain Italian food and indifferent wine, which had been supplied on easy credit, the restaurant would have struggled to make an impression but for the garrulous personality of its owner.

Romano's enthusiasm for taking bets and his habit of mixing with the diners caught the attention of a group of journalists working in the nearby offices of *The Sporting Times*, colloquially referred to as 'The Pink 'Un'. Friendly bets were placed on the outcome of sporting events and, of course, the hacks typically won back the money they had been charged for their meal.

Word spread and the Café Vaudeville – now universally known as Romano's – was attracting not just the sporting fraternity but actors, artists and bohemians eager to savour the atmosphere. Romano expanded by buying the next-door premises and converting the space at his disposal into one enormous dining room and ballroom. The main dining hall was given a high ceiling and decorated in the Moorish style with oriental arches in the style of the Alhambra Palace in Granada. With his name in bold letters and an awning decorated with copper cupids above the door, Romano's summed up the optimism of the 1890s.

By the 1890s Romano's prices were no longer cheap:

If his charges for main dishes – 2s. 6d for lamb cutlets, 3s. 6d. for an entrecote, 6s. for a portion of partridge – seemed not unreasonable, he certainly made it up on the 'etceteras'. Soup or *hors d'oeuvres* were 2s. vegetables and salad were between 1s. and 2s.[8]

He charged 13*s* 6*d* for a bottle of non-vintage champagne. A dinner costing £1 3*s* 6*d* in 1890 would today cost in the region of £77, which is not unreasonable for a top West End restaurant.

Romano's drew a lot of its trade from the Strand's many theatres and music halls. A theatre hub in its own right, the Strand could boast the Gaiety Theatre, the Savoy Opera Comique, the Adelphi and the Lyceum, not to mention many lesser theatres and music halls including Terry's, the Olympic, the Tivoli and the Vaudeville, after which Romano named his original restaurant.

Famous music-hall stars lent Romano's a dash of glamour. Bessie Bellwood was a regular, as was Marie Lloyd. George Edwardes, the 'Guv'nor' of the Gaiety Theatre, paid Romano a retainer to give his famous Gaiety Girls a 50 per cent discount on their lunch. The presence of so many glamorous starlets drew custom both to Romano's and publicised the Gaiety. Who wouldn't want to be seated at the next table to Miss Gertie Millar or Marie Studholme? A vaudeville act known as the Sisters Leamar immortalised Romano's with their song 'Romano's Italiano, Paradise in the Strand'!

The diminutive Italian with the thick accent and the waxed moustache placed one final bet on the Derby and, for one of the few times in his life, picked the winning horse at long odds and stood to collect several thousand pounds. He died in June 1901 before he could collect his winnings. With his death, much of Romano's unique character was lost. It soldiered on through the interwar years but was destroyed by enemy action during the Blitz.

A CULTURAL MELTING POT

In his book *The Night Side of London*, Robert Machray explores the cafés, restaurants and bars in the side streets around Piccadilly Circus. In Glasshouse Street just off Regent Street he walks into a café:

> which rejoices in a Latin name, and which is determinedly foreign [the Tivoli]. Here you will unquestionably imagine you have transported your-self into a German beer garden. The majority of its frequenters, you will see, appear to hail from the Vaterland ... By this time, you will understand that the centre of London is cosmopolitan.[9]

Nowhere in London's West End was more cosmopolitan than Soho, an enclave of decaying Georgian streets whose overcrowded dwelling houses and workshops lay at the northern edge of Piccadilly Circus. It was bounded by Shaftesbury Avenue, Regent Street and Oxford Street to the south and west, and Charing Cross Road to the east. Since the mid-nineteenth century the tiny parish of St Anne's, Soho, had attracted poor migrants from across the world with significant communities of Germans, French, Italians, Jews, Spanish, Greeks, Poles, Hungarians, Turks and many other nationalities. Some were fleeing political persecution, while others were in search of opportunity. Together these migrants made a significant contribution to the West End's hospitality industry.

From the late nineteenth century to the outbreak of the First World War, the West End was a cultural melting pot. There were French waiters, Indian and Chinese cooks, Swiss proprietors and Italian chefs. The restaurant trade was supported by big expatriate communities, which acted as pools of tal-ented chefs, managers and waiting staff. Cultural cross-fertilisation led to an abundance of exciting regional dishes and hybrid menus based on French and Italian cuisine.

Virtually all of the top West End restaurants were owned and run by migrants, starting with the Café Royal, Romano's, Monico's and Gatti's, founded by an Italian Swiss Carlo Gatti, who rose through the ranks from ice-cream seller to restaurateur. Many of the most successful restaurateurs had risen through the ranks, and being head waiter of the Savoy appears to have launched the careers of several of the most famous restaurateurs like Ernesto Quaglino and Carlo Gatti.

Soho was a hotspot for small and exciting restaurant start-ups. This included Kettners in Church Street, which was launched by Auguste Kettner, former chef to Napoleon III, and those set up by more recent migrants like the fascist sympathiser and Mussolini supporter Peppino Leoni, who opened the Quo Vadis Restaurant in Dean Street in 1926. He named his restaurant after a famous silent-film epic then showing in the West End.

As the largest and one of the richest cities in Europe, London was a magnet for foreign waiters. In 1885 *The Caterer* estimated there were 7,000 German waiters in London as well as 4,500 other foreign nationals. Less than ten years later, that same publication calculated there were over 5,000 Italians in the capital and 27,000 Germans. As many as 40 per cent of the Italian nationals and a quarter of the German expatriate population were engaged in catering in some form.[10] But at the outbreak of the First World War, London's German waiters left en masse to enlist. The vacancies were filled almost immediately by an influx of Belgian refugees fleeing German oppression. It was not uncommon for former waiters to turn up as captured prisoners of war where they were often recognised by the British officers they once served at the Criterion, the Café Royal or Romano's, where head waiter Otto once held sway.

Now almost ubiquitous, Indian restaurants got off to a slow start in London's West End. Although authentic Indian cuisine was a well-established staple for members at the East India and the Oriental Club, Indian dishes started to appear on the menus of several of Piccadilly's top restaurants late in the nineteenth century. In 1896, Spiers and Pond's Criterion Restaurant started employing an Indian chef. Former Indian army officer and restaurant critic Colonel Nathaniel Newnham-Davis writing in his culinary guide to London, *Dinners and Diners,* praised the 'genuine Indian curry and chutnees galore at the Criterion, where a sable gentleman is charged with its preparation'.[11] Clearly possessing a rare appreciation of curries, Newnham-Davis recounts that after the meal he summoned the cook from the kitchen and cross-examined him about his culinary skills in his native Hindustani.

The first recognisable Indian restaurant was Veeraswamy's in Regent Street, Piccadilly. Starting out as an Indian food importer and subsequently official caterer for the Indian Pavilion at the 1924 British Empire Exhibition, Veeraswamy's opened its famous restaurant that same year. It is still trading today on the corner of Regent Street and Swallow Street.

The first Chinese restaurant to open in the West End was the Cathay, established in Piccadilly Circus in 1908. By the 1930s, a few Chinese restaurants had started appearing. Maxim's in Wardour Street was said by Anthony Powell to have been the inspiration behind his novel *Casanova's Chinese Restaurant*, part of the *Dance to the Music of Time* series. Published in 1960, the novel is set in the year 1933, at a time when Chinese entrepreneurs were taking over failing restaurants and offering Chinese dishes sometimes mixed with European cuisine.

The novel's narrator Nick Jenkins scours Soho with his friend, composer Hugh Moreland, and the down-at-heel music critic Maclintick, looking for somewhere cheap to eat. Powell takes up the story:

> Further up the street was the Amoy, called by some Sam's Chinese Restaurant. The New Casanova went into liquidation. Sam bought it up and moved over their pots and pans and chopsticks, so now you can eat eight treasure rice, or bamboo shoots fried with pork ribbons, under panels depicting scenes for the career of the Great Lover.[12]

One of the best known of the pre-war Chinese restaurants was Ley-On's Chop Suey Restaurant on the corner of Wardour Street and Brewer Street, believed to have been founded in the late 1930s. It survived until the 1950s.

BENTLEY'S OYSTER BAR

Once a working-class staple, oysters became a luxury item after pollution began to wipe out coastal oyster beds, sending prices rocketing.

As a boy, Will Bentley had sold oysters from a barrow on Clacton pier in around 1890. By 1899 he was earning a precarious living as a stand-up comedian and singer at Clacton's open-air theatre and on the concert party circuit. He was moderately successful as in 1899 he and two partners formed a stage act: Graham, Russell and Bentley. After Russell's early death in 1910, aged just

34, the remaining performers formed Graham and Bentley's Concert Party, Russell's place being taken by a young Stanley Holloway, famous for his 'Lion and Albert' monologues.

Ambitious for financial security, Will's wife Rose Godwin, from a wealthy family of ship's chandlers, asked her parents to stake her husband in buying the oyster beds at West Mersea near Colchester. Finding he now owned some of the best-quality oysters in England, Will decided to open his own seafood restaurant in London.

He established his first restaurant in Piccadilly Place in 1916 and was joined by his sons Bill, Derek and Roy, who waited and took turns shucking the fresh oysters ready to be served up to customers. Within two years he had repaid his parents-in-law's loan and was ready to expand.

Still hankering after fame as an entertainer, Will Bentley would work in the restaurant during the day before travelling back to Clacton each evening to appear on stage. In May 1928 Will opened Bentley's Oyster Bar at 8–11 Swallow Street. By now, his Mersea oyster beds were so productive he opened another business, Fred Bentley Ltd, described on the firm's headed paper as 'Oyster Purveyors to the Principal Hotels and Clubs'. The company's title was derived from Will's middle name, Fred; he and four of his five sons were listed as directors.

Surprisingly, given the workload running a restaurant and a wholesale supplier must have entailed, Will continued with his stage career, performing comic songs like 'Have a Little Bit of my Wife's Cake' and 'I Do Look a Lad in Plus Fours'. But in 1934 he retired from the stage to focus on becoming one of Piccadilly's best-loved restaurateurs.

CATERING FOR THE MASSES

The success of the West End in attracting the crowds was in part due to a new development – mass catering. Commuters travelling to work by train, or working-class families visiting the West End to watch a film or see a show, needed somewhere cheap to eat out and the arrival of the Lyons teashops and 'Corner Houses' played a major part. Tea shops appealed across the social spectrum and were more woman friendly than their male-dominated counterparts, the coffee houses.

J. Lyons opened its first tea shop in Piccadilly in 1894, serving tea, cakes, sandwiches and a limited range of hot meals, all to the accompaniment of a Gypsy violinist or string quartet. It was called 'The Popular Café', soon nicknamed 'The Pop'. As Walter MacQueen-Pope recalled, 'You got luxurious surroundings, excellent service and a remarkably good table d'hôte dinner for 2s.6d. with a first-class orchestra thrown in.'[13]

Looking to expand, the firm moved into restaurants and hotels, opening the Trocadero Restaurant on the site of the old Trocadero Music Hall at the junction of Shaftesbury Avenue and Piccadilly Circus in 1896. Under the stewardship of maître d' Louis Monbiot, the Trocadero set high standards of respectability. Known criminals, underworld types and prostitutes were barred.

Service and quality dining at low prices were a major part of Lyons's success, as were its waitresses. A contemporary advertisement for Lyons's Trocadero Restaurant boasts, '... young fellows will go where there are the prettiest girls to wait on them.'[14]

The army of attractive young waitresses who wore black alpaca dresses with starched white caps, detachable collar, and cuffs were dubbed 'nippies' on account of the speed with which they took customers' orders. Their dazzling white starched aprons underlined Lyons's commitment to hygiene and efficiency.

By 1909, the company presided over a growing chain of tea shops as well as prestige hotels, the Strand Palace, which opened in 1909, and the Regent Palace, 1915. The Cumberland Hotel followed in 1933.

So, how had J. Lyons, an unknown outsider, managed to expand so rapidly? The answer is it was financed by the very successful chain of tobacconists and cigar merchants founded in 1855 by two entrepreneurs, Barnett Salmon and Samuel Gluckstein.

Samuel's sons, Montague and Isidore, identified catering as a growth market. Looking for a business partner, Montague found one in the shape of a distant family relation, Joseph Lyons, setting up J. Lyons in 1887. The stage was set for the launch of one of catering's most iconic brands. Lyons took as its business model the centralised purchasing and accounting that underpinned the Spiers and Pond catering empire and improved on it.

Lyons supplied all of its shops from Cadby Hall, a 10-acre factory and office complex in Hammersmith, which grew to include butchers' shops, a bakery, cold storage, administrative offices, a tea and coffee importers, and food production facilities. In a market dominated by small independent cafés and eating houses, a reliable and affordable chain of tea rooms was destined for success.

By 1910 Lyons was feeding half a million customers from around 150 branches throughout London. But the company did not have the market entirely to itself. Competitors included Pearce's Dining and Refreshment

Rooms, the British Tea Table Co. and the Aerated Bread Company, which had almost as many tea rooms as Lyons itself.

Lyons's biggest competitor, the Aerated Bread Company, had opened its first bakery in Islington in 1862 and by the 1890s was running a chain of what we might now call 'greasy spoon' cafés. By providing a better quality of service, Lyons came to occupy pole position. With popular prices, and bright and comfortable surroundings, Lyons was set to conquer London's West End.

CORNER HOUSES

Lyons Corner Houses made their first appearance in 1909 at Coventry Street, extended in 1923 to create four floors containing a food hall, restaurants and a tea room, all with their own musicians. The Lyons Trocadero Restaurant was of a similar size and able to seat 2,000 customers.

Following the craze for jazz bands, Lyons's original Popular Café, which had boasted a palm court orchestra in the 1890s, now introduced jazz, and in the summer of 1931 Harry Singer and his Band entertained diners.

Further Corner Houses opened in Tottenham Court Road, Oxford Street and the Strand, each of which was arranged over at least three floors and able to seat 2,500 diners. Not serving alcohol, the Corner Houses stayed open late into the night. The jazz singer Al Bowlly met his first wife Freda one night in early December 1931 at the Strand Corner House; after a whirlwind romance the couple married at St Martin's register office on 18 December and returned to the Corner House for their wedding reception.

Referred to as the 'Lilypond', the Lyons Corner House in Coventry Street and the long bar at the Trocadero were well-known pick-up points for gay men. Male prostitutes who cruised openly for men were known as 'Dilly Boys'.

WHAT MAKES THE WEST END?

The nature of the West End is for business models to intertwine and support and then occasionally destroy each other or expire. It is this constant expansion and contraction driven by the energy of ambitious entrepreneurs, often economic migrants, whether from Italy or Clacton, that generates the unique business model that is the West End. The growth of tourism and the West End's theatre hub led to a corresponding explosion in fine dining. The Café Royal and Romano's were legends. The characterful Romano's is now a distant memory, while the Café Royal traded on its original site and continued until recently to set an international gold standard for luxury. Comprehensively rebuilt in the mid 1920s when Regent Street was redeveloped by its freeholder Crown Estates, the Café Royal has sadly lost some of its quirky character and atmosphere. Nevertheless, its name lives on as an exemplar of luxury.

Another healthy survivor is Rules. Founded by Thomas Rule in 1798 and serving English fare with an emphasis on game, Rules Restaurant in 35 Maiden Lane is London's oldest restaurant. Together with Simpson's in the Strand, a former cigar divan and famous for its roast beef carvery, these two restaurants keep tradition very much alive.

7

NIGHTLIFE

Up the West End, that's the best end, where the night clubs thrive
Down into a dive you go
There's a jazz queen, she's a has been, has been Lord knows what
Every night she's there on show
She dances underneath a magic spell
She's full of charm and beer and stout as well
She's 66 but looks 16, her friends don't know her now her face is clean
Fanlight Fanny, the frowsy night club queen.

George Formby, 'Fanlight Fanny'

ATTEMPTS AT REGULATION

The Early Closing Act of 1874 decreed that all licensed premises were to close at half past midnight. All West End pubs and restaurants had to observe the rules and, come 12.30 a.m., frantic waiters and publicans would begin ushering reluctant guests out onto the street. The author Robert Machray paints a vivid description of this late-night exodus of gentlemen and their mistresses from St James's Hall Restaurant at Piccadilly, 'Jimmy's':

About half-past twelve a crowd of demi-mondaines and men pour forth, but by this time there are four policemen outside the door to preserve order … Hansoms dash up, and the porter helps the Faustines who climb into them with as much care as if they were duchesses.[1]

Written in 1901, *The Night Side of London* hints at widespread vice and a crackdown on nightclubs which had 'practically become impossible thanks to the ceaseless raiding of such dens ... Only a few years ago there were many of them open, furnished with ballrooms, bars and supper rooms.' The introduction of the Early Closing Act considerably curtailed the opportunities for Londoners intent on pleasure.

But the urge to party into the night was unabated and demand was filled by a succession of clandestine clubs that operated in cellars, frequently switching locations to evade the law. Unlicensed, these illegal clubs would be the focus of illicit gambling, drug taking and prostitution.

By the early years of the twentieth century, an uneasy truce was called, allowing licensed clubs to become venues for late-night dancing and cabaret. Some fell victim to the Defence of the Realm Act (DORA), passed in 1914, which gave the state virtually unlimited power over people's lives. As new restrictions were added, licensing hours were cut to 11 p.m. and nightclubs suffered progressive curbs as late-night excess was regarded as harmful to public morals during the dark days of the First World War.

SODOM AND GOMORRAH

In the early nineteenth century, gentlemen bent on pleasure did not have far to look for ladies of 'easy virtue' among the music halls and song and supper rooms of the West End.

Questionable entertainments supplemented by hot meals washed down with copious amounts of alcohol were a staple of late-night West End dining. The moral crusaders who compared music halls to Sodom and Gomorrah certainly had a point as there was an undoubted link to the sex trade among disreputable song and supper rooms, such as the Coal Hole in the Strand and the Cyder Cellars in Maiden Lane, and less reputable theatres, like the Alhambra Palace of Variety and the Empire Theatre in Leicester Square, whose stage productions loosely described as 'ballets' boasted lavish stage sets involving hundreds of scantily clad dancers. There was also an alternative attraction that would set female hearts a-flutter: 'The Man on the Flying Trapeze', a Frenchman, M. Leotard. His physical prowess, shown to perfection in his eponymous figure-hugging tights, was admired almost as much as the dancing troupe and inspired a well-known music-hall song.

Built in 1854 when it opened as the Royal Panopticon of Arts and Science, the Alhambra was a lofty terracotta-clad building whose Moorish-inspired domes and minarets represented the pinnacle of West End entertainment. In 1869, the author J. Ewing Ritchie described it in glowing terms as 'the greatest success in London; it has set the fashion. One of the first places visited by strangers to London is the Alhambra.'

But the Alhambra held a dark secret. Surface impressions of respectability masked a male-dominated culture, which treated young women as commodities. This was no place to take your wife or family. The 'ballet dancers' wore flesh-coloured tights and flimsy petticoats, sometimes appearing virtually naked in tableaux known as *poses plastiques*. They also danced the cancan, hoisting their skirts to reveal their nether regions.

In this degraded and corrupting atmosphere, prostitutes would openly ply their trade in the promenade area where drinks were served to men seated at tables throughout the show. In true Victorian form, Ritchie passes judgement:

> I boldly declare the ballet to be unmitigatedly sensual, and to offer young men amusement in its most dangerous form. Scanty costume and liberal display of female development – 'ripe and real', as Byron writes, may attract the men but that is all.[2]

There was worse. Patrons, if admitted to the basement green room, were free to mingle with the ballerinas as they squeezed into and out of their flimsy outfits. Furnished with bare boards and benches, the changing room, known as 'the Canteen', served alcoholic refreshment:

> Looking through a dense haze of tobacco-smoke you will see some forty or fifty ballet-girls standing or seated in company with their male admirers … No wonder that the girls are bold and brazen, intent chiefly on a liberal display of personal charms.[3]

It's small wonder Victorian moral crusaders were outraged.

EVANS'S SONG AND SUPPER ROOMS

Evans's Song and Supper Rooms at 43 King Street in Covent Garden was one of the great West End institutions. Superficially, all appeared above board. Built as a London townhouse for Admiral Edward Russell in 1772, the mansion subsequently became a hotel and was bought by Welsh music-hall comedian W.C. Evans in 1840, who converted the hotel's dining room into an informal 'song and supper room'. A music hall was added to the rear of the property in 1856, cementing its reputation as a destination for night owls.

In 1859, journalist and social commentator George Augustus Sala wrote of an expedition to Evans's at one o'clock in the morning in his book *Twice Round the Clock*. After returning from seeing a play and consuming oysters at a stall in the Haymarket, Sala moved on to Evans's where he was dazzled by the 'steaming succession of red-hot chops, serene kidneys weltering proudly in their noble gravy and corpulent sausages all to be washed down with pints of stout or sparkling pale ale'.[4]

Also known as 'The Cave of Harmony', Evans's establishment was much more than a late-night watering hole. One of its star attractions was a group of youthful glee singers wearing short school jackets and Eton collars, singing in close harmony. Inside the supper room, a rowdy audience seated at tables dined lavishly while downing copious amounts of 'sparkling pale ale … or brownest Burton' as they watched a succession of music-hall acts. C.B. Cochran enthuses about this knockabout theatre: 'kidneys and baked potatoes were the staple diet, and one great star of the programme was Sam Cowell who sang "The Ratcatcher's Darter", "Vilikins and his Dinah" and other Cockney creations.'[5]

But there was another side to Evans's Supper Rooms. A contemporary journalist describes the late-night scene where 'inhabiting the supper rooms' well cushioned corners, female diners displayed a greater and yet greater expanse of bare flesh'. The writer goes on to observe that as the evening progressed two elegantly dressed girls, having ordered their supper, could be seen 'waiting for some mug to come along and pay for it'.[6]

The implication is that, having found a man to buy them dinner, one of the 'elegantly dressed girls' would transact business and the couple would retire to become better acquainted in one of the establishment's many empty bedrooms. The presence of such ladies is clear evidence of a financial arrangement between the manager of Evans's Supper Rooms and the better class of prostitutes who plied their trade in Covent Garden.

Evans's closed in 1880 but was sorely missed by late-night revellers who then switched their custom to the night haunts of Piccadilly Circus. In 1891 the old supper rooms and music hall were taken over by the National Sporting Club as a clubhouse and boxing ring. Number 43 King Street still exists as an exemplar of Georgian architecture.

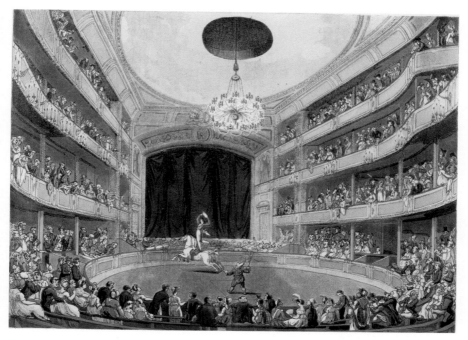

Spectacular scenes at Astley's Amphitheatre in 1808. (Wikimedia Commons)

Chess diplomacy: Benjamin Franklin playing chess with Mrs Caroline Howe in London, 1774. (Wikimedia Commons)

Bullock's Museum in Piccadilly housed a strange and exotic collection of stuffed animals, natural curiosities and militaria. (Wikimedia Commons)

A sneak peek inside one of London's most exclusive addresses, Albany in Piccadilly. (Author's photograph)

West Country mail coaches wait to depart from outside Piccadilly's Gloucester Coffee House. (Author's collection)

Founded in 1797, Hatchards in Piccadilly has been trading from the same premises since 1801. (Author's collection)

A vintage advert for Maskelyne and Cooke's performance at the Egyptian Hall, Piccadilly. (British Library)

Depicting bohemian London's café society, 'The Cafe Royal at London' was painted by Sir William Orpen in 1912. (Wikimedia Commons)

A postcard depicting the Embassy Club, the West End's foremost dinner and dance venue. (Author's collection)

Piccadilly at war. The Shaftesbury Memorial Fountain was removed for safekeeping. (Author's collection)

Clockwise from left: Nothing like a Dame! Dan Leno plays Widow Twanky in the pantomime *Aladdin* (Wikimedia Commons); a 1968 advert from *Country Life* magazine for Simpson's of Piccadilly (the building is now Waterstones) (Author's collection); a vintage programme for the Windmill Girls' farewell performance in 1964. (Author's collection)

Customers enjoying al fresco dining in Soho's Chinatown during the summer of 2020. (Author's photograph)

A deserted Piccadilly Circus during the Covid-19 pandemic. (Author's photograph)

DINNER AND DANCE

During the early twentieth century, the jazz age led the fashion for dinner and dancing, prompting a number of West End restaurants to convert their spacious dining rooms by adding a sprung dance floor and a small stage for an orchestra. Seating and tables were arranged around the edges of the room enabling couples to dine and dance.

But the craze for dancing and partying could only ever be satisfied by nightclubs, which were licensed to provide drinks and entertainment beyond the 12.30 a.m. cut-off and were where the fashionable elite could let their hair down. Nightclubs pushed boundaries as the clubbers could indulge in drug taking and extramarital affairs away from the prying eyes of a censorious press.

One of the very first was Murray's Jazz and Cabaret Club, which opened in 1913 in Beak Street. Owned and run by American Jack Murray and his English partner Ernest Cordell, Murray's opened late, had a cabaret and floor show and an orchestra that played the latest tango dance tunes – a fashion then sweeping Europe. Entering at street level, wealthy patrons in evening dress descended a grand staircase to a massive basement ballroom and dining room illuminated by chandeliers. The finest French cuisine was served and the club could accommodate around 400 guests in style.

Ciro's nightclub opened in Orange Street in 1915. Part of an international chain that ran dance restaurants in Paris, Monte Carlo and Nice, Ciro's operated as an exclusive private members' club to comply with London's strict licensing laws. Members of fashionable high society dined and danced until 2 a.m. to the syncopated jazz music of a West Indian dance band led by Jamaican Dan Kildare.

Ciro's brought in the head chef from Les Ambassadeurs Restaurant in Paris and hired professional exhibition dancers dressed in tails and evening gowns to perform the tango, foxtrot and other fashionable dances. Ciro's had the look and feel of a sophisticated Parisian haunt as the celebrated French singer Odette Myrtil gave intimate cabaret performances.

Some thought her act was too decadent to be staged when so many young men were dying for king and country. The authorities moved swiftly and, in March 1917, they revoked Ciro's licence, citing the Defence of the Realm Act (DORA) and forcing it to close. For the duration of the war Ciro's was converted into a temporary hospital for wounded officers. But this repressive piece of legislation did not end the problem; it merely drove late-night drinking and dancing underground to unlicensed clubs where drugs, gambling and prostitution were added to the excessive pleasures.

The West End's post-war revival got under way with the arrival of a younger generation, intent on hedonism and partying, known as the 'Bright Young Things'. Many fashionable West End restaurants became private members' clubs. One of the first to convert was Maxim's restaurant in Wardour Street, which since 1914 had been holding sedate early evening 'dance suppers'. In 1923, and now renamed Revelle's Club, Maxim's was granted a licence to open until 2.30 a.m. on two nights of the week.

HAUNTS OF THE RICH AND FAMOUS

During the roaring twenties, the favourite West End nightspots comprised a new breed of restaurant nightclubs. The attractions included four-star gourmet menus prepared by celebrity chefs, the exclusivity of mixing with high society and the intimacy afforded couples on the dance floor. Undesirable characters were barred from entry into this world of privilege.

Restaurant nightclubs began to attract young men who in earlier times might have become members of the traditional gentlemen's clubs of St James's. This trend reflected the priorities of a new generation who preferred the shared pleasures of dining and dancing with a lady friend rather than male society. Furthermore, women were allowed to become members in their own right, enjoying freedom and equality denied to earlier generations.

Foremost among the new breed of nightclubbers was that leader of fashion, the fun-loving Edward, Prince of Wales, who would gather a group of friends for a nightly tour of the West End nightspots. The party would typically include a lady friend – Freda Dudley Ward or Thelma Furness – his trusted equerry Major Edward 'Fruity' Metcalfe, Lady Alexandra 'Baba' Curzon, his brother George, Duke of York, and Lady Edwina Mountbatten. The prince's patronage conferred a stamp of respectability on nightclubs, on top of the added frisson of excitement that one might actually bump into him.

These riotous outings to places like the Embassy Club in Old Bond Street might end with the prince leaping onto the stage and joining the band, before commandeering the drum kit and executing a solo performance to much applause. The Duke of Windsor's memoirs relate a particularly memorable occasion at the Kit Kat Club when Fred Astaire and his sister Adele were invited back to the duke's St James's residence, York House, to join the royal party along with Paul Whiteman's Orchestra, then on tour from the USA. When it was pointed out to the prince that this might be a breach of security, 'Baba' Curzon invited everyone back to her family home in Carlton

House Terrace. Her father, Foreign Secretary Lord Curzon, was away on official business.

The prince duly had several crates of champagne brought over from York House and the royal revellers proceeded to dance the night away with gay abandon. Matters got out of hand when couples started dancing on the top of Curzon's prized antique dining table. A mahogany leaf of the table finally snapped under the weight of George, Duke of York, the future King George VI. It took all of Lady 'Baba's' tact and diplomacy to smooth things over with her father when he returned from overseas.

The top clubs were the Kit Kat Club, the Embassy Club, the Café Anglais, Café de Paris and of course Ciro's. Each restaurant/nightclub had its own resident dance band, many of which were famous in their own right as recording artists and radio stars, like Al Starita and the Kit Kat Band.

The fashionable Kit Kat Club was opened in the summer of 1925 as a dance hall and restaurant, which was part of the newly built Capitol Cinema complex in the Haymarket. It was a major project to rebuild the West End's reputation and its owner Sir Walter Gibbon had a major financial interest in the Piccadilly Hotel. Both the Piccadilly Hotel and the Kit Kat Club were particularly favoured by American visitors and film stars.

Occupying the cinema's deep basement, it had seating for 1,700 people and was the only club in London to have been purpose-built. A glass-fronted entrance led into a large lobby and a cloakroom and then through to a lounge. Two floors below the street level were located the ballroom, restaurant, grill room and American bar, accessed by a wide staircase that went down to the balcony and then down to the dance floor. Diners seated around the balcony overlooked a large ballroom, which also had two rows of tables and seating around the dance floor. Pillars rose right up to the roof. At the height of its popularity the club had around 6,000 members.

Then came the Wall Street Crash in 1929, which sparked a worldwide slump, the Great Depression. The Kit Kat Club's American visitors dried up. The club was too lavish and had too many overheads to succeed in a new climate of austerity. It closed down in 1931 and the dancing moved elsewhere.

HOLLYWOOD COMES TO LONDON

During the interwar years, dance orchestras reigned supreme in London's West End. One of the most famous venues that became an exclusive private club was the Monseigneur Restaurant, which stood on the corner of Lower Regent Street and Jermyn Street.

A vanity project, the Monseigneur was financed by Jack Upson, the managing director of the high-street shoe-shop chain Dolcis. Upson aspired to create the most luxurious dance club in London, if not the world! To achieve this, he invested his entire fortune in creating a fantasy world where he would mingle with the rich and famous.

His first step towards living the dream was to hire leading American bandleader Roy Fox from Hollywood and to introduce a strict dress code of white tie and tails. Roy Fox had recently fronted a band at Hollywood's Coconut Grove restaurant and was musical director of Twentieth Century Fox, although no relation to the film mogul.

Fox had arrived in London in 1930 when he was booked for an eight-week season at the Café de Paris. Waving a chequebook and giving Fox carte blanche to plan his own programme and hire the most talented musicians, Upson managed to secure the famous bandleader known as the 'Whispering Cornettist'.

Roy Fox and his Orchestra debuted at the Monseigneur on its opening night, 27 May 1931. Playing his muted instrument, the soft-spoken Fox, clad in white tie and tails, launched into his signature tune, 'Whispering'. Similarly attired, his dance band included some of the best jazz musicians of the period, such as clarinettist Billy Amstell, later to star in his own right as bandleader of Ambrose, trumpet player Nat Gonella, Lew Stone on piano and vocalist Al Bowlly, who also played acoustic guitar.

The marble-clad and rococo carved interior of the basement club was the last word in luxury as couples made their way down a grand marble staircase to a cocktail bar or tables that surrounded the huge ballroom where the orchestra would perform on a raised podium. At 10.30 p.m. the music would start.

Very soon the Monseigneur started to attract attention. Edward, Prince of Wales, is said to have dined there on several occasions and Upson offered free entry to the prince and his circle of friends. Royalty aside, the club attracted names like Jack Buchanan, Noël Coward, Hoagy Carmichael, Lady Diana Cooper and the Maharanee of Sarawak.

Always eager to further his career, Fox got Upson to agree to an arrangement with the BBC to broadcast music live from the Monseigneur every Tuesday night. By now the band had become nationally famous and was one of the highlights of London's nightlife. These live concerts elevated the band's singer Al Bowlly to cult status.

A crooner, Al Bowlly's mellow voice provided a string of musical hits including 'Love is the Sweetest Thing', 'Night and Day' and 'The Very Thought of You'. The long-anticipated last waltz was a cue for Bowlly to sing 'Goodnight Sweetheart'. He recorded a string of hits with the Ray Noble Orchestra on HMV. Emerging as the pre-eminent British vocalist of the 1930s, his reputation for a while eclipsed that of the rising US singer Bing Crosby. Al Bowlly left the band to tour the USA where he made guest appearances at New York's Radio City.

Meanwhile, a punishing work regime, including live performances at the Paramount Cinema Regent Street and the Carlton Cinema in the Haymarket, took a toll on Fox's constitution. After less than a year at the Monseigneur, Fox's health broke down and he was sent to a Swiss sanitorium to recover. Lew Stone took over as bandleader. Three months later Fox was fired from the Monseigneur and moved with a re-formed orchestra to the Café Anglais.

The resulting contractual dispute with Fox and the stresses of dealing with volatile musicians drained the last of Jack Upson's reserves of money and patience. In September 1934 he quit. The Monseigneur was converted into a cinema, which it remains to the present day.

CHEZ VICTOR

One of the most exclusive and notorious nightclubs, Chez Victor was owned and run by Italian Victor Perosino. Opened in 1924 at 9 Grafton Street, Chez Victor attracted the international smart set, including stars like Fred Astaire, Jack Buchanan, US star of stage and screen Tallulah Bankhead, and royalty, including the Prince of Wales, his brother, the Duke of York, King Alfonso of Spain and England's glamorous power couple Dickie Mountbatten, a rising naval officer and cousin to the king, and his wife Edwina, Lady Mountbatten.

Edwina was frequently unescorted when her husband was away at sea and at some point in 1926, either in America or Paris, she became the lover of the black singer and pianist Leslie Hutchinson, better known as 'Hutch'. Handsome, well-endowed and with a powerful libido, 'Hutch' was at the very top of his fame when he performed in C.B. Cochran's revue *One Dam Thing After Another* at the London Pavilion from May 1927.

Matters swiftly came to a head after 'Hutch' became resident singer at Chez Victor in 1927. The lovers were frequently seen together in public.

Joan Vyvyan, a young socialite, recalled, 'At Chez Victor, he used to sing directly to Edwina Mountbatten who, on one occasion, took off her chiffon scarf and put it round his neck and kissed him while he was playing.'[7] According to historian Andrew Lownie, the affair was 'an open secret'. Mountbatten was reported to have exploded in public, 'If I ever catch that man Hutch, I'll kill him.'[8]

BOTTLE PARTIES

If guests wanted to drink alcohol long into the night, there was little that could be done to enforce antiquated licensing laws. Many nightclubs, including Chez Victor, were prepared to break the law or at least bend the rules. This involved hosting what were known as 'bottle parties'. Under this system, guests added to an invitation list were credited with pre-ordering a bottle of spirits before the official time for last orders. They were thus able to carry on drinking and enjoying the bottle they had ordered but not yet paid for.

Revellers might begin the evening at one club, but when it closed they would head for a 'bottle party'. Bright Young Things would dance at the Café de Paris until 1.30 a.m. and then head to Chez Victor's to continue their festivities. Chez Victor was said not to have really come alive until after two in the morning. The fact that rules were flagrantly breeched was an embarrassment to the government, especially since royalty was involved.

But on the morning of Saturday, 12 November 1927, matters took an unhappy turn when the police raided Chez Victor. The dragnet was carefully timed to avoid trapping the Prince of Wales, who was known to be taking an evening off. He was booked on the following day to lead a delegation to the Cenotaph to honour the dead of the Great War and so would be absent.

A few weeks later, Victor was summoned for unlawfully selling tobacco, wine and spirits by retail without a licence. A fine of £250 was imposed and on 9 February 1928 the name of the club was struck off the registry and the doors closed. Victor was ordered to be deported – a decision that was not only harsh but also unprecedented. Perhaps it was because he knew too many scandalous secrets of his rich and influential clientele.

Away from the haunts of high society, some nightclubs were regarded as hotbeds of criminality. Many of these clubs were located in Soho basements and were similar to the 'speakeasies' of New York and Chicago. Bohemians mixed with the criminal underworld and drugs and girls were freely available. Dancing partners could be arranged for single men and women prepared to pay for sexual favours.

Louche clubs like Murray's Jazz and Cabaret Club, famous for its scantily clad dancers, the 43 Club at 43 Gerrard Street and the Silver Slipper Club just off Regent Street thrived as fronts for illicit drinking and sex. For many years, these and other basement clubs were able to operate under the radar as local police turned a blind eye to such activities. Indeed, there are reports that senior officers accepted bribes. In December 1936 a police raid of Soho nightclubs discovered twenty-seven bottle parties in full swing.

The Astor Club, which operated in Mayfair from the 1930s, became the haunt of royals, car dealers and career criminals. The Astor was one of the most prestigious of a number of nightclubs and 'hostess clubs', which spanned a period from the mid 1930s to the 1960s, and enjoyed popularity during the Second World War as a late-night watering hole. It was owned by Bertie Green, a businessman and impresario who had the habit of cheating cabaret performers out of the fees they were owed.

THE QUEEN OF CLUBS

When toothy Lancashire ukulele player George Formby launched into his popular comedy hit 'Fanlight Fanny', audiences would have immediately recognised who he was referring to. When the song was written in the 1930s, Formby's raddled club hostess would have been an almost literal description of Kate Meyrick, queen of West End nightclubs in the roaring twenties.

Meyrick's slide into notoriety had started gradually. A genteel Irish woman brought up in middle-class Dublin, Meyrick had been married to a doctor who ran a private mental asylum in Brighton for shell-shocked soldiers. When her husband abandoned her, Meyrick upped sticks and left for London with six children in tow. In London she invested her divorce settlement in buying a partnership in a shady tea-dance venue in Leicester Square called Dalton's. The tea dances turned out to be a prostitution racket based on the exhibition dancers whose time could be booked by patrons for a variety of purposes, including dancing.

With six hungry mouths to feed and school fees to pay, Meyrick quickly learned that nightclubs could provide an unlimited source of ready money so long as you had no moral scruples, were prepared to break the law and had the right connections.

Meyrick opened her first club at 43 Gerrard Street in 1923. The 43 Club was an after-hours drinking club, which became a magnet for film stars, gangsters, good-time girls, jazz musicians and aristocrats. The alcohol flowed freely as jazz musicians like Nat Gonella, Billy Amstell, Teddy Brown and Manny Klein dropped in to 'have a blow', playing improvised jazz to relax after an evening playing with a band at a West End restaurant. After last orders the crowd, now in a party mood, were served drinks, which Meyrick would claim had been pre-ordered.

Known to her wealthy patrons as 'Ma', Meyrick made a healthy profit selling champagne at £2 a bottle. The Lancashire millionaire Jimmy White once turned up with an entourage of six Daimlers full of showgirls to a late-night champagne party. This extravagance cost him £400.

Meyrick opened the Silver Slipper Club off Regent Street. This was a dancing establishment whose claim to fame lay in its mirrored dance floor which encouraged downward glances as the men tried to spy a flash of their dancing partner's expensive lingerie.

Meyrick's clubs have been accused of being a front for prostitution. Attractive dance hostesses were employed to persuade gullible men to buy them bottles of vastly overpriced house champagne or cuddly toys in the hope of sexual favours to come. Sex was rarely forthcoming and the men would leave the club in the early hours of the morning with an empty wallet and a severe hangover.

One of Ma Meyrick's inner circle, Mildred Hoey, left to set up her own club, the Bag O' Nails at 9 Kingly Street, just off Carnaby Street. The club offered a warm welcome to black jazz musicians and call girls. The club survived in a different incarnation during London's swinging sixties, when it reopened as an intimate music club hosting stars like Paul McCartney and Jimi Hendrix.

Despite the customary and flagrant breaches of the law, Ma Meyrick appeared to lead a charmed life. Her clubs were seldom targeted by the law, and on the odd occasion they were raided, plenty of advance warning would be given. It was rumoured that Ma had bribed the local police and, in any case, club members included prominent politicians and lords for whom a scandal would have been damaging.

Nevertheless, the 43 Club and the Silver Slipper were raided on a number of occasions and Ma received a total of five prison sentences and countless fines. In 1929, she received a fifteen-month prison sentence for bribing a police sergeant and was sent to Holloway Prison. Prematurely aged, Meyrick's health never fully recovered from this ordeal and she died of pneumonia in January 1933.

The Queen of Clubs left an undisputed legacy, marrying two of her daughters into the aristocracy. Nancy Meyrick married Baron de Clifford in 1926, and two years later her sister May was led to the altar by the 14th Earl of Kinoull.

LONDON'S JAZZ HOTSPOT

The West End's love affair with black musicians, singers and dancers, which started with touring New York vaudeville acts and the successful staging of musical revues like *In Dahomey* and *Blackbirds*, changed and enriched the cultural landscape. It embraced a wave of talent coming from the West Indies that included pianist and nightclub singer Leslie 'Hutch' Hutchinson, the bandleader Ken 'Snakehips' Johnson and many others.

Serving London's growing black diaspora, clubs like the Nest, Jig's Club in Wardour Street, the Blue Lagoon and the Frisco in Frith Street, and the Big Apple and the Cuba Club in Gerrard Street, Soho, were central to the development of black jazz and bringing it to a wider audience. Many clubs were run by black entrepreneurs with connections to the music industry; some like Ike Hatch had close links to Pan-African politics.

While clubs like the 43 and even Chez Victor openly flouted licensing laws, the police regarded Soho's edgy jazz-oriented clubs with suspicion, if not outright hostility. Quite apart from their late-night partying, clubs run by black proprietors were said to turn a blind eye to dancing between same-sex couples and encouraged relationships between black men and white women.

The most famous of the 'black clubs' was the Shim Sham at 37 Wardour Street, owned by Jewish businessman 'Flash' Jack Isow and black American jazz musician Ike Hatch. Founded in 1935 and named after a lively tap dance originating from Harlem, New York, the Shim Sham ran a night cabaret featuring dancers, the Trinidadian drummer George 'Midnight' Blake and his band and Hetty Booth and her Palm Beach Stompers. A small ad appearing in *The Stage* and dated 22 April 1937 reads: 'BEAUTIFUL GIRLS Wanted for West End Floor Show. Height 5' 2" to 5' 6". Must be good Tap Dancers. Apply Shim-Sham, 37 Wardour Street.'

The Shim Sham held a special place in the hearts of jazz afficionados. It was the real deal according to the *Melody Maker*, which ran an article titled 'Harlem in London', published on 7 March 1936 and illustrated with a photograph of Ike Hatch, resplendent in white tie and tails. Written by Spike Hughes, the article gushed, 'Jazz is the music of Harlem gin mills, Georgia backyards and New Orleans street corners – the music of a race that plays, sings and dances because music is its most direct medium of expression and escape.'[9]

Representing the cutting edge of African American jazz, musicians like Duke Ellington, Dizzy Gillespie and Louis Armstrong were frequent visitors to the Shim Sham when in London. Despite critical acclaim, West End hotels refused to accept these talented black musicians as guests. They faced wide-spread discrimination and racial abuse except when on stage.

Later in his career, Louis Armstrong would be accused of setting back the cause of black rights when he appeared with white entertainers, employing his gravelly voice to make schmaltzy sentimental hit records like 'It's a Wonderful World'. But in the 1920s and '30s, the jazz trumpeter from New Orleans paved the way for his fellow African American musicians.

Like many of Soho's diverse nightspots, the Shim Sham was tolerant of people's ethnicity and sexuality. It set out to break down barriers and appealed to the broad-minded constituency unafraid of playing with the expression of non-standard sexual orientation. Inside the club, through a haze of marijuana smoke, '"pale faces" from the suburbs jostled with prostitutes and pimps, single-sex dancing couples, lesbian waitresses who were visited by rich white women, international black stars, black working people and representatives of high bohemia'.[10]

The Shim Sham's customers were designated 'persons of interest' by the Metropolitan Police who attempted on many occasions to infiltrate the club using undercover police officers. According to a report that appeared in the *Daily Herald* of 1 October 1935, just weeks after opening, the club and named individuals were fined a total of £449 for holding a 'bottle party', and for keeping a disorderly house. Appearing on the same charge sheet and described as a 'dance hostess', Josephine Trittle was fined £6 for soliciting.

In 1936, the Florence Mills Social Parlour at 50 Carnaby Street was the club to go to. Named after the black dancer and actress Florence Mills, who had starred in C.B. Cochran's revue *Blackbirds*, the Social Parlour was run by Amy Ashwood, the first wife of black activist Marcus Garvey. Part jazz club, part restaurant and part social centre, this club attracted many of the leading Afro-Caribbean figures of pre-war London.

By early 1940, the Social Parlour was under new management and was operating as the Blue Lagoon Club, and had acquired a dubious reputation. It was said that guns had to be handed in at the cloakroom along with coats.

Three murders and several serious assaults were reported by the contemporary press as being linked to the club.

A WARM WELCOME FOR BLACK SERVICEMEN

During the Second World War, black American GIs stationed in Britain found a warm welcome at these clubs and no shortage of white women eager to dance with them. Many at the time were accused of being prostitutes but were in fact a mix of shop girls and young women serving with the armed forces or volunteer ambulance drivers looking for a good time. Black soldiers brought their own brand of music with them, and some were jazz performers in their own right.

A wartime West Indian drinking club, the Bouillabaisse International in Old Compton Street, Soho, open between 1941 and 1943, is credited with being one of the first to hold freestyle jamming sessions for jazz musicians. At this time, most African Americans were moving away from the big-band jazz sound that had been commercialised by mainstream bandleaders such as Glenn Miller, Tommy Dorsey and Benny Goodman in favour of complex and virtuoso jazz arrangements known as bebop, championed in the States by Dizzy Gillespie, Charlie Parker and Miles Davies.

The Bouillabaisse became home to bebop jazz and guests danced to the beat of the resident West Indian rumba band led by Clarry Wears. Very soon British luminaries such as Ronnie Scott, Johnny Dankworth and his wife Cleo Laine would be performing there.

While the US Army was segregated along racial lines, Soho's jazz clubs offered black American GIs a space where they could be among friends. Word quickly spread of the warm welcome they could expect. Subsequently, a subculture of clubs and entertainment venues emerged to cater for black soldiers. Many white British club owners also resented the colour bar and welcomed black troops.

In 1943, *Picture Post* magazine published an exposé of the moral dilemma posed by interracial dancing. Illustrated with a series of dramatic photographs taken inside the Bouillabaisse International in Soho, white girls were seen embracing and dancing with black American GIs. The article was titled 'Inside London's Coloured Clubs'.

Later the same year the club closed and was replaced by a new club, the Fullado, under new management, where jazz was played from 3 p.m. till midnight. It was a free and easy place for musicians to drop in and jam, and where 'off the cuff' bands would be formed. Musicians such as Ronnie Scott, Tommy Whittle, Don Rendell, Denis Rose, Johnny Dankworth, Hank Shaw and Tommy Pollard all played there regularly.

The Fullado closed in 1955, by which time a new generation of jazz clubs was taking over, including the 100 Club in Oxford Street, the Jamboree in Wardour Street and Ronnie Scott's, which originally opened in October 1959 on Gerrard Street, before moving to its current location at 47 Frith Street in 1965.

In the 1930s and '40s, the existence of the pioneering black jazz clubs in Soho paved the way for modern jazz. Without the freedom of musical expression fostered by places like the Shim Sham and the Bouillabaisse, clubs like Ronnie Scott's would not exist.

THE GAY SCENE

Soho, Leicester Square, Piccadilly and Covent Garden were areas of the West End most accepting of gay men and lesbians. London's cosmopolitan heart offered a natural camouflage for people fleeing political or racial persecution. Soho's narrow streets and enclosed courtyards were home to a variety of basement clubs and dive bars where minorities could find a welcome. Homosexual acts were against the law and anyone found engaging in them could be imprisoned under harsh laws that were only repealed in 1964.

The Cave of the Golden Calf, located beneath Heddon Street in Mayfair, was the first recorded gay club in London's West End. Eric Gill designed the club's motif of a phallic Golden Calf, which was a symbol of biblical dissipation. When it opened in 1912, the bohemian hangout pushed boundaries and almost immediately started alarm bells ringing in law-enforcement circles.

Philip Hoare describes the Golden Calf in his book *Oscar Wilde's Last Stand*. 'Down a dark cul-de-sac lurked a new and devilish sort of place where Futurists cavorted,' he wrote. The founders' own stated aim was to create 'a place given up to gaiety ... a hideout brazenly expressive of the libertarian pleasure principle'. The Golden Calf was closed down in 1914.

Although many of the Soho nightspots of the 1930s and '40s were tolerant of gay men and lesbians, and turned a blind eye to same-sex couples dancing, homosexuality was against the law and to be seen openly encouraging same-sex couples could land any club in a lot of trouble. Many chose to defy the law.

Sandy's Bar at 25 Oxendon Street, off the Haymarket, was a sandwich bar set up by the actor Kenelm Foss and inspired by a trip to New York, where coffee and sandwich bars enjoyed popularity during the Prohibition era. Open all hours, Sandy's attracted actresses and revue dancers as much as it did gay men, lesbians and transvestites. The *Weekly Dispatch* described the crowd thus: 'Women in gorgeous lamé cloaks sit on high stools and rest their feathered fans upon the bar counter while their escorts sit holding their silk hats, waiting for the sandwiches of their choice.'[11] This was a tolerant, easy-going place.

The Long Bar at the Trocadero in Shaftesbury Avenue and Lyons Corner House in Coventry Street were well-established pick-up points for gay men. Lyons was referred to by those in the know as 'the lily pond' – probably a reference to the Aesthetic movement.

Gay men and lesbians needed their own clubs where they could celebrate their sexuality and let their hair down in the same way that heterosexual couples could. Opened on 14 July 1934 at 81 Endell Street, Covent Garden, the Caravan Club became for a while a haven for London's gay community. It was run by eccentric entrepreneur Jack 'Ironfoot' Neave. Neave's right leg had been permanently shortened as a result of an accident. To compensate he wore a metal device on his right boot, hence the nickname. When inebriated, his dragging foot reputedly caused sparks to fly. He gave a range of colourful and frankly unbelievable accounts of how his injury had been sustained: being bitten by a shark while pearl diving, being injured by an avalanche in Tibet, to name a couple.

Situated in the basement of a warehouse building with a discreet entrance in a courtyard off the main street, the Caravan relied for its publicity on business cards handed around within the gay community. A surviving calling card advertised the club as 'London's Greatest Bohemian Rendezvous, said to be the most unconventional spot in town' and further promised a 'Night of Gaiety'. Expressions such as 'bohemian' and 'unconventional' were regarded as synonymous with homosexuality.

Almost immediately, the club came to the attention of the police. Letters were sent from residents who noticed the comings and goings, one of whom described the club on little evidence as an 'absolute sink of iniquity'. In late July, plainclothes police officers visited to find out what was going on. One constable reported seeing mainly male couples dancing and had spoken to a cross-dressing man named 'Josephine'. Female couples were seen dancing together and 'importuning by predatory individuals' was observed.

The club was raided in the early hours of 25 August and 103 people were arrested. A cache of firearms was found. Reports in the tabloid press sparked prurient interest in some of the sensational details of the charges – men discovered kissing other men, women soliciting, as well as 'divers lewd, scandalous, bawdy and obscene performances and practices to the manifest corruption of the morals of his Majesty's liege subjects'.

Eager for amusement, the public gathered outside Bow Street Magistrate's Court on the day of the trial. *The Illustrated Police News* of Thursday, 6 September, reported a crowd of over 300 composed of 'shirt sleeved Covent Garden porters, young women who were obviously typists and men on their way to business'. The police formed a cordon. As the accused were led through the throng they were subjected to 'cheers, jeers and ribald comments'. As each male defendant arrived, they were met with calls from the crowd such as 'What ho, Gerald' or, for women, ''Ere comes Tilly'.

The Hambone Club in Ham Yard, Soho, located at the site of the new Ham Yard Hotel, flouted convention. The club was said to be a 'cauldron of homosexual promiscuity' and a breeding ground for extramarital affairs of every flavour. Lesbian and male couples danced intimately. Ethel Mannin's 1925 novel *Sounding Brass* makes a veiled reference to the Hambone's famously androgynous performers – one pianist is described as 'either a masculine woman or a feminine man'.

HIGH BOHEMIA

Financed by Welsh matinee idol Ivor Novello and Gaiety Girl-turned-Shakespearian actor Constance Collier, the Fifty-Fifty Club in Wardour Street opened on 1 October 1923. The club was intended as an exciting new venue for theatrical people and bohemians, and invitation was by word of mouth.

The name Fifty-Fifty provoked much speculation at the time. Some said it was a reference to Novello's ambivalent sexuality, others that it was intended to attract equal numbers of gay men and lesbians.

The Fifty-Fifty had a cocktail bar and a large room for dancing and cabaret acts. Events and club nights were advertised discreetly in *The Era* or *The Stage*, and membership fees were minimal as Novello ran the loss-making business as a social enterprise and party venue, which attracted many of theatre's leading lights including Noël Coward, Ernest Thesiger, Michael Arlen, John Gielgud, Gertrude Lawrence, Gladys Cooper, Fay Compton and Tallulah Bankhead. Novello's Canadian boyfriend Bobbie Andrews was a frequent visitor.

Plays were discussed, connections made, gossip exchanged and actors or singers might make impromptu performances. While Oscar Wilde and his coterie were happy to conduct their private lives and affairs at the Café Royal, confident that privacy would be respected, the Fifty-Fifty was essentially a bohemian world whose members referred to one another as 'Us', a charmed theatrical inner circle.

David Tennant, son of 1st Baron Glenconner, established the Gargoyle Club at Meard Street in 1925. Famous artists, literary types and gay men rubbed shoulders with socialites and peers of the realm. The walls of the club were decorated with mirrored tiles and paintings by the French impressionist Matisse, who was an honorary member. A rooftop garden overlooked theatreland.

Besides the founder's younger brother, poet Stephen Tennant, the club attracted a galaxy of literary and artistic talent, many of them gay: Noël Coward, Virginia Woolf and the artists Augustus John and Duncan Grant, a leading member of the Bloomsbury Set.

After performing in his first major breakthrough as a stage actor when he starred in *The Vortex* at the Royalty Theatre, Coward and members of the cast would come and eat sausages and bacon at the Gargoyle Club and listen to the dance band. Joining the mix were the socialite Nancy Cunard and her companion Iris Tree, daughter of the celebrated manager of His Majesty's Theatre, Herbert Beerbohm Tree.

Headstrong daughter of shipping magnate Sir Bache Cunard and his young American wife Emerald, Nancy Cunard was a rebel who smoked cigarettes, wore her hair in a severe bob and sported trousers. A well-known presence in the West End's top restaurants and nightclubs, Nancy Cunard lent glamour and a seal of approval to the Gargoyle.

As a teenager she had made a dramatic entrance into the Café Royal accompanied by Iris Tree in the early summer of 1914. Diners were scandalised that two young society women could appear in public unaccompanied. This freedom was reserved for prostitutes and *demi-mondaines* who were brazen enough to defy convention. Piccadilly played by its own rules.

Nancy and Iris and their sexually liberated artist friend Nina Hamnett showed their contempt for the bastions of male privilege by walking into clubs and restaurants unchallenged. Their insouciance helped define the West End of the roaring twenties and encouraged other independent-minded young women known as 'flappers' who came to colonise a social sphere that had always been customarily male.

A CRUCIBLE OF CREATIVITY

Soho's nightclubs were a crucible of creativity. New forms of jazz music and experimentation fed the music and film industries with ideas. In these exciting places, black jazz musicians, dancers and actors mingled with celebrities, bohemians and the avant-garde. During the repressive and conformist interwar years, nightclubs were an important safety valve and a social space where London's cosmopolitan talent could feel at home and forge its own identity.

8

THE THEATRE

The drama's laws the drama patrons give
For we that live to please, must please to live.
…
Bid scenic Virtue form the rising age,
And Truth diffuse her radiance from the stage.

> Prologue to the opening night of the Theatre Royal,
> Drury Lane, by Dr Johnson, 1747

THE RESTORATION

Regarded as sinful, London's bright and bawdy theatres, including the famous Globe in Southwark, were closed in 1640 by order of Oliver Cromwell and demolished. There followed twenty years in which all festivities, including dancing, were banned. The Restoration of the Monarchy in 1660 unleashed a pent-up desire for pleasure.

The theatre that had thrived during the time of Shakespeare was revived and, with it, a welter of plays that explored previously taboo subjects such as sexual attraction, marital infidelity and high living. Known today collectively as 'Restoration Comedies', the plays by William Wycherley, William Congreve and Oliver Goldsmith were for a brief time not subject to censorship.

Two companies were licensed by the Lord Chamberlain, the Duke's Company and the King's Company, who first performed in converted buildings like indoor tennis courts. Under royal patronage, the Theatre Royal opened in 1663. Sadly, it was destroyed by a fire nine years later and replaced by a new structure designed by Christopher Wren. This lasted for almost a century, until 1791, when it was replaced by a much larger building by actor-manager Richard Brinsley Sheridan. This survived for a further fifteen years before it too burnt down. The current Theatre Royal, Drury Lane, dates from 1812 and is the West End's oldest theatre.

THE ITALIAN OPERA

In the early eighteenth century, the craze for Italian opera was sweeping Europe. Cities like Dresden, Milan, Madrid and Naples all had thriving opera houses as their royal families vied with each other to attract Italian composers and operatic stars. London could only look on in envy.

In 1703, the playwright and architect Sir John Vanbrugh launched a subscription among aristocratic members of the Kit Kat Club to fund an opera house. Raising the sum of £2,000, Vanbrugh bought a stable yard and a long leasehold at the corner of Haymarket and Pall Mall, which was cleared to build a theatre.

Known as the home of the Italian Opera, and named in honour of the reigning monarch, Queen Anne, the Queen's Theatre in the Haymarket opened on 9 April 1705. The opening night saw a performance of the opera *Gli amori di Ergasto* (*The Loves of Ergasto*) by Jakob Greber, performed by a group of Italian singers. It was a commercial flop that struggled on until May before finally closing. Undeterred, Vanbrugh ploughed time and money into the project for a further four years before finally cutting his losses and selling the lease. Vanbrugh was both a poor theatre manager and, on this occasion, an indifferent architect.

While the proscenium arch and the columns and lofty spaces made a bold statement, actors struggled to make their voices heard amid the echoing auditorium. Colley Cibber described the drawbacks thus:

> The Front-boxes were a continued Semicircle to the bare walls of the House on each Side: This extraordinary and superfluous Space occasion'd such an Undulation from the Voice of every Actor, that generally what they said sounded like the Gabbling of so many People in the lofty Isles in a Cathedral.

The arrival of George Frideric Handel in 1711 saved the Queen's Theatre from certain bankruptcy. Performed in English, his opera *Rinaldo* featured two fashionable castrati, Nicolò Grimaldi and Valentino Urbani, whose piercing high notes overcame the theatre's acoustic limitations. Castrati were able to sing countertenor parts and were highly popular with audiences. All of the early Italian operas featured castrati and famous names Farinelli, Senesino and Gaetano Berenstadt drew large audiences. These stars were often paired with female singers whose range was versatile enough for them to play 'breeches' parts'. Early opera often played on sexual ambiguity. Handel's rivals in popularity were the composers Attilio Ariosti and Giovanni Bononcini, who between them wrote a string of successful operas all performed in Italian.

On the accession of King George I in 1714, the opera house changed its name to the King's Theatre. Handel received royal assent to open the Royal Academy of Music, an operatic company that lasted from 1719 until his departure in 1734 to direct music and opera at the Covent Garden Theatre. A subscription led by Lord Burlington and a group of noblemen including the Dukes of Kent, Newcastle, Grafton, Portland, Chandos and Manchester raised more than £17,000, enabling Handel's Royal Academy of Music to build a permanent pool of talented singers, recruited from across Europe. These singers formed the basis of the Haymarket's Italian opera and gave the King's Theatre the boost it needed among London's beau monde.

Unlike today's polite connoisseurs, Georgian audiences were rowdy and badly behaved. Theatres were noisy, chaotic places where the aim was to see and be seen. During performances the entire auditorium and stage would remain lit, enabling people to mingle freely and young rakes to flirt shamelessly with the ladies. It was not unknown for gentlemen to have a table in the box for a game of cards during the performance, pausing only to listen to their favourite arias. Furthermore, members of the audience who had paid for the privilege were allowed to stand at the edge of the stage only a few feet from the action, thereby adding to the general confusion.

Then, as now, the opera was an expensive luxury. Seats had to be booked ahead for the entire coming season and boxes were available for an annual subscription of 20 guineas per person. Prices varied and, while a pit seat might typically be had for half a guinea, an individual might pay up to £5 if a popular diva was performing.

Despite this elitism, opera houses made an attempt to broaden their appeal. There were occasionally concessionary standing places available for footmen at a few shillings, but it was a contentious issue. When the Theatre Royal, Covent Garden, removed the low-priced seats concession in 1762, a riot broke out as the audience invaded the stage and started hurling missiles, and members of the orchestra and cast had to flee for their lives.

DIVA WARS

Huge sums were paid to attract the best talent from across Europe and, over the coming decades, a succession of divas such as Francesca Cuzzoni, Faustina Bordoni and the hugely talented singer impresario Regina Mingotti graced the West End stage, their talent winning them scores of male admirers.

Born in Parma, the Italian soprano Francesca Cuzzoni sang in Bologna, Florence and Turin before being lured to London in 1722 to play the lead in Handel's opera *Ottone*. She was paid £2,000 for the season in spite of being described by the diarist Fanny Burney as being 'short and squat with a doughy cross face but fine complexion'. This record salary was soon topped by the £2,500 offered to her Venetian rival Faustina Bordoni several years later.

Bordoni's London debut came in 1726 when she took the role of Roxana in Handel's *Alessandro*. Cuzzoni and Bordoni divided male opinion as fan worship developed into an unhealthy obsession. The following year, both sopranos sang in Bononcini's opera *Astianatte*. At a performance attended by Princess Caroline on 6 June, rival fans came to blows and the opera house erupted into pandemonium.

A report in *The British Journal* described the incident:

> The Contention at first was only carried on by Hissing on one side, and Clapping on the other; but proceeded at length to Catcalls, and other great Indecencies: And ...[the two singers] pull'd each others' coiffs. It is certainly an apparent Shame that two such well-bred ladies should call each other Bitch and Whore, should Scold and Fight like any Billingsgaters.[1]

The curtain came down, the audience was ushered off the premises and the rest of the season was cancelled. Faustina Bordoni left England never to return.

Cuzzoni herself stayed on but left England in 1737, shortly before Handel moved on. She sang in Florence and Vienna, but her reputation took a dive when she was accused of poisoning her husband, a charge which was never substantiated. Returning to the West End briefly in 1750, she attempted to revive her career but to little avail as she was arrested that same year for a debt of £30. Bailed by the Prince of Wales, Cuzzoni sang her final benefit concert on 20 May 1751 and vanished from public life.

MASQUERADE

In 1719, a Swiss businessman, John James Heidegger, was appointed stage manager of the King's Theatre. Sent by a relative to England to sell stage machinery, Heidegger insinuated himself into the theatre and quickly made himself indispensable. Styling himself 'Count', the ambitious Heidegger proceeded to conquer London society.

Heidegger's real talents lay as an organiser of masquerades, a popular European pastime where attendees dressed up in exotic costume and engaged in even more exotic behaviour. These were imported into London and their venues needed to be somewhere discreet. The King's Theatre was ideal both in terms of location and privacy. Extending the stage into the auditorium, Heidegger created a dance floor that could be used in the winter season when opera performances ceased. Hanging cloths painted with rustic scenes covered the walls, creating a backdrop, and a false ceiling completed the effect of this improvised ballroom. Dancers could retire to a long gallery on the first floor, which had been fitted out as a fashionable tea room. Between 1729 and 1734, Handel joined Heidegger as joint manager in this enterprise.

Heidegger's masquerade balls subsidised Handel's high art. Heidegger's involvement with the King's Theatre lasted right up until his death in 1749. During the last seven years Heidegger had formed a partnership with Robert Arthur, the proprietor of the exclusive St James's gentlemen's club White's to run 'balls, masquerades and assemblies'.

THE FINAL YEARS OF ITALIAN OPERA

Attracting audiences to see cultural entertainments has always been a risky business. Bankruptcy was never far away. The 1770s was a particularly hard time for playwright Richard Brinsley Sheridan and Thomas Harris who took over the lease of the King's Theatre. Ballet was performed, but as it proved hard to keep a corps of professional dancers, the new owners hired a group of amateurs. In 1788, members of the cast fled for their lives after an angry audience stormed the stage demanding their money back. Sheridan filed for bankruptcy.

A year later a mysterious fire broke out, which burned the theatre to the ground. In 1789 opera was staged at the Pantheon in Oxford Street and for a time the two companies existed under a single management: the Pantheon took over the royal patent while the King's Theatre was being rebuilt. A new King's Theatre was opened in 1791 – a more substantial building with an auditorium able to seat 2,500. It began by staging ballet and dance performances.

From 1794, Italian opera returned to the Haymarket, coinciding with the popularity of a new style of baroque opera. Mozart's first London performance of *La clemenza di Tito* was performed in 1806, swiftly followed by *Così fan tutte* and *Die Zauberflöte* (*The Magic Flute*). Gaetano Donizetti and Vincenzo Bellini also premiered in London.

The season 1824–25 was the most successful ever as the celebrated soprano Giuditta Pasta arrived from Paris to take London by storm in an outstanding season of opera, and on 24 April 1824 she premiered in *Otello* with its composer, Rossini, himself directing. A theatre critic wrote, 'This lady inspires it [her voice] with such eloquence of the mind, and by mere management, distributes it with the variety of light and shade that she renders it the medium of extraordinary dramatic effect.'[2]

Improvements by the architects John Nash and Humphrey Repton gave the King's Theatre a new stuccoed frontage to blend in stylistically with Nash's architectural vision for London's West End. This included an arcade formed of a continuous portico of Doric columns. It was renamed the Italian Opera House in 1830.

Fashions began to change to embrace a new romanticism and the Italian Opera House attracted operatic composers Felix Mendelssohn, Giuseppe Verdi and Gaetano Donizetti. The final and perhaps best-known prima donna was Jenny Lind, whose melodious singing voice earned her the soubriquet the 'Swedish nightingale'.

This great building burned down in 1867 and was replaced with a theatre in the Gothic style. Italian opera was off the menu. But part of Nash's remodelled building survives in the form of the Opera Arcade on Pall Mall, now home to a row of boutiques and an art gallery, but at the time, a covered walkway and entrance to the theatre.

Opera moved to the Theatre Royal, Covent Garden – a playhouse that had been built in 1732, which along with its near neighbour the Theatre Royal, Drury Lane, had been given letters patent by Charles II, giving both theatres exclusive rights to present spoken drama. Handel moved to Covent Garden to stage a series of operas and oratorios after falling out with the management of the King's Theatre, Haymarket, and his disreputable former business partner Heidegger.

Fire ravaged the Theatre Royal, Covent Garden, on two successive occasions, but after its final rebuilding in 1858 it was reborn as the Royal Opera House.

Beside the ever-popular Italian opera, the 1870s saw the arrival of an entirely home-grown oeuvre: the comic operas of the librettist W.S. Gilbert and composer Arthur Sullivan. The succession of popular operas that premiered in London's West End between 1871 and 1893 drew upon English themes. They became known as the Savoy Operas because all bar the first five premiered at the Savoy Theatre in the Strand. On 10 October 1881 *Patience* was the first Gilbert and Sullivan opera to be performed at the newly built Savoy Theatre, owned and managed by the impresario and hotel entrepreneur Richard D'Oyly Carte, whose name is indelibly associated with the opera for his close artistic control.

Beginning with *Thespis*, which opened at the Gaiety Theatre on 26 December 1871, popular works like *H.M.S. Pinafore*, *The Pirates of Penzance*, *The Mikado* and *The Yeoman of the Guard* are still performed today. Many were satirical in content. *Patience*, for example, poked fun at Oscar Wilde and the Aesthetic movement, while *H.M.S. Pinafore* took a sideswipe at government cronyism in appointing the newsagent W.H. Smith to become First Lord of the Admiralty despite his complete ignorance of naval matters.

NO LEG TO STAND ON

Standing opposite the King's Theatre stood a small brick-built playhouse. The Haymarket Theatre was jokingly referred to as 'the little theatre' on account of its size and lack of significance. Dating from 1720, the theatre specialised in acerbic political satire, which led to its being temporarily shut down under the 1737 Licensing Act.

It had survived in hand-to-mouth fashion by acquiring a succession of temporary licences allowing it to compete with the Theatre Royal, Covent Garden, and the Theatre Royal, Drury Lane, who both operated under letters patent granted by the king, which conferred on them a monopoly on spoken drama. But the subversive Haymarket Theatre managed to circumvent the licensing laws by staging short musical entertainments and adding a play free of charge.

The Haymarket Theatre became indelibly associated with the flamboyant Cornishman, actor and playwright Samuel Foote, best known for a wooden leg that he used to great comic effect. Foote had lost the lower part of his right leg in a riding accident in 1766. Having made an impression as a serious actor – he played Shylock in Shakespeare's *Merchant of Venice* and Othello at the Haymarket – Foote realised his acting was no match for that of the star of the Georgian theatre, David Garrick. He turned to comedy, both writing satirical plays and acting in them.

Foote secured a lease on the Haymarket Theatre in 1746 and a year later staged his first play, *Diversions of the Morning*, a satire on the acting fraternity in which all of the main parts were played by Foote himself. Foote's popularity as a mimic put the theatre's finances on an even keel. Two satirical revues followed in quick succession, *A Dish of Chocolate* and *A Cup of Tea*, which later earned Foote the nickname of the Tea Party Man and birthed the expression, 'to give tea', meaning to give offence.

Foote's string of successes and flair for publicity finally earned him enough money to buy the theatre outright in 1766. He set about demolishing the old, little theatre and building a vastly improved theatre with the capacity to seat 1,000 people. Foote's affability and value as an entertainer enabled him to move in exalted circles and he set about cultivating a friendship with the king's brother, the Duke of York. As a result of tireless campaigning, he was granted a royal patent in 1767 enabling him to name his new playhouse the Theatre Royal, Haymarket.

The Man of Pleasure's Pocket Book of 1780 lists the cost of a single box ticket as 5s while a seat in the pit was priced at 3s. These prices compared favourably to the astronomical ticket prices charged by the Italian Opera opposite where a box was priced at 20 guineas for the season.

Foote came to a sad end. In 1777, he was arrested for a homosexual assault on a footman. The case came to court, and although he put up a spirited defence and was acquitted of the charge, his health gave out. He died the following year.

DAVID GARRICK, INVENTOR OF MODERN THEATRE

In October 1747 a rising star of the Georgian stage took over as manager of the Theatre Royal, Drury Lane. His arrival revolutionised acting and theatre management.

David Garrick was just 30 when he was offered this plum position. He was already regarded as the foremost Shakespearian actor of the age, since playing the title role of Richard III in the 1741–42 season at Drury Lane to sell-out audiences and critical acclaim. An 'unknown' from the provinces, Garrick had arrived in London from Lichfield, Staffordshire, with Dr Samuel Johnson, his former tutor who was eight years his senior. This connection with the great man of letters was to prove useful in getting established in his career. Dr Johnson wrote the 'Prologue' for his protégé that was read out on the opening night of the Theatre Royal season in 1747.

Yet it had been no easy journey. Contemporary theatre was stuck in a rut as plays were written or adapted to showcase the leading actor, who would stand centre stage and deliver his lines loud and clear like an orator, using a limited range of gestures and facial expressions. Above all, actors were chosen for their height and build. Garrick did not fit the mould: he was short, just over 5ft 2in, and of slight build. But he had one important advantage: he could act.

Garrick's strength was in the range of emotion he portrayed. He studied each part he was to play and interpreted the character's psychology. His Richard III was utterly believable; just as importantly, he went back to a version of the play closer to Shakespeare's original. Within two seasons Garrick was being paid £500 a year – a fortune for an actor at that time. By then, he had acted the parts of King Lear, Benedick in *Much Ado About Nothing* and Macbeth, often playing opposite his leading lady and sometime lover, the irrepressible Irish actor Peg Woffington.

In Georgian times, theatres were open for a season, which ran from the beginning of October to the beginning of June the following year. This followed the convention by which landed gentry retired to country estates during the summer and Parliament and the law shut down.

Garrick's main competition came from the Theatre Royal, Covent Garden, under the lacklustre management of John Rich, who one theatre historian describes as a 'semi-literate philistine ... but an excellent showman'.[3] Rich is credited with introducing pantomime to London audiences – a low form of comedy based on the Italian Commedia dell'arte.

Both venues were competing to attract an audience of no more than 12,000 people who comprised the *haute monde* of London society. Astute businessman Garrick worked hard to cater for all tastes and frequently changed programmes to offer variety. The evening programme began with a serious drama at 6 p.m., when many people would still be at work. But when the play was over Garrick would charge half price for the next part of the programme, the afterpiece, usually a three-act comedy or farce. In this way, he maximised the theatre's takings. Over the 1747–48 season comprising 190 evenings, Drury Lane massively outshone Covent Garden, staging a total of sixteen tragedies, thirty different comedies and twenty-five afterpieces.

Garrick is credited with rediscovering Shakespeare and staging plays that were true to the spirit of the original text performed in the Elizabethan theatre. It has to be remembered that at the time many different versions of Shakespeare's plays were circulating, many abridged or adapted for contemporary audiences. Garrick was invited to found a theatre at Shakespeare's birthplace in Stratford-upon-Avon and actually built an amphitheatre on the banks of the Avon.

When Garrick took over the management of the Theatre Royal, Drury Lane, a building which had been designed by Sir Christopher Wren, the theatre was in decline. In 1774, he commissioned the architect John Adam to design a new enlarged theatre in the classical style. Garrick cashed in his share of the theatre's mortgage and retired. His retirement enabled a new generation of Shakespearian actors, notably John Kemble and Mrs Siddons, to shine.

If Garrick had one weakness, it was a desire to hog the limelight and to dominate conversations, a trait that made him unclubbable and led to a falling out with his mentor Dr Johnson, who said cuttingly of him, 'No wonder, Sir, that he is vain, a man who is perpetually flattered in every mode that can be conceived. So many bellows have blown the fire, that one wonders he is not by this time become a cinder.'[4] Garrick's legacy, however, was to set new standards for acting, professionalise theatre management and lay the foundations for the Shakespeare industry.

THE DARK CHARISMA OF HENRY IRVING

On 25 November 1871 a play opened at the Lyceum Theatre that took London's West End by storm. It was a melodrama entitled *The Bells* and it turned its leading actor Henry Irving into a household name. On its opening night a woman fainted, the audience sat in stunned silence and Irving was given a standing ovation. The play saved the theatre from financial ruin and launched a superstar of the stage.

Born John Henry Brodribb and from Somerset, Irving was the pre-eminent actor-manager of his day. A tall, gaunt individual with very exaggerated mannerisms and a deep booming voice, Irving's acting style was ideally suited to the Victorian stage and to melodrama in particular. In real life, Irving's complex and charismatic character is said to have inspired Bram Stoker's 1897 Gothic novel *Dracula*. There is overwhelming evidence to support this claim. There is a notable physical similarity between the two men that is apparent in Irving's craggy face and nervous energy.

Melodrama was a formulaic, over-simplified form of drama, which was performed in three acts during which the innocents are threatened and good finally triumphs over evil. Melodrama involved stock characters – the aged parents, a daughter, her suitor and an evil villain who might attempt seduction.

Melodrama was the staple of the West End theatres of the mid to late nineteenth century and includes plays like *The Corsican Brothers*, *A Legend of the Devil's Dyke*, *The Colleen Bawn* and *The Vampire*, all of which were written by Irish playwright Dion Boucicault.

Hugely popular in its day, *The Bells* was a translation of *Le Juif Polonais* by Leopold Lewis, set in a Polish village. Irving played the part of Burgomaster Matthias, a respectable man with a guilty secret. Fifteen years earlier he had robbed a wealthy Jewish merchant to pay off his debts. Now wealthy, married and with a daughter about to be wed, Matthias is haunted by the sound of the bells from his victim's sleigh, audible only to him. In a dramatic finale Matthias suffers a violent hallucination in which he hears the ghostly bells and confesses his guilt. He dies of a heart attack. Irving went on to reprise the part many times throughout his stage career.

On the cab journey home following that dramatic debut, Irving got into a fierce argument with his wife, who had poured scorn on his acting, he got out of the cab and disappeared into the night. He chose never to see his wife again, abandoning both her and their two young sons.

A few years later, following a performance of Shakespeare's *Hamlet* in which he took the starring role, Irving granted an interview to a Dublin journalist named Bram Stoker, who was rapturous in his appreciation. The two men forged a friendship that would endure, and in 1878, when he had assumed artistic control at the Lyceum, Irving invited Stoker to be the Lyceum's business manager. He also persuaded the flame-haired actor Ellen Terry, a woman as talented as Irving himself, to be a partner in his enterprise.

There followed a decade in which Irving and Terry became the star attractions of the West End theatre. While Irving and Terry wooed audiences with *Hamlet*, *The Merchant of Venice* and *Much Ado About Nothing*, Stoker was the affable front-of-house manager, always on hand to meet and greet and ensure the finances were in order. Henry Irving was knighted for services to theatre in 1895, the first British actor to be so honoured.

Both Stoker and Irving joined the private members' institution the London Library in 1890 and their names are listed in the club records as having joined on the same day. Whereas Irving may have wanted to study the works of obscure playwrights and research some of the complex roles he was starting to play, Stoker delved deep into Gothic horror, researching folklore, vampires and the topography of Transylvania and the Carpathian Mountains.

One of the few individuals who ever got close to Irving, Stoker's characterisation of Count Dracula has amazing similarities to Irving, who he describes as being 'compact of steel and whipcord. His energy and nervous power were such as only came from a great brain; and the muscular force of that lean, lithe body must have been extraordinary.'

Dracula was published to great acclaim in 1897. Irving was unimpressed by his friend's novel and subsequently turned down the opportunity to act the title role in a dramatisation of the book. Stoker's Gothic masterpiece has gone on to inspire plays and films enjoyed by successive generations and remains a tribute to Sir Henry Irving's own dark charisma.

THE CRITERION PUTS PICCADILLY CENTRE STAGE

The Criterion on Piccadilly Circus was a new addition to West End theatres when completed in 1873. Its first production, *An American Lady*, opened a year later on 21 March 1874 under the management of H.J. Byron, who wrote and acted in the play, which featured incidental music by W.S. Gilbert.

In 1875, Charles Wyndham took over as manager and lessee of the Criterion and turned its fortunes round by establishing it as the home of farce and light comedies. Wyndham, a light comedy actor turned manager, had a very interesting career. From Liverpool, Wyndham had begun his career by training as a doctor. He subsequently abandoned his medical training and tried his hand at acting. He made his stage debut in 1862 at the Royalty Theatre, playing the juvenile lead opposite Ellen Terry. Emerging as a versatile actor, he learned his craft acting alongside famous names of the Victorian stage.

Spurred on by wanderlust, Wyndham left a promising stage career to travel to America at the time of the American Civil War, determined to join the Union Army as a medic. He served for two years. He made some guest appearances in an acting company led by John Wilkes Booth, who later achieved notoriety by assassinating US President Abraham Lincoln in a theatre.

Back in Britain, a succession of minor acting roles saw him embark on a new phase of his career as an actor-manager. His understanding of what made West End audiences tick resulted in his translating French farces for the London stage, having toned down their more risqué humour. It was a successful formula.

Wyndham was well connected. He acted in plays produced by that other great actor-manager, James Albery. Wyndham's son Howard went into a business partnership with Albery's son Bronson James Albery, later Sir Bronson Albery. Together, the duo ran the Criterion in addition to both the Wyndham and Albery Theatres. They founded a dynasty of owner-managers who shaped West End theatre and established a formula that would last right up until the 1960s.

In 1919, Charles Wyndham's career was cut short when he died of influenza during the Spanish flu epidemic of 1918–20, a health crisis that claimed more lives than the Great War.

The Criterion Theatre remained open for the duration of the Second World War. It was requisitioned by the BBC as an underground theatre, making an ideal wartime studio safe from the London Blitz. Light entertainment programmes were both recorded and broadcast live from this underground theatre.

OSCAR WILDE AND THE *VISION OF SALOME*

Renowned as London's 'literary couple', Oscar Wilde and his wife Constance arrived in London from Dublin and enjoyed cult status through being in the vanguard of the Aesthetic movement, a group of influential writers and artists that included Algernon Charles Swinburne, James McNeill Whistler and Sir Edward Burne-Jones. It is often forgotten that Constance was a well-regarded writer of poems and short stories as well as journalism.

Oscar Wilde published his first collection of short stories in 1887 and a novel, *The Picture of Dorian Gray*, in 1890. His first play *Lady Windemere's Fan*, a comedy of manners, was performed to critical acclaim when it debuted at the St James's Theatre, King Street, St James's, on 22 February 1892. His next plays, *A Woman of No Importance* and *The Importance of Being Earnest*, cemented Wilde's reputation as playwright and a writer of epigrams (witty asides).

But Wilde the Aesthete wanted to push artistic boundaries. At the same time *Lady Windemere's Fan* was being performed he was in Paris working on *Salome*, a risqué dramatisation of King Herod's daughter Salome's beheading of St John the Baptist. Heavily laced with eroticism, the play's central character performs the dance of the seven veils. In an effort to appease the censors and preserve artistic integrity, Wilde wrote his play in French. The internationally famous actor Sarah Bernhardt collaborated with the playwright and had even promised to take the lead part. It all looked set to go.

Sadly, the censor was of a different opinion. *Salome* was blasphemous and obscene and could not be staged. Wilde decided to have a limited edition printed, bound with purple cloth covers, which he distributed widely to his friends.

He approached his publisher John Lane of the Bodley Head of Vigo Street, Piccadilly, who commissioned a lavishly illustrated English translation of the play. Already well known for his eroticism, Aubrey Beardsley was chosen to provide the artwork. Today, Beardsley's sinuous Salome triumphantly bearing aloft the saint's severed head is regarded as an iconic masterpiece reflecting the decadence of the 1890s.

That decadence extended to Wilde's own bisexuality. Despite being married and having a son, Wilde's dalliance with the young Oxford scholar Lord Alfred Douglas, nicknamed 'Bosie', was an open secret. Bosie's father, the Marquess of Queensberry, was furious and demanded that Wilde end the relationship. Wilde's response resulted in him being sued for libel.

The Importance of Being Earnest was playing in St James's Theatre when the scandal hit. The trial of Oscar Wilde on 26 April 1895 and the surrounding moral panic prompted his publisher John Lane to terminate all of his book contracts. Wilde was found guilty, sentenced to two years' hard labour and imprisoned in Reading Gaol. In 1896, as Wilde was languishing in prison, *Salome* premiered in Paris. Wilde died in Paris on 30 November 1900.

There is a further twist to the story. A dance version of the play entitled *The Vision of Salome* was put on at the Palace Theatre, London, in 1908. Salome was played by the celebrated American dancer Maud Allan. Long-limbed and with golden hair, Allan performed her Dance of the Seven Veils in a sheer skirt with a strategically placed string of pearls covering her breasts. An Edwardian sex goddess, Maud Allan's dance broke box-office records. A contemporary account reported, 'Her slender and lissom body writhes in an ecstasy of fear, quivers at the exquisite touch of pain ... London has never seen such graceful and artistic dancing.'[5]

The Vision of Salome still had the power to shock and in 1918 it sparked a libel action that became a national cause célèbre at Court Number One, the Old Bailey. That April, two private performances in aid of charity had been put on at the Prince of Wales Theatre in Coventry Street. Moral crusader Noel Pemberton Billing wrote a review entitled 'The Cult of the Clitoris', which appeared in *The Vigilante* magazine, accusing Allan not only of being a lesbian but of being a German conspirator to boot.

The flimsy chain of evidence rested on Maud Allan's close friendship with Margot Asquith, whose husband Herbert Asquith had until recently been the prime minister. Furthermore, she was rumoured to have compiled a 'black book' naming all of the German sympathisers in Britain at the time prepared to act against the government. Major Evelyn Rothschild, a so-called double agent Mrs Villiers-Stuart and Admiral Hall, the Director of Naval Intelligence, were among the many worthies called upon to give evidence.

At the end of a protracted and at times surreal trial, Allan was found guilty. Her dancing days were effectively over. Among Oscar Wilde's many entertaining *bons mots* is an epigram which might serve as a warning to anyone attempting to stage *Salome*: 'Moderation is a fatal thing. Nothing succeeds like excess.'

THERE IS NOTHING LIKE A DAME

Christmas would not be Christmas without a pantomime. The tradition of staging pantomimes over the festive season goes back to the Theatre Royal, Covent Garden, during the 1830s. Reliant on slapstick comedy, topical jokes and cross-dressing, pantomime was written to appeal to children but also to provide entertainment for parents who were able to spot double entendres and laugh at smutty jokes. Pantomime showcased music-hall talent and children were admitted for half price – a marketing ploy that ensured packed houses and would secure a new generation of theatregoers.

There evolved a set of rituals without which no panto is complete. A male comedian acts the part of the pantomime dame – a matronly figure of fun who scolds her offspring. Then there is the prince charming – usually played by an attractive young woman dressed in tights and knee-high boots who makes a great show of slapping her thighs. There would also be a villain – a miserly landlord whose arrival on stage to collect rent from the poor widow would prompt boos and hisses from the audience. A princess, also played by a young woman, and a couple of clowns to provide comic business in the interludes between dramatic set pieces brought the romantic plot line down to earth.

The great age of pantomime came with the late Victorian and Edwardian era when West End theatres all vied with each other to stage these star-studded seasonal comedies. Competition between the Theatre Royal, Drury Lane (manager Augustus Harris), and the Theatre Royal, Covent Garden, was especially fierce. In the Christmas of 1888, Covent Garden's *Jack and the Beanstalk* was pitched against Augustus Harris's *Puss in Boots*.

During the season there would be competing shows drawn from a wide range of possible options. *Puss in Boots, Cinderella, Babes in the Wood, Aladdin and the Forty Thieves, Dick Whittington, Humpty Dumpty, Mother Goose, Sinbad the Sailor, Treasure Island* and *Jack and the Beanstalk* were all based on children's fairy tales. There would normally be a matinee performance in the early afternoon and an evening performance at 7.30 p.m.

To keep the shows current there would be innovations like magic effects and novelty acts. New pantomimes used a basic plot line adapted with special parts written for star performers. New characters were sometimes added, like the giant in the Drury Lane Theatre's 1899 production of *Jack and the Beanstalk* called Blunderboer, which was a reference to the South African President Kruger, the villain of the Anglo-Boer War.

The 1910 production of *Aladdin* at Drury Lane featured a circus act called 'The Salambos'. An advertisement for the show promised a 'great electrical specialty in the grand palace scene playing the slave of the lamp with effect and much success'. When Aladdin rubbed his old lamp, not only would a genie appear in a puff of smoke but there would be dazzling special effects.

The 1908 production of *Cinderella* at the Adelphi Theatre kicked off on Christmas Eve. A preview intended to whet the appetite of theatregoers praised the production directed by Mr Robert Courtneidge and George Edwardes with its cast of West End stars including Gaiety Girl Miss Phyllis Dare making a guest appearance:

> Cinderella becomes the embodiment of self-effacing sweetness, a loveable nature garbed in the rags of drudgery, her rewards the triumph of summer over the snows of winter. It is this picture of Cinderella that Miss Phyllis Dare presents. Daisy the mother to be played by Mr John Humphries is on the other hand designed on the lines of ordinary flesh and blood. In her composition she has a good deal of the unforgettable Mrs Malaprop, and the authors have endeavoured to provide her with a liberal supply of quotations for distortion.[6]

Stars were paid huge sums to make guest appearances. In 1861, actor-manager Henry Byron created the character of Widow Twankey in *Aladdin* at the Strand Theatre, starring James Rogers as the widow, named after 'Twankay Tea', a popular type of green tea imported from China.

The best-loved dame of all was the comedian Dan Leno. Born George Wild Galvin but adopting the stage name of Dan Leno, he first played a pantomime dame in the 1888 production of *Babes in the Wood* and would continue to play the role for the next fifteen years. Leno had risen to fame as a clog dancer and variety artist. A small, thin man with a wistful face and husky voice, he was said to have 'the saddest eyes in the world'. What he brought to the dame was a talent for the 'patter song', a type of music-hall entertainment in which a song was interrupted in mid-flow with a comedy routine.

The part of the principal boy was traditionally played by a young woman. The curvaceous and diminutive Rita Presano, a star of Richard D'Oyly Carte's English operas, starred in *Jack and the Beanstalk* at the Theatre Royal, Drury Lane, in 1899.

A FINANCIAL LIFELINE

However offbeat the pantomime appeared, to West End theatre managers it was a lifesaver. Sometimes a successful pantomime could enable cash-strapped theatre companies to recoup losses from an unsuccessful season. With packed houses and two shows a day, the pantomime might be all that stood between profitability and bankruptcy.

John Beckett, one of the first intake of Labour MPs and subsequently a member of the Independent Labour Party, turned his hand to theatre management after losing his seat at the 1931 general election. He accompanied Arthur Bourchier's theatre company on a tour of South Africa, where the unfortunate impresario and owner of the Strand Theatre died unexpectedly of a heart attack. Marrying Bourchier's young widow, actress Kyrle Bellew, with whom he had been conducting a discreet affair, Beckett suddenly found himself tasked with managing the Strand Theatre.

He booked Leslie Henson's musical comedy *Nice Goings On*, but it was not a success and the expense stretched the theatre's meagre resources to breaking point. Beckett recalled in an unpublished memoir, 'Each week the theatre had to find £250 to pay the mortgage regardless of whether the theatre was empty or full.'

Beckett recouped his losses by staging one of the theatre company's successful pantomimes at the Comedy Theatre. He wrote:

At Christmas I was instrumental in presenting a special season of *Treasure Island* at the Comedy Theatre. It proved much to the liking of the public and for the customary three weeks the theatre was packed every afternoon. ... business was so good that not only was the play rehabilitated in public esteem, but it actually paid for the whole of the [Strand Theatre's] new production.

SURVIVING THE GREAT DEPRESSION

The 1930s was a torrid time for theatres in London's West End. They were in competition with a new entertainment that had moved on considerably from the primitive moving pictures first shown in Piccadilly's Egyptian Hall during the 1890s and 1900s. Silent film progressed rapidly from short comedy sketches and melodramas to tackle ambitious subjects including biblical epics like *Quo Vadis* and *Ben Hur* made by W.D. Griffiths and also Fritz Lang's *Metropolis*.

The game changer was the introduction of talking pictures in 1932 when Al Jolson starred in *The Jazz Singer*. This was followed by a string of popular musicals featuring matinee idols supported by chorus lines of high-kicking young women in tights. Musicals like *The Gold Diggers of 1934*, with its hit song 'We're in the Money', and *Footlight Parade*, a Busby Berkeley spectacular from 1933 featuring Dick Powell and Ruby Keeler singing 'By a Waterfall', easily translated to British audiences whose spirits were in need of a lift.

Very soon a British film industry emerged, famously Ealing Studios and Gainsborough Pictures of Islington, which made some very successful films with rising British stage star Laurence Olivier. Some theatres bowed to the inevitable, closed their doors for the last time and were converted into cinemas like the London Pavilion in 1934 and the Empire, Leicester Square, in 1927.

Theatres, still reliant on drama, adopted different strategies to attract and retain their audience share. The Aldwych Theatre became synonymous for its farces – light-hearted comedies involving mistaken identities, characters dashing in and out of bedroom doors and a chaotic denouement. The great comic actor of the 1930s Ralph Lynn, known for his monocle and 'silly ass' demeanour, was partnered by bumbling straight man Tom Wall in the long-running Aldwych farce *Rookery Nook*.

Noël Coward played opposite Gertrude Lawrence in the light comedy *Private Lives*, which opened at the Phoenix Theatre, London, on 24 September 1930. The play, involving two lovers married to different partners who meet on a hotel balcony in Deauville, had premiered in Edinburgh before moving to the West End.

The show was such a resounding success that it transferred to Broadway in 1931, for once reversing the trend of American cultural dominance. Coward, easily the most talented and influential stage actor of his generation, followed his success with a string of theatrical hits including *Blithe Spirit*, *Hay Fever* and *Present Laughter*. *Private Lives* has been revived regularly ever since and is now a staple of theatres.

As the stakes got higher, theatres turned to musicals to win large audiences. For one theatre, the Coliseum in St Martin's Lane, owned by Stoll Theatres, the gamble paid off. With a musical score by Ralph Benatsky and featuring 300 extras on stage including a herd of cows, a river steamer, an 'oompah' band and a Tyrolean choir, the Austro-Hungarian spectacular *The White Horse Inn* was the talk of the West End. It was, of course, pure coincidence that another White Horse Inn had been one of Piccadilly's oldest coaching inns.

The show had premiered in Berlin in 1930 but incurred the Führer's wrath for perpetuating outdated stereotypes. When the English version opened at the Coliseum on 8 April 1931, English audiences lapped up the show's mixture of Ruritanian charm and *Sound of Music* style schmaltz. *The White Horse Inn* ran for 625 performances in London before touring the provinces, easily recouping Oswald Stoll's investment in the lavish production.

Oswald Stoll and Edward Moss, both subsequently knighted, joined forces to create a theatre conglomerate, Moss Empires, a company that owned and ran most of the major West End theatres of the 1930s and the immediate post-war years, as well as the leading theatres in cities from Leeds, Manchester and Birmingham.

The White Horse Inn proved lavish musicals could return a huge profit. It would be the forerunner of the string of West End successes that over the years have attracted huge audiences and been a major boost to London's tourist economy. Contemporary musicals like *Jesus Christ Superstar, Evita, Phantom of the Opera* and *Les Misérables* have followed where *The White Horse Inn* had led. The commercial success of the West End's theatreland is inextricably linked to the fortunes and the appeal of huge musicals featuring international singing stars.

9

SHOW TIME!

He's very well-known is Algy, to the ladies on the stage
Such a jolly good chap is Algy, just now he's all the rage
And a jolly good favourite Algy, with the barmaids at the 'Cri'
He's very well-known is Algy,
As the Piccadilly Johnny with the little glass eye.
Vesta Tilley, 'The Piccadilly Johnny with the Little Glass Eye'

POPULAR CULTURE

From the bawdy comic operas and masquerade balls of the eighteenth century, through Victorian music-hall, variety shows featuring lines of high-kicking chorus girls, to salacious theatrical revues like *Oh Calcutta!* and the musical *Hair*, London's West End has provided entertainment for the wealthy and for the masses. During this development, one can also trace the intersection between the 'leg shows' popular at the Empire and Alhambra, Leicester Square, and the West End sex trade.

The construction of Shaftesbury Avenue in 1885 added seven theatres and music halls to the West End, starting with the London Pavilion and the Trocadero and ending with the Palace Theatre of Varieties on Cambridge Circus, now renamed the Cambridge Theatre. Piccadilly Circus was now the hub of a vast entertainments network whose spokes radiated outwards to include the Gaiety Theatre and the Savoy in the Strand, the Aldwych, the Coliseum in St Martin's Lane, the Shaftesbury Theatre, and the London Palladium at Argyll Street, Oxford Circus. All of these buildings have survived as landmarks reflecting popular culture in an age before cinema, television and the internet.

PENNY GAFFS, POPULAR ENTERTAINMENTS AND THE LONDON PAVILION MUSIC HALL

Piccadilly spans the class divide – a chasm that separated the lives of the wealthy elite from the mass of working people. In the mid-nineteenth century a new form of theatre began to emerge spontaneously in the back rooms of public houses or in vacant shop premises. Known as 'penny gaffs', these were unlicensed performing spaces where working men and women would gather to enjoy home-grown entertainments, paying an entrance fee of a penny.

These impromptu theatres were often no more than a bare room containing a stage made of packing cases, screened off by a rough curtain. Sitting on whatever seats were available, the audience would drink and cheer at amateur conjurers and acrobats, song and dance acts and stand-up comedians. If the act did not live up to expectations, rotten fruit might be thrown. The White Bear on Kennington Park Road preserves something of this feel and a former penny gaff theatre can still be found among the back rooms at the Cock public house on Kennington Road.

Penny gaffs were unapologetically working-class haunts that held a strong appeal to the thousands of people who lived in often overcrowded tenements in St Giles, Soho or St Martin-in-the-Fields. Social histories of the West End frequently ignore the 'invisible' working classes, but the West End offered respectable employment to vast armies of people of both sexes from cleaners and laundry women to grooms and stable boys, and from shop assistants to cooks. The West End world of the upper classes existed only thanks to the labour of these unrecorded multitudes.

In 1859 the Black Horse Inn at Tichborne Street, Piccadilly, turned its back on coaching and created an entertainments room built over the old inn yard and stables. The Black Horse was rechristened the London Pavilion Music Hall and amateurs were invited to come up on stage to try their hand at singing, dancing or comedy. If the crowd enjoyed the act, they were hired and given a contract. In the early days, admission was free and the profits were made by adding 6*d* to every glass of liquor sold. Eventually, admission to the Music Hall was by ticket.

Similar transformations of pubs into music halls were already taking place across the West End. Built on the site of the old Boar and Castle pub at 6 Oxford Street in 1861, the Oxford Music Hall rivalled the London Pavilion in popularity. The Canterbury Theatre of Varieties and the Bedford Music Hall were among the first music halls to appear in London's West End. Competition for talent was fierce as the West End's halls tried to outbid each other to attract the best acts and the biggest stars.

Combining the copious consumption of alcohol with popular entertainment that included young women dancing and singing, early music halls were fast acquiring a reputation for drunkenness, disorder and immorality. This perception was hard to shift even when the halls became more gentrified.

One of the biggest stars of this period was the cockney Bessie Bellwood, a feisty dame who belted out songs like 'Wot'cher Rita', 'He's Going to Marry Mary-Ann' and 'Woa' Emma!' Famed for her ability to shut down any hecklers in the audience, Bellwood epitomised a less deferential age when singers could be booed off the stage by drunken audiences.

Born in south London to Irish parents, Catherine Mahoney adopted the stage name of Bellwood when she began her stage career in 1876 at the Bermondsey Music Hall. Her alcohol-fuelled lifestyle ended in an early death at the age of 40. She is remembered for her unsuccessful court action against the Duke of Manchester to whom she lent a considerable sum of money that was never repaid.

Her character was reprised in the 1946 film *Champagne Charlie*, starring Tommy Trinder and Betty Warren. The film was based on the life of George Leybourne, whose celebrated song 'Champagne Charlie' reflected the heavy drinking culture of early music halls and his rivalry with Alfred Vance, known popularly as 'the Great Vance'. The duelling singers' alcohol-fuelled lifestyle gave rise to a string of popular ballads including 'We are the Brandy and Seltzer Boys' and 'An 'arf of 'arf 'n 'arf' and they were played in the film by Tommy Trinder and Stanley Holloway respectively.

In 1862, the London Pavilion was enlarged and refurbished – a scheme that included adding galleries on two sides of the auditorium. With an orchestra in the pit providing the music and frequently changing backdrops, the music hall provided fun, excitement and a shared experience. The plush new seating, gas lighting, mirrors and crystal chandeliers were a marked contrast from the early halls and penny gaffs with their spit and sawdust floors. It is no wonder music halls were referred to as 'working-class palaces'.

MINSTREL SHOWS

From 1860 to 1904, St James's Hall was home to an unimaginably insensitive form of popular entertainment known as the minstrel show. Song, dance and comic routines were all performed by white actors in blackface to enthusiastic applause. It is almost impossible to comprehend the twisted morality and unthinking prejudice that created such spectacles. Like the freak shows staged by P.T. Barnum and countless vaudeville acts, 'minstrelsy' was an American import that played well with British audiences. It was oblivious to the idea of a common humanity that demands respect for all members of society.

As this antebellum plantation-based, slavery-infused entertainment demonstrated, West End productions evolved in lock step with the USA where novelty and brash sensationalism appeared to point the way towards mass-market commercial success. It was to become a recurring theme from now on.

The first touring company to leave New York for England were the Christy Minstrels, founded by the entrepreneurial showman and comedian George Christy. The minstrel show followed an unvarying three-part formula. The first act featured an exaggerated walkaround known as the 'cakewalk' containing a dialogue between two comics, Mr Tambo and Mr Bones. Their apparently hilarious arguments and misunderstandings were mediated by a master of ceremonies known as Mr Interlocutor. The second act involved egregious slapstick comedy performed by a stock character known as Jim Crow, as well as song and dance routines and banjo solos like the popular plantation song 'Old Folks at Home', the copyright of which Christy bought from its composer Stephen Foster.

The final act, a scene from *Uncle Tom's Cabin* purporting to show the joys of plantation life, was a travesty of historic fact as well as an insult to the sensibilities of any decent member of society, particularly black Americans. It is salutary to know that contemporary critics were also outraged at the misrepresentation and the hypocrisy involved. The black American social reformer, writer and abolitionist Frederick Douglass described blackface performers in a 1848 *The North Star* newspaper as 'the filthy scum of white society, who have stolen from us a complexion denied them by nature, in which to make money, and pander to the corrupt taste of their white fellow citizens'.

By 1874, George Christy's son Edwin had died and a troupe had regrouped around two surviving cast members, 'Pony' Moore and Frederick Burgess, who renamed their company the Moore and Burgess Minstrels, performing regularly until the closure of St James's Hall in 1904. At the same time, other minstrel troupes rode the wave of this popular music and comedy, such as the Imperial Minstrels and the Mohawk Minstrels, who performed at the Agricultural Hall, London. The Mohawk Minstrels wrote countless novelty comic songs and ballads, which were published by Francis, Day and Hunter and enjoyed a massive following.

'Minstrelsy' translated to the silver screen and to talking pictures with the famous film *The Jazz Singer* starring the Jewish entertainer Al Jolson. Indeed, the tradition was so ingrained and so much a part of popular culture that the BBC actually ran a series on Saturday night prime-time television called the *Black and White Minstrel Show*, performed live by the George Mitchell singers. A clearer indictment of institutionalised racism could hardly be found. This series was last aired in 1967, the same year that the legendary black American rock star Jimi Hendrix toured Britain, appearing at the Round House and the Hammersmith Palais to packed audiences of young people.

AN ENTERTAINMENTS HUB

The construction of Shaftesbury Avenue in 1885 – a new road linking Piccadilly with New Oxford Street – brought sweeping changes that would pave the way for the further development of theatres and restaurants, and which would cement Piccadilly's place as the hub of London's West End.

The road-widening scheme at Piccadilly Circus necessitated the demolition of the south side of Tichborne Street, a small lane to the north. This clearance meant that the Monico Café and Restaurant now faced directly onto Piccadilly Circus and its thronging crowds – an opportunity its owners seized upon to upgrade and modernise, while its near neighbour, the old Black Horse coaching inn and its entertainments room, known as the London Pavilion Music Hall, was acquired by the Metropolitan Board of Works and scheduled for demolition. It closed on 25 March 1885.

A vastly enlarged and improved London Pavilion was built on the corner site at the junction of Shaftesbury Avenue and Coventry Street. It was more than double the size and capacity of the music hall it replaced. Occupying an island site with its rear entrance on Great Windmill Street, and with tall porticos supported by classical columns facing onto two main thoroughfares, the magnificent theatre, designed in the Italian style by Harold Peto, was the centrepiece of the enlarged Piccadilly Circus.

Standing opposite and overlooking the Criterion Theatre and restaurant on the south side of Piccadilly Circus, the new London Pavilion opened on

Monday, 30 November 1885, under the management of impresario and lessee Robert Edwin Villiers. Commonly known as 'The Pav', the London Pavilion was a step change from the rough-and-ready music halls' drunken audiences and rowdy behaviour that had survived from an earlier era.

In their place, the London Pavilion boasted marble-topped tables, waiter service, crystal chandeliers, soft carpets and electric lighting. It was said that the new variety palace:

> ... outstrips every rendezvous of the kind in England, and possibly the European continent. The exterior of the hall, the noble proportions of which are enhanced by its commanding site and airy surroundings, is imposing ... the whole gamut of modern architectural and decorative art has been drawn upon to make this hall beautiful.[1]

The first night's line-up included comic turns, singers, acrobatic troupes, impressionists, a choir and much else besides. The comedians Arthur Lloyd, Harry Randall and the eccentric yodelling violinist G.H. Chirgwin, known as 'The White-Eyed Kaffir', entertained the audience with songs and comic patter. Also appearing on the bill were the Frediani Troupe, Madame Garetta and her Pigeons and cockney music-hall legend Bessie Bellwood.

The proceedings kicked off in style and with a patriotic flourish. A contemporary review wrote gushingly:

> Mr. Villiers is a loyal citizen, and it goes for saying that the initial feature of this programme was a performance of 'God Save the Queen', followed by 'God Bless the Prince of Wales', sung by the Pavilion Choir, Miss Constance Loseby singing the solo verses.

Acts were introduced by the 'president' Mr Sam Adams from a throne to one side of the stage while an army of aproned waiters scurried around bearing trays of drinks to seated customers during the show.

The spacious auditorium could seat 1,500 people in comfort and the entertainments on offer reflected a new era. The music hall had not only become an accepted mass entertainment but it had morphed into something else – a variety theatre:

> The Programme just now of the London Pavilion, Piccadilly in excellency and variety thoroughly deserves the title 'the best in London', including as it does such artistes as the great and only McDermott, the genial Sam

Redfern and the beauteous Katie Seymour ... and a host of other 'stars too numerous to mention. Good old Pav!'[2]

CULTIVATING RESPECTABILITY

Around the time of its transformation from public-house entertainments room to variety theatre, the London Pavilion began introducing culture in the form of operatic selections, which showcased the talents of visiting opera singers backed by the London Pavilion chorus. This review appeared that same year:

> Amongst the more recent changes in the programme of the Business proper of the Hall has been the introduction of an Operatic Selection from Der Freischutz, embracing the whole strength of the Pavilion corps, and under the able, painstaking and effective Conductor, Mr Russell Grover is a delightful feature in the amusements.[3]

This formula was copied by other music halls, exploding the myth that opera could only be enjoyed by the middle and upper classes.

Despite the music halls' efforts to cultivate respectability, there were a great many enemies who preached against their corrupting influence. Attempts were made to persuade magistrates to revoke music-hall licences by, among others, the temperance movement, the Methodist Church, the Band of Hope, evangelical Baptists and various non-denominational sects. These organisations believed the working classes should be set an example of sobriety and hard work.

Notable moral crusaders included purity campaigner Laura Ormiston Chant, parodied in the popular press as 'Mrs Prowlina Pry', and Henry Varley, a Baptist minister, both of whom campaigned tirelessly to have music halls closed down. In *The Era* magazine, Varley is quoted as complaining, 'No less than twelve great houses of pleasure, so called, have been licensed in the West-end and are contributing factors to the great flesh market of the world.' He added that audiences were 'attracted thither by the hope of meeting immoral women' and music halls were, as he put it, 'a blind for sexual commerce'.

The Era's editorial firmly rebutted his claim:

> If this were so, how is it that proprietors of music halls go to the expense of securing the cleverest singers, dancers, acrobats and ventriloquists? And why do the music-halls attract so many respectable couples? Is the husband who

takes his wife, and the young man who accompanies his sweetheart to one of the numerous Classical Concerts, to a music-hall, or a public exhibition to be debarred of their lawful recreation?[4]

In spite of constant efforts to keep prostitution at bay and to create an environment where women and families would feel safe, the music halls and variety theatres of the West End were inextricably linked with commercial sex and depended on the sexual exploitation and degradation of defenceless young women. Some theatres, such as Evans's Song and Supper Rooms in King Street, Covent Garden, the Empire Theatre of Varieties and the Alhambra in Leicester Square, were notorious haunts for ladies of the night. Others, like the Gaiety Theatre, featured scantily clad chorus lines.

The opening of the new London Pavilion on Shaftesbury Avenue and Coventry Street in 1885, however, went against this narrative, tapping into a wave of female talent and helping shape a respectable working-class identity. Female comic singers like Marie Lloyd, Florrie Forde, Vesta Victoria and Ella Shields often got top billing. They were as famous and as well loved as their male counterparts like Dan Leno, George Robey, Albert Chevalier, Gus Elen and Harry Champion.

As outwardly respectable as the music hall had become, popular comic songs tackled taboo subjects like infidelity, bigamy, drunkenness and illicit sex. Songs like 'There was I Waiting at the Church', 'Our Lodger's Such a Nice Young Man' and 'I'm Following in Father's Footsteps' were delivered with a nudge and a wink to audiences who understood the innuendo behind the innocent-sounding lyrics.

The music hall broke down barriers surrounding sexual identity as many of the top female stars had acts featuring cross-dressing. Sporting a monocle and evening dress, Vesta Tilley aped Piccadilly's high society with her song, 'The Piccadilly Johnny with the Little Glass Eye'. A long list of male impersonators included Miss Hetty King ('All the Nice Girls Love a Sailor') and Ella Shields, the original 'Burlington Bertie'. The upper classes who visited Piccadilly late at night on the prowl for women were mocked for their double standards and hypocrisy.

THE GAIETY THEATRE

While the music hall treated women as equal participants and played to mixed audiences, a new genre of musical comedy showcased female beauty, objectifying women and removing their right to respect. The Gaiety Theatre was a decidedly escapist enterprise appealing to male fantasy. The female stars of musical comedy boosted a fast-growing entertainments industry as new techniques in mass marketing began to satisfy a public demand for images and news stories of their beloved stars. The Gaiety Girl phenomenon, which gathered pace in the 1890s, influenced women's fashion as titled men bombarded their favourite singers and chorus girls with offers of marriage, many of which ended at the altar. It is not for nothing that Gaiety Girls were dubbed the 'actress-stocracy'!

John Hollingshead established the Gaiety Theatre in the Strand as a home of musical comedy and farce in 1868. It was Hollingshead who created the chorus line, which subsequently became the hallmark of musical comedy. Hollingshead was succeeded at the Gaiety Theatre in 1892 by the young producer and impresario George Edwardes, who ran the Gaiety Theatre from 1893 to 1914.

The fashion for burlesque comedies and musical revues originally staged by the Gaiety Theatre were copied by the Adelphi in the Strand, the Apollo and Lyric Theatres in Shaftesbury Avenue and packed regional theatres when the Gaiety company took its shows on tour.

Known always as 'the Guv'nor', Edwardes took the musical revue to a new level, recruiting potential leading ladies for their beauty, physique and an ability to sing and dance. Putting together talented songwriters, lyricists and choreographers, Edwardes produced a string of box-office hits including *A Gaiety Girl* (1893), *The Shop Girl* (1894) and *A Runaway Girl* (1898). The wealth he amassed was spent owning and breeding racehorses and on staking huge sums at the racecourse.

In 1902 an opportunity presented itself of moving to a new and bigger theatre. Slum clearances and a new road linking the Strand with Holborn – Aldwych – involved road widening and the demolition of a stretch of buildings opposite Waterloo Bridge, which meant the theatre had to be re-sited on the junction of Strand and Aldwych. Designed in the Italian Renaissance style, the new Gaiety Theatre opened on 26 October 1903 with a special performance of a musical comedy, *The Orchid*, attended by King Edward VII and Queen Alexandra. The stellar cast included Gaiety Girls Gertie Millar, Marie Studholme and Gabrielle Ray.

Theatre manager Edwardes realised that his female leads were starting to attract publicity and he manipulated this to his advantage. Licensing images for postcards provided a lucrative source of income for himself, the stars and their agents. Edwardes further understood that the costumes worn by his stars were a crucial part of a show's success, whether it was chorus girls dressed in revealing bathing suits or the actresses showing a modicum of stockinged leg. His ladies were crowd pleasers and a morale boost for a public weary of reading about mounting British casualties in the disastrous Anglo-Boer War.

GAIETY GIRLS

Many young women modelled themselves on the Gaiety Girls, following a dress code borrowed from the actresses and chorus girls who appeared at the Gaiety Theatre. Playing to packed houses, Gaiety Girls enjoyed a huge fan base and attracted offers of marriage from young scions of the nobility. These women were confident and unafraid to reject their parents' prudish Victorian values. Bypassing the women's suffrage movement led by social pioneers like Sylvia and Christabel Pankhurst, the Gaiety Girl was a reflection of a patriarchal and highly conservative society. The phenomenon spanned the 1890s and lasted throughout the Edwardian era up until the outbreak of the First World War in 1914. Edwardes himself was interned as an enemy alien for part of the First World War after he had unwisely travelled to Germany for his annual spa break just as war broke out.

Former theatre doorman James Jupp wrote a memoir, *The Gaiety Stage Door*, in 1923. Paying a lively tribute to the Edwardian beauties who had graced the stage, he wrote:

> There was a time when police had to marshal the crowds that gathered round the theatre to catch even a glimpse of Gertie Millar, as, with her Pekingese, she darted from stage-door to motor-car.[5]

But were Gaiety Girls really liberated or merely willing dupes participating in a male fantasy? In the male-dominated world of the Edwardian theatre, there is little doubt that their freedom was illusory. Nevertheless, for some the rewards could be great – expensive jewellery, offers of marriage from stage-struck earls and possibly the start of a serious acting career. At least one Gaiety Girl – Constance Collier – made it all the way to Hollywood. Though their names are mostly forgotten, the Gaiety Girls were the West End forerunners of Hollywood stars and the present-day cult of the celebrity.

Despite the glamour, the Gaiety Girls were part of what can only be described as a balletic boot camp. There were endless rehearsals, a taxing fitness regime and a nightly appearance as well as taking the show on tours of provincial theatres. Edwardes also produced a series of musical comedies at the Apollo Theatre, Shaftesbury Avenue, which opened on 21 February 1901.

On stage, Gaiety Girls might wear a succession of exotic costumes including bathing suits, frilled petticoats, flesh-coloured body stockings and Pierrot outfits. When out on the town and escorted by a gentleman, Gaiety Girls would appear corseted to create the ideal wasp waist. With their luxuriant hair piled up in a halo, they typically wore a chiffon blouse with leg-of-mutton sleeves, a figure-hugging floor-length skirt and button boots. Accessories like a muff or an extravagant hat, ornamented possibly with the plumage of exotic birds, projected the image of idealised femininity.

The heady excitement of the Gaiety Theatre in its heyday is captured by the 1949 black-and-white film *Gaiety George*, starring Richard Greene and Ann Todd. Loosely based on the life story of Edwardes and his lavish productions, the film features a fictitious musical comedy 'The Tom-Boy Princess' which culminates in the female lead stripping down to her frilly underwear before ducking behind a screen and re-emerging minutes later in satin ballgown and tiara, aided by a bevy of ladies in waiting.

Images of Edwardian beauties or Gaiety Girls were mass produced and formed the staple of the cheap photographic postcards that were avidly collected by young men and women. The craze for sending cards was fuelled by the Post Office's decision in 1904 to approve postcards with a picture on one side and the reverse divided in two to allow for the stamp, address and a brief message. Prior to this date, only the address could be written on the back of the card.

This concession sparked a boom in communication, doubling postcard mail in Britain from around 400 million a year at the turn of the century to over 800 million by 1905. With up to six postal deliveries a day in large towns and cities, postcards could be sent and replied to the same day in what would be the equivalent of today's instant messaging.

BREAKING DOWN BARRIERS

In casting his famous musical comedies, George Edwardes had established an accidental marriage bureau. Many of the talented and ambitious young women who auditioned for the chorus of the Gaiety and who worked hard to achieve star billing undoubtedly did so in order to secure a wealthy or even an aristocratic husband. In this manner, attractive young working-class women might find themselves propelled into the ranks of the aristocracy.

In 1901, Connie Gilchrist quit the Gaiety Theatre to marry the 7th Earl of Orkney and that, same year, chorus girl Rosie Boote married the 4th Marquess of Headfort. May Gates, a chorus girl from *The Beauty of Bath*, married Baron von Ditton of Norway, while Sylvia Storey became Countess Poulett.

The stage door was zealously guarded to protect the Gaiety Girls from male intrusion. Their dressing rooms were regarded as a target for ardent suitors, and it was the rare breach of security and possibly the result of a hefty bribe that enabled a man to enter this holy of holies. When a show was on, men would gather at the stage door trying to catch a glimpse of the objects of their desire. They were referred to as 'stage door johnnies' and the lengths to which they would go to contact their favourite actress was no mere cliché.

James Jupp, the doorman of the Gaiety, describes how bouquets, expensive jewellery and boxes of chocolates were customary tributes. As he recalls in his memoir:

> My stage door was a miniature Covent Garden on the occasion of a First Night. Baskets of the most exquisite flowers from Bond Street, Regent Street, Piccadilly … and they were taken to the dressing rooms of the ladies to whom they were sent.

Even staid middle-aged men were not immune to the appeal of a Gaiety Girl. Jupp describes how on one occasion Gaby Deslys was on stage and a member of the audience went mad, emptied the gold sovereigns from his pockets, adding his gold watch and cigarette case, and threw them at Mlle Deslys' feet:

> The show was stopped and attendants rushed to eject the miscreant. The man's worldly goods were scooped up and returned to him and he was bound over to keep the peace.[6]

Aristocratic families tried their best to nip romance in the bud and ensure wayward sons were kept in line to marry within members of their own class. Young men had their allowances cut off or were sent away on lengthy foreign holidays in an attempt to get the infatuation out of their system. Nevertheless, there were cases of genuine love and many of these marriages succeeded. Olive Mary Meatyard – stage name Olive May – was billed as 'the Lass with the Lasso' after an act that involved lassoing a series of handsome men in the manner of steers at a rodeo. She ended up 'roping' Lord Victor Paget, who she wed in 1913; divorced in 1921, she subsequently married the Earl of

Drogheda. Gertie Millar, the most famous Gaiety Girl of all time, ended her career as the Countess of Dudley.

The turnover of leading ladies threatened the viability of popular shows so that the Guv'nor got new arrivals to sign a contract stipulating a minimum length of service and containing a clause banning marriage. But this did little to halt the turnover of talent.

Chorus girls found themselves being invited to upmarket Piccadilly restaurants and exclusive clubs like the St James's Restaurant – 'Jimmy's' – or the Criterion Restaurant – 'the Cri'. No gentleman would take his wife to 'Jimmy's', but he would certainly take a Gaiety Girl. Edwardes had an arrangement with Romano's Restaurant in the Strand whereby any member of the Gaiety cast would be given a 50 per cent reduction on production of Edwardes's business card. Out of town, Gaiety Girls might also be invited to punt on the Thames at Maidenhead at Skindles Hotel – a notorious rendezvous for seductions – a cliché that resurfaces in the Ealing comedy *Kind Heart and Coronets*.

Not all Gaiety Girls were set on an advantageous marriage. More than a few had serious acting ambitions and none were more successful than Constance Collier. Born in 1878, Constance joined the Gaiety in 1901 before switching to star in a series of Shakespearean stage plays after being talent-spotted by the manager of His Majesty's Theatre, Haymarket, Herbert Beerbohm Tree. An established actress, Constance moved to Hollywood at the dawn of the movie industry, eventually becoming a voice coach when the talking pictures were developed at the end of the 1920s.

GERTIE MILLAR

The daughter of a mill worker and a dressmaker in Bradford and born in February 1879, Gertrude 'Gertie' Millar was one of the most celebrated Gaiety Girls of her generation. Starting out as a shop girl, her stage career started at the age of 13 when she took a minor role singing in the pantomime *Babes in the Wood* in Manchester. Her precocious talent was recognised. Tall and slender, with attractive features and an impressive head of luxuriant hair, Gertie was given starring roles. She danced and sang at local music halls but, keen to make a name for herself, she started appearing with touring theatre companies playing light comedy before finally ending up in London in 1897.

She was talent-spotted by the Gaiety Theatre's George Edwardes who began by casting her in his revue *The Toreador* in 1901 and later in *The Messenger Boy*.

In 1903, with the opening of the new Gaiety Theatre, Gertie Millar was given top billing as the Hon. Lady Violet Anstruther in *The Orchid*. She starred in a string of musical hits including *The Girls of Gothenburg* in 1907.

What really cemented Gertie's fame was being picked to play the lead in the Gaiety Theatre's biggest ever hit, *Our Miss Gibbs*. First staged in 1909, the musical comedy had a continuous run for two years and even transferred to Broadway with an all-American cast. Set in a department store called 'Garrods', the comedy charted a rise from rags to riches that paralleled Gertie Millar's own route to stardom from being a shop girl.

In 1902, she married the composer Lionel Monkton who had written the scores for many of her top hits. But on Monkton's death in 1924, Gertie married the 2nd Earl of Dudley, retiring from the stage to become Countess of Dudley.

LEG SHOWS AND CENSORSHIP

The first recorded incidents of nudity on the West End stage were intimate cameos staged in the Walhalla Gallery, Leicester Square, during the 1840s, where discerning gentlemen could admire 'Mme Warton's *tableaux vivant* and *poses plastiques*'. Naked women could be regarded as art so long as they remained completely motionless.

Instead of admiring the nude statuary by sculptors like Canova, the theatre took the nude to its logical next step by hiring actual women to pose naked in reconstructions of classical subjects. Shows like *A Night with Titian* and *Venus Arising from the Sea* give an indication as to what the male audience might be getting for its 2*s* 6*d* entrance fee.

The Alhambra and the Empire Theatre of Varieties, Leicester Square, which opened in the 1870s, began with the lofty ambition to stage ballets. But in short order, the ballets became more and more risqué and were dropped in favour of the Parisian cancan and 'leg shows', which were choreographed to display as much female flesh as possible. The *poses plastiques* had become much more animated! A predominantly female cast wore gauzy costumes or flesh-coloured tights to simulate nudity for the benefit of male audiences.

The Empire navigated a fine line, pushing what was allowed under the terms of its licence granted by the London County Council. Sex was seen as good for business in every sense of the word. At the back of the dress circle was a promenade – an area where members of the audience could stand or sit drinking at tables. Throughout the show and especially during the intervals, ladies of the night would glide past, swinging their hips. Arrangements were made and couples would pair off as the management turned a blind eye to these seedy transactions.

In October 1894, feminist reformer Mrs Laura Ormiston Chant successfully challenged the terms of the Empire's music and dancing licence. Concessions to decency were made but the theatre remained open. On 27 October, a cartoon appeared in *Punch* lampooning the elderly black-bombazine-attired lady barred from entering the Empire by a forbidding doorman. A placard read, 'Three thousand employees will be thrown out of work if this theatre is closed by the LCC.'

Music-hall and theatre promenades continued to operate as zones for commercial sex until the Defence of the Realm Act (DORA) banned them in 1916, along with tighter restrictions imposed on nightclubs, stage acts and pub licensing laws. The First World War had generated a moral panic.

Something positive was needed to lift the nation's sombre mood and family values were back in fashion. West End theatres staged a number of commercially successful musical revues, which were watched avidly by troops home on leave. One of the biggest box-office hits of the war years was the musical comedy *Chu Chin Chow*, which opened on 3 August 1916 at His Majesty's Theatre, Haymarket, and enjoyed a run of over five years. *The Bing Boys are Here* drew large audiences at the Alhambra, Leicester Square, with popular songs like 'If You Were the Only Girl in the World' and 'Let the Great Big World Keep Turning'.

Starring comedian George Robey and Violet Lorraine, the show's plot revolves around two brothers from Binghampton who go to seek their fortune on the London stage. Emma, a cook and sweetheart of the younger brother, follows in their wake and trumps the boys' adventures by ascending to the top rung of London society, marrying an aged duke who promptly dies, leaving the two young lovers to be reunited.

Using the same winning formula, the Alhambra then staged *The Bing Girls Are There* and, following the Armistice, *The Bing Boys on Broadway*. *The Maid of the Mountains* opened on 10 February 1917 at Daly's Theatre and proved one of the three most popular shows of the period, creating another hit with the song 'A Paradise for Two'.

CULTURAL TRANSFORMATION

As musical comedies were drawing audiences to the Alhambra Theatre, powerful cultural influences from the USA were waiting to take London by storm. A series of actors, entertainers and musicians made their way across the Atlantic to entertain West End audiences, establishing a link between Broadway and the West End that has remained to this day. The West End in particular provided an opportunity for talented African American singers and performers.

In 1903, the cast of a successful Broadway revue, *In Dahomey*, arrived to tour the UK. The show opened at the Shaftesbury Theatre on 18 April 1903 to instant acclaim. With music and words by two black Americans, Will Cook and Paul Dunbar, *In Dahomey* was a milestone celebration of black culture and was the first musical to feature an entire cast of black artists, who included comedians George Walker and Bert Williams and the singer Adah Overton Walker.

With two tours in the USA and one in Britain, *In Dahomey* ran for over four years, popularising a new dance called 'the cakewalk'. There was even a performance at Buckingham Palace in honour of the king's nephew, the future Prince of Wales' ninth birthday before the show went on a tour of the provinces.

Broadway's hugely popular *Ziegfeld Follies* combined singing and dancing with comedy sketches, a formula that proved irresistible to British audiences. In 1912, *Hullo Ragtime* was based around Irving Berlin's *Ziegfeld Follies'* smash hit 'Alexander's Ragtime Band' featuring the black singer and vaudeville comedienne Emma Carus.

By the end of the First World War rigid social and class barriers were breaking down as young people danced to jazz music, with its strong roots in African American culture. In 1919, the arrival of the Original Dixieland Jazz Band in England on tour from the USA led the charge. Playing a number of sell-out concerts, the band of black musicians appeared at the London Hippodrome in a revue titled *Joy Bells*. Like *In Dahomey* fifteen years earlier, the cast was invited to stage a royal command performance for King George V at Buckingham Palace.

The showman C.B. Cochran was so excited by the energy and creativity of black performers that he devised revues that showcased their talents. In 1923, his revue *Dover Street to Dixie* at the Palace Theatre had an all-white cast in the first half of the programme followed by an all-black cast who took the stage for the second half. The audience went wild as the 'frenetic black chorus and dancers galvanised the house with their delirious high spirits'. Star of the show Florence Mills, a cabaret singer known in the USA as the 'Queen of Happiness', received a standing ovation for her rendition of the show's signature song 'Bye-bye Blackbird'.

In 1926, Florence and an African American cast headlined in Cochran's revue *Blackbirds*, which opened at the London Pavilion. Edward, Prince of Wales, was reported to have seen the show eleven times. Cochran sums up the singer's appeal:

> Florence Mills was an artist pure and simple ... She possessed a bird-like voice with a throb in it such as I have never heard in any other ... There has not been in my time a coloured woman performer of anything approaching the quality of Florence Mills.[7]

Black dancers and bands were suddenly popular in the fashionable society cafés of the West End, while the arrival of black musicians, artists and entertainers en masse transformed the Soho club scene, which was already one of the most cosmopolitan in the world. Nightclubs like the Nest, the Cuba Club and the Shim Sham Club, run by black American singer and pianist Ike Hatch and businessman Jack Isow, drew mixed audiences, and stars like Dizzy Gillespie, Louis Armstrong and the cast of *Blackbirds* mingled freely with socialites and musicians.

C.B. COCHRAN AND THE LONDON PAVILION

Born in Brighton in 1872, the impresario and showman C.B. Cochran dominated the West End theatre of the interwar years. Over a long career, Cochran was lessee or manager at thirteen West End venues, including the Adelphi, the Aldwych, the Ambassadors, the Palace, the New Oxford and the London Pavilion. On occasion, he would have six shows running at different theatres simultaneously.

The *Oxford Dictionary of National Biography* paints a pen portrait of C.B. Cochran in late middle age as 'short and red-faced, a well-fed country squire in appearance. He wore a bowler hat, a monocle, and elegant double-breasted suits, and leant heavily on a walking stick made necessary by the crippling pain of an arthritic hip.'

Aged 18, Charles Blake Cochran travelled steerage on a liner bound for New York where he lived on his wits while attempting to make a career on the stage. Returning to England in 1902, he turned fight promoter and publicist, boosting the career of an aspiring escapologist called Harry Houdini. A successful hustler, Cochran saw an opportunity in producing light-hearted musical comedies.

Cochran leased the London Pavilion in Piccadilly and his first show, *As You Were*, opened in August 1918. The ever more daring revues he staged owed their popularity to what he would describe as 'perhaps the prettiest collection of girls ever seen on any stage in the world'.[8] Nicknamed 'Cocky', Cochran enjoyed brief flings with many of his nubile chorus-line recruits.

Cochran's revues and comedies at the London Pavilion from 1918 until 1934 were written by many of the famous songwriters of the period including Cole Porter, Rogers and Hart, Jerome Kern and George Wimperis. Despite bouts of near bankruptcy, Cochran had a knack for discovering a new generation of stars, including Noël Coward, Gertrude Lawrence, Jack Buchanan, Jessie Matthews and Anna Neagle.

The high-kicking chorus lines created by Cochran became a fixture of all West End variety shows. Troupes of dancers such as the Tiller Girls, who performed at the London Palladium, remained in fashion well into the 1960s.

On With the Dance opened on 30 April 1925 at the London Pavilion with Noël Coward in the starring role. Just days earlier, Cochran had been discharged from the London Bankruptcy Court. Coward was reported to have remarked in awe after his first night, 'Oh Cocky, I've just seen my name in lights.'

A long-standing collaboration between Cochran and the gay singer-songwriter Coward resulted in some spectacular stage successes at the London Pavilion, including *Bitter Sweet*, *This Year of Grace*, *Private Lives* and *Cavalcade*. But in 1934 Cochran's relationship with Noël Coward turned sour in a dispute over the authorship and rights of a play, *Conversation Piece*, which Coward wrote for the French star Yvonne Printemps. Cochran tried to take all of the credit. Coward terminated his contract and ended their relationship.

In 1947 Cochran's final stage triumph was *Bless the Bride* at the Adelphi Theatre, which ran from April 1947 to December 1949. The showed earned him enough money for a comfortable retirement. In 1948 he was awarded a long-overdue knighthood, followed two years later by a French honour, the *Chevalier de la Legion d'Honneur*. In his final years, Cochran managed the Royal Albert Hall. He died on 31 January 1951 after having been scalded in his bath.

MRS HENDERSON PRESENTS

In 1931, newly widowed Mrs Laura Henderson was looking to invest her nest egg in an enterprise that would benefit the arts. In the middle of an economic depression and at a time when music halls were being converted into 'talking picture' cinemas, Mrs Henderson decided to go against the flow. She bought a cinema with the intention of converting it into a theatre, which would stage avant-garde productions.

Her tiny theatre in Great Windmill Street, Piccadilly, got off to a shaky start, but a chance meeting with Vivian Van Damm, son of a Whitechapel solicitor who had married into the wealthy Lyons catering dynasty, changed all that. Van Damm had ambitions to become a theatre manager and his vision for the Windmill involved nude girls and comedians.

Mrs Henderson, despite her prim appearance, went into partnership with Van Damm, giving him carte blanche to realise his vision. The shows would be artistic. They would involve dance routines ending in tableaux showcasing nude girls in tasteful poses. There would be none of the bawdy eroticism of US strip shows and burlesque theatres or Parisian cabarets, let alone the unspeakably lewd Berlin nightclubs. A comedian would warm up the audience, and comic turns punctuated the stage routines.

Van Damm worked out a series of dances, exotic costumes, choreographed moves and dramatic lighting. Young girls aged around 18 were auditioned. They had to be a typical English rose – slim, with long legs and a small bust. Many were out-of-work dancers.

Provocatively titled *Revudeville*, the Windmill's first show went live in 1932 and the theatre was to operate until it finally closed in 1964. The revue included comedians, a chorus line of scantily clad dancing girls and a *tableau vivant* featuring one or two nude women who held a motionless pose. Van Damm would have been unaware that the *tableau vivant* or *poses plastiques* was merely a revival of a Regency entertainment that had inspired an earlier generation of thrill seekers.

At first the haunt of furtive clerks whiling away their lunch hours, jaded businessmen with an hour or two to kill or tourists up in London for the day, the Windmill came into its own during the Second World War.

WORLD WAR RUDE

Sex was in the air, as the *Daily Mirror's* long-running 1940s comic book heroine 'Jane' was to prove. Weekly cartoon strips of the curvaceous blonde secret agent titillated readers with Jane's daring exploits – most of which seemed to involve running around in scanty lingerie or losing all of her clothes. The cartoon strip was pinned up in barracks and officers' messes, and Jane's image was even painted on the nose of one of Britain's iconic Lancaster bombers. Jane typified the leggy Windmill dancer.

Exotic dancers and burlesque acts may have been common fare in the USA but in wartime London strict censorship rules laid down by the Lord Chamberlain applied. With their diet of exotic dancers, intimate cabaret theatres like the Windmill and the Whitehall Theatre stretched censorship rules to the limit.

Van Damm gave away up to 500 tickets weekly to British soldiers home on leave. The presence of huge numbers of US GIs billeted in London from 1943 led to a rise in demand for risqué adult entertainments. While other theatres and cinemas were closed during air raids, the Windmill stood firm. And so the legend of 'the Theatre that Never Closed' was born. *Picture Post* ran stories of dancers caught in air raids bedding down together in the Windmill's basement changing rooms. Photos showing the showgirls huddled under a blanket like 'Babes in the Wood' revived public spirits.

Journalist Vivien Goldsmith, daughter of Windmill dancer Joan Jay, recounted in *The Daily Telegraph* on 25 November 2005 an amusing story told by her mother:

> The only time a nude moved was when a bomb dropped on the Regent Palace Hotel. The theatre shook and the 'statue' ran for her life as a dead rat fell out of the rafters. The nudes were never allowed to sing as that would involve too much deep breathing and heaving of their fulsome chests.

The Windmill offered an audience starved of female company a brief glimpse of flesh and frilly underwear. Timed at around an hour and a half, non-stop performances started at noon and went on until 10.35 p.m. The front six rows of the tiny 300-seat theatre were the most popular and, whenever anyone got up to leave the front row, men would scramble over the seats to try to secure a better view of the 'action' near the spotlights, where it was almost possible to touch the dancers.

Dancers did their best to excite male libido. One American-style performer known as 'The Platinum Goddess' performed an African jungle routine and 'got around the strict censorship laws by allowing her bra and skirt to be torn off by savages',[9] while male dancers were dressed in loincloths. Britain's most feted stripper, Phyllis Dixey, entertained with her famous fan dance.

Sashaying around the stage while holding an enormous fan made of ostrich feathers, the diminutive blonde would gradually remove items of her apparel until at the climax of the act she would appear nude for a split second before the stage lights were switched off. Dixey had a string of shows at the Whitehall Theatre including *Peek-a-Boo*, *Piccadilly to Dixie* and *Step Out with Phyllis*.

Post war, a gradual relaxation of censorship saw attempts to recreate the faux sophistication of Las Vegas nightclubs or Parisian Folies through a rash of seedy striptease shows. This dead end has done little to enhance the West End's enduring cultural appeal and has more in common with the area's seamier side.

10

THE BUSINESS
OF PLEASURE

My right hon. Friend the Minister of Transport and I have set up a Working
Party with the following terms of reference:
'To determine the area which is of significance in relation to the traffic
passing through Piccadilly Circus, and to consider probable developments
in that area affecting the volume and composition of that traffic in the
foreseeable future …'

Sir Keith Joseph's address to Parliament, 20 February 1954

AUSTERITY BITES

The immediate post-war years saw Piccadilly and the West End reeling in the
aftershock of war. Britain's economy had been devastated; bomb damage had
to be repaired and transport infrastructure patched up. The statue of Anteros,
which had been mothballed for safekeeping, was restored to its rightful place
on its plinth in the centre of Piccadilly Circus in 1949 – a symbol of the capital edging back towards a semblance of normality.

The blackout that had plunged Piccadilly and the West End into darkness
was finally banished when the neon advertising lights were switched back on
in January 1949. The stage was set for the ageing star to make a comeback.

Post-war austerity exacted a heavy toll. Food and clothes rationing continued and Attlee's Labour government imposed a swingeing purchase tax
on luxury items. Trade and tourism were slow to revive, although the upper
classes continued to frequent exclusive West End bars and nightclubs. This

upper-class patronage, in some senses a hangover from the Regency Grand Tour when the scions of the aristocracy developed a taste for the better things in life – food, art, women, sculpture, the salon, gambling … whatever took their fancy – continued. It was a vigorous lifeline stretching across the palm of the West End.

Christmas lights made a tentative arrival when stores in Regent Street clubbed together to install illuminations in 1954, signalling the start of the pre-Christmas shopping season. The idea spread to Oxford Street in 1959. Confidence was starting to build in the West End.

A BIGGER VISION

In the aftermath of the Second World War, planners came up with radical solutions for dealing with the depopulation of city centres caused by the bombing. They believed ravaged city centres presented a once-in-a-lifetime opportunity to remodel the urban environment and make cities attractive places to live and work. Considering the threats of closure, this creativity and innovation is the approach required in London today.

Sweeping away historic buildings and characterful nooks and crannies, visionary architects drew up plans to modernise Piccadilly and the West End with new road layouts, concrete-and-glass shopping arcades, rooftop gardens, water features and much more. This was nothing less than a full-frontal assault on London's much-loved cityscape.

A 1954 plan by Geoffrey Jellico, Ove Arup and Edward Mills involved piecemeal demolition of Soho with a platform then built above with twenty-four-storey towers on top alongside landscaped gardens and glass-bottomed canals that followed the path of the streets, as well as concert halls and tennis courts.

Piccadilly Circus would have been altered beyond recognition if London County Council had got its way in 1958. Plans drawn up by its appointed architect Sir William Holford envisaged the wholesale demolition of Piccadilly's historic theatres, shops and restaurants to create an entirely new elevated pedestrian precinct with a road system at street level designed for fast-moving traffic.

This scheme, unwelcome to some, proposed four concrete-and-glass tower blocks between Piccadilly and Leicester Square, containing hotels, offices, flats and restaurants. It sounds not dissimilar to modern Tokyo or the usual cityscape presented in sci-fi films.

The schemes would need the approval of Crown Estates, the freehold owner of Regent Street, but promised to enhance the value of properties by extending upwards and maximising retail floorspace. As a first step in the wholesale destruction of Piccadilly, developer Jack Cotton bought up the Monico Restaurant from its then owners Forte Group in order to demolish it and replace it with a modern office block.

Londoners were outraged. A huge groundswell of organised protest forced the planners and developers into headlong retreat. To the consternation of progressive architects, ordinary members of the public and local businesses responded that they were quite happy with the Circus the way it was. Piccadilly's core buildings, the London Pavilion, the Criterion, and Swan and Edgar's had escaped the bombing and could be refurbished. After more than a decade of wrangling, both plans were ditched in the early 1970s.

A similar fate awaited Covent Garden, London's old fruit, vegetable and flower market, which was now too small and outdated to function as a modern wholesale market for an expanding metropolis. Covent Garden would move lock, stock and barrel to Nine Elms in south London while the historic early nineteenth-century covered market would be razed to the ground and replaced with concrete and glass. This boorish and ill-conceived scheme devised by greedy developers and financed by offshore investment funds was overturned at the last moment only after a determined public backlash and a well-orchestrated conservation lobby. It had been a very close call.

Thus, the Royal Opera House, the Lyceum and the Theatre Royal, Drury Lane, were allowed to flourish within the context of a vibrant new quarter where characterful streets of modest Georgian and Victorian buildings were transformed into boutiques and smart restaurants to become one of the West End's prime tourist destinations. One monstrosity the planners were able to inflict, however, was the construction of 'Centrepoint', the tall, narrow office block between Tottenham Court Road and New Oxford Street. Centrepoint was to remain vacant for more than a decade as office space was simply not needed in that location.

LET THE GOOD TIMES ROLL

The West End's revival took off at the start of the swinging sixties, when full employment began to create a new sense of optimism. The consumer revolution was led by young people, able for the first time to save more of their pay packet to spend on pop records, fashion, going out to the cinema or dance halls and having a good time.

Carnaby Street became a mecca for fashion, attracting confident mini-skirted girls and well-groomed 'mods' and encouraging them to become serious shoppers. Boutiques Lord John, Lady Jane, Kleptomania and I was Lord Kitchener's Valet, where guitarist Jimi Hendrix bought his famous tight-fitting military jacket, became synonymous with the latest trendy gear. Nigel Waymouth's psychedelic-inspired boutique Granny Takes a Trip opened at 488 King's Road, Chelsea, in February 1966. The front end of a bright orange Cadillac was installed bursting through the shop front, inspiring hippiedom and making the shop and the King's Road the place to be seen and an outlier for the West End.

Garish and outrageous, camp or retro, many of Carnaby Street's colourful designer clothes were produced by the local rag trade in Berwick Street. The tiny but influential street revived the British fashion industry, boosting the reputation of a new wave of designers including Ossie Clark, Mary Quant, Jeff Banks, Vivien Westwood and 'queen of punk' Zandra Rhodes.

A hugely influential force in women's fashion, former art student Bárbara Hulanicki opened a boutique named Biba in Abingdon Road, Kensington, in September 1964. Simple and sophisticated, Biba shops were welcoming though dimly lit, encouraging young women to explore and find clothes and beauty products. In 1973 Biba had grown so big that it took over Derry and Toms department store in High Street, Kensington, where it was attracting over a million visitors a week. In 1975, Biba closed. It had grown too big and unwieldy to manage. Since then, there have been many attempts to revive the iconic brand.

Oxford Street and Regent Street were starting to enjoy a boom. The busiest time was the run-up to Christmas when spectacular displays of Christmas-themed lights were strung across both main shopping streets. Miss World, Venezuela's Pilín León, was invited to the first ceremonial switching on of the West End illuminations in 1981. Since then, a celebrity has always been a focus of this event in late November. To date, stars including Cliff Richard, Sir Lenny Henry, the Sugababes and the Spice Girls have all taken turns at flicking the switch.

In January 2021, the store group Debenhams was forced into administration, hastened by successive lockdowns intended to slow the spread of the Covid-19 pandemic. The group, whose 200-year history could be traced to the drapers Debenham and Freebody and had been a presence in London's West End and across Britain, was bought by online retailer Boohoo, who simply wanted to acquire the trading name and website. As a physical bricks-and-mortar store, Debenhams would cease to exist.

The pandemic has speeded up a trend for online shopping as the Topshop fashion chain that includes Miss Selfridge has been snapped up by online fashion retailer ASOS. The future of West End shopping will depend heavily on luxury brands like Burberry, Alfred Dunhill and Fortnum and Mason. Many sell online or have franchised operations around the globe. These businesses have survived and will continue to thrive by continuing to innovate and by providing a unique and unbeatable customer experience – something that simply cannot be replicated online.

THE CIRCUS

The giant illuminated advertising billboards of Piccadilly Circus are an essential part of the West End's claim to international recognition, like the similar displays in Times Square, New York, or the Shinjuku district of Tokyo. From the late 1950s, Piccadilly's neon signage reflected Americanisation, aspirational tastes and an end to austerity. The most visible products were now Coca-Cola, Max Factor, Cinzano and Skol Lager.

But advertising was continually evolving and technology has ensured the Circus moved with the times. Visitors to Piccadilly Circus today will notice that much is left unchanged. Buildings have been cleaned and given a facelift. The famous statue of Anteros was fully restored in 2000 and is now accessible as part of a pedestrianised plaza linking the statue with the Criterion and its neighbouring buildings, including the fountain which stands at the corner of Haymarket. A Congestion Zone introduced by the Mayor of London has reduced a lot of central London's traffic and the new road layout sweeping from Regent Street to Haymarket speeds up bus traffic, leaving Coventry Street as a much narrower one-way thoroughfare.

The haphazard collection of huge illuminated billboards on every build-ing facing the north side of Piccadilly Circus underwent a radical makeover. In January 2017 the existing hotchpotch of neon advertising billboards that had grown up over the years was replaced by a single ultra-high-definition electronic screen that is one of the most technically advanced in the world. At around 790 square metres, the screen occupies a single site on the corner between Regent Street and Shaftesbury Avenue where the old Monico once stood. The remotely controlled display screen can be configured to show a single image or to break into a set of smaller advertisements.

Controlled by advertising agency Ocean Outdoor, the Piccadilly Circus illuminated screen offers live video streaming, news updates, weather reports and sports fixtures. Images and text can be updated in real time, creating new opportunities and formats for brands and advertisers. It is even said that a sensor can log vehicles passing through Piccadilly Circus and then tailor the advertising to the most frequently observed passing makes of car.

The palimpsest of neon signage that once covered the exterior of the London Pavilion has been stripped away and the building now stands proud, its classical facade revealed. The Pavilion was given a complete refurbishment in 1985 and is now an exhibition centre.

On the other side of the Circus, major social changes and changes in shopping habits are in evidence. Swan and Edgar's no longer stands on the corner of Regent Street. It was replaced by Tower Records, subsequently a Virgin Megastore, then Zavvi and now a fashion shop called The Sting.

The shift from formal business attire and tailored clothing has swept away reassuring and familiar names like Simpson's of Piccadilly, Austin Reed, Aquascutum, Edinburgh Woollen Mill and Viyella – quality brands that have been replaced by bland leisurewear franchises like J Crew, Superdry, Abercrombie and Fitch, Uniqlo and Hollister. In the process, the street has lost much of its exclusivity and is now sadly starting to resemble an upmarket version of a suburban high street.

SEX AND THE SWINGING SIXTIES

Murray's Jazz and Cabaret Club had a long history of dissipation. Founded in 1913 at 16–18 Beak Street, a side street just off Regent Street, the club was one of the first to introduce exotic dancers. In the post-war years it boasted 'Over 50 minutes of the largest and most lavishly staged floorshow in London'.

Guests were invited to dine from 7.30 p.m. with dancing until 3 a.m. and, in its 1950s and '60s heyday, Murray's Cabaret was one of the most discreetly risqué establishments in London with a membership of 60,000. It was a place where royalty, film stars and leading politicians rubbed shoulders with gangsters and the demi-monde. Princess Margaret and the Kray twins were members.

One of Murray's discoveries was a statuesque young showgirl called Christine Keeler and her bottle-blonde companion Mandy Rice-Davies. Christine Keeler had joined the club in 1958 and would later claim to have been employed to 'walk around naked', though in fact hostesses wore elaborate but revealing Cleopatra-style costumes with strategically placed gold and feathers.

It was here that Keeler first became acquainted with rackety society osteopath Stephen Ward. Through Ward, Keeler was introduced to Defence Minister John Profumo at a poolside party at Cliveden, the Astor family's stately home where Ward rented a cottage in the grounds. Her subsequent simultaneous sexual relationships – simultaneous in time but not in location – with both Profumo and Soviet naval attaché Captain Yevgeny Ivanov would spark a national scandal that toppled Harold Macmillan's government in October 1963.

In her autobiography *Secrets and Lies*, Keeler described her duties at the club with disarming honesty:

> We star showgirls walked bare-breasted on to the stage, and the hostesses, all cleavage and chat, moved among the wealthy and aristocratic middle-aged [clientele] … It was only after I left Murray's and returned to the real world that I realised the strange underground fantasy life I had been leading.

The Profumo scandal, combined with the *Lady Chatterley's Lover* trial conducted at Court Number One, the Old Bailey, from October to November 1960, which ruled that D.H. Lawrence's classic could finally be published in Britain, marked the beginning of the permissive sixties.

THE KING OF SOHO

A stone's throw from Piccadilly, Soho in the 1950s and '60s was the centre of London's film, advertising and music-publishing industry. Soho was lively. Cheek by jowl with the cheap cafés, gourmet restaurants, noisy pubs and Italian grocery stores, basements and courtyards provided cover for illegal gambling dens, drinking clubs, dive bars and clip joints. The latter were shady establishments where a hostess would lead her nervous client to a table in a darkened alcove where he would be persuaded to buy overpriced bottles of champagne on the hint of sexual favours to come. If the man was drunk, he risked losing his wallet into the bargain.

Post-war austerity may have put a crimp in the sex trade, but streetwalking persisted until the Street Offences Act became law on 16 August 1959. Prostitution went underground. Discreet calling cards popped up in newsagents' shops advertising red-light services with notices such as 'large chest for sale', 'white mini' or 'artist's model'. As the police regime relaxed in the 1980s, these calling cards became more explicit and migrated to the old red telephone boxes, in some cases obscuring most of the glass panes.

Soho vice had strong links to Malta, and the Messina family in particular. Gangster and pimp Alfredo Messina had arrived in London from Malta in 1934 and set up a network of prostitutes. After the war, helped by his sons Carmelo and Eugenio, he established many of the clip joints, and the rented rooms above shop fronts were typically accessed by a steep set of stairs and advertised by a red light and a scrawled notice pinned to the door frame. Over several decades the police battled to contain the Maltese mafia. Some things never change: the sexual and economic exploitation of women has always been a feature of London and the West End.

By the late 1950s, seedy members' clubs operating without a public music and dancing licences were popping up all over the place. The first such establishment, the Irving Strip Club, opened at 17 Irving Street just off Leicester Square in 1957. Run by former barrister Dhurjati Chaudhuri, the club's turnover was more than enough to enable its owner to pay the monthly £100 fine and still show a healthy profit. Less than a year later, Paul Raymond's Revuebar opened in Brewer Street, Soho.

From Liverpool and christened Geoff Quinn, Paul Raymond had gone on the run to avoid national service, eventually gravitating to Soho where he operated as a spiv or dodgy dealer in black-market goods. A budding stage career failed but provided him with the contacts to try his hand as an impresario. Changing his name to Paul Raymond, he started making serious money as the producer of nude revues, touring provincial theatres.

Realising regional theatre was in decline, Raymond looked for the opportunity to set up in London. He discovered empty premises in Brewer Street, which he transformed into a sophisticated nightspot where members would drink at a bar and dine at table while watching the floorshow.

The Revuebar opened at 2.30 p.m. on 21 April 1958. Very soon the venue was attracting showbiz personalities – household names like Peter Sellers, Michael Redgrave, Trevor Howard, John Mills, the blonde bombshell Diana Dors, and singers Alma Cogan and Dickie Valentine. The list of the rich and infamous included Billy Hill, the villain who had pulled off the Eastcastle Street job, a million-pound mail-van robbery, and gangland royalty Ronnie and Reggie Kray.

The club's black-marble facade, cocktail bar and red plush seating was in stark contrast to the dowdy Windmill Theatre, which struggled on until the death of its owner-manager Vivian Van Damm in 1964. For one thing, it was explicit. Paul Raymond, self-styled 'King of Soho', put on his 'International Striptease Spectacular' featuring dozens of naked showgirls flown in from Paris, Hamburg and even Chicago. One of his star performers was the Las Vegas stripper Annie Banks, aka 'Tempest Storm', famous for her overt sexuality and rumoured affairs with Frank Sinatra, Elvis Presley and President John F. Kennedy. In January 1961 Raymond signed Miss Storm to appear for a run of seventeen weeks at £1,000 a week, making her the world's highest-paid striptease artist.

Soon other seedier enterprises were joining the fray, exploiting newly liberal licensing laws, as well as the young women themselves. On the same day the Revuebar launched, the Casino de Paris opened its doors in nearby Denman Street, becoming Raymond's closest rival. These became places where businessmen with generous expense accounts could entertain their clients.

A family man with wife Jean and daughter Debbie, Raymond's business activities stood in sharp contrast to his Catholic upbringing. When casinos were given the green light by the passing of the Betting and Gaming Act in 1960, it was game on for the West End. Paul Raymond installed a roulette wheel and a *chemin de fer* table at the Revuebar and at his newly acquired Bal Tabarin Club in Hanover Square. As Raymond realised, most of the exclusive gaming clubs and nightclubs were shifting further west – far enough away from the protection rackets that threatened their prospects in Soho.

In 1965 Hugh Hefner, publisher of the upmarket girlie magazine *Playboy*, expanded his empire by opening a Playboy Casino at 45 Park Lane, Mayfair, in partnership with his English agent Victor Lownes. The club featured a Living Room, a Playmate Bar, a Dining Room and a Club Room. Members and their guests were served food and drinks by Playboy Bunnies – girls in tight-fitting 'waspie' corsets, fishnet tights, high heels and wearing bunny ears and a powder-puff tail.

In 1971, Paul Raymond published his own top-shelf magazines, *King* and *Men Only*, appointing actress and glamour model Fiona Richmond, the daughter of a Church of England clergyman, as its editor. Richmond had previously starred in the West End's first nude play, Paul Raymond's *Pyjama Tops*, which had opened at the Whitehall Theatre in August 1970. Richmond went on to star in soft-porn films *Women Behind Bars* and *Let's Get Laid*.

Meanwhile, the ever-astute Paul Raymond was building an empire of his own that included gaming clubs, casinos, strip clubs, theatres and a gay bar called the Pink Pussycat. After he divorced his wife Jean, Raymond and Fiona Richmond were briefly in a relationship. By the late 1980s, the 'King of Soho' had built up a significant property portfolio, mostly consisting of valuable freeholds yielding a significant annual rental income. In 1994, the *Sunday Times* Rich List estimated Paul Raymond's wealth at £1.5 billion, putting him above the Duke of Westminster as Britain's wealthiest man.

Raymond's daughter Debbie, a shrewd businesswoman, ran Soho Estates Holdings, the property side of the family enterprise. Raymond withdrew from the day-to-day running of his many clubs, living in a penthouse apartment near the Ritz Hotel and becoming more and more of a recluse. He died of prostate cancer in March 2008.

FAST FOOD AND CHAIN RESTAURANTS

Much has changed since J. Lyons opened its first Wimpy Bar in Coventry Street in May 1954, where it shared premises within the Corner House. Diversifying, Lyons had bought the UK franchise for this hamburger restaurant from a US company founded by Edward Gold in Bloomington, Indiana. Wimpy struggled to compete with more recent US franchises McDonalds and Burger King, as well as new kids on the block, Byron Burger and Gourmet Burger Kitchen.

Once a solid and reassuring presence on West End streets, Lyons teashops and Corner Houses vanished overnight in 1976. By now a vast conglomerate that owned and ran a range of businesses from luxury hotels to a substantial food-distribution business with its own brands of tea, coffee, cakes and fruit pies, J. Lyons and Co. had fallen victim to the international oil crisis.

Its hotel portfolio was haemorrhaging cash as overseas visitor numbers plummeted. The Strand Palace, the Cumberland Hotel at Marble Arch, the Royal Palace Hotel in Kensington and the Tower Hotel, St Katherine's Dock, were costly to operate in a recession. Unable to provide sufficient liquidity to meet its obligations, the overextended firm went bankrupt. In its day, Lyons had been a pioneer of modern management practice, having installed the first computerised payroll system in the UK.

Now a familiar sight, Spaghetti House made its first appearance in Goodge Street off the Tottenham Court Road in 1955. In the days before cheap package holidays broadened their horizons, most people's only acquaintance with spaghetti was the type that came pre-cooked in a Heinz tin. Spaghetti

House cheerfully disabused its customers with a cheeky sign: 'Spaghetti but not on toast!' Situated close to London University, the original Spaghetti House was highly popular with hungry and impecunious students.

That other great West End standby, Pizza Express, has claimed a place in the affections of Londoners ever since Peter Boizot opened his first pizzeria with its cast-iron marble-topped tables in Bloomsbury in 1969. The chain has expanded rapidly and gone from strength to strength with its reliable customer-service ethic, changing seasonal menu, well-chosen Italian wines and special deals.

From the 1970s onwards, mid-range restaurants like Pizza Express, Spaghetti House and London Steakhouses saw the growing demand for eating out and expanded into successful chains along with a host of similar eateries. Few today realise how unusual eating out was after years of post-war austerity, when most families relied on home cooking. London Steakhouses and Berni Inns, with their waiter service, soft lighting, prawn cocktails, fried rump steak, button mushrooms and chips, followed by Black Forest gateau and cream, accompanied by a bottle of cheap red wine or a schooner of sherry, offered affordable luxury that enabled a generation of young men to impress their girlfriends with their suave sophistication.

LA DOLCE VITA

Before the war, milk bars were a popular rendezvous for the cash-strapped young. Black and White Milk Bars and Strand Milk Bars had branches across the West End. But by the early 1950s, milk bars gave way to a new and fashionable rival, the espresso coffee bar. Rather than harking back to an eighteenth-century tradition, coffee bars were an Italian import and came equipped with Gaggia coffee machines whose jets of superheated steam would froth the milk to create perfect cappuccino coffee or deliver an espresso.

In 1953 pneumatic Italian starlet Gina Lollobrigida created a stir when she opened the Moka Bar at 29 Frith Street, Soho. Young people perched on stools at a long Formica counter on which stood one of the new Gaggia coffee machines. Soon coffee bars were opening across the West End, including the upmarket Coffee Inn in Park Lane, the Chalet in Grosvenor Square, the Boulevard in Wigmore Street and the Cabana in Prince's Street near Oxford Circus.

Appealing to a youthful demographic, some Soho coffee bars became music venues. The hippest places to be seen in 1950s Soho were two adjoining coffee bars in Old Compton Street called Heaven and Hell and the 2i's. Here people jived to a new kind of improvised folk music called 'skiffle'. Foremost among the new stars that rode this trend was Lonnie Donegan and his Skiffle Men, famous for hits such as 'Rock Island Line' and 'My Old Man's a Dustman'. The Beatles started their musical career in Liverpool clubs as a skiffle band known as The Quarrymen.

Soho's basement nightclubs drew a new generation of music fans. The 100 Club in Oxford Street had hosted a galaxy of jazz greats during the war years and for the duration of the 1950s it was renamed the Humphrey Lyttelton Club after the saxophonist who kicked off the craze for 'trad jazz'. Ronnie Scott's jazz club at 47 Frith Street went from edgy to mainstream with its candlelit basement auditorium and bar where diners seated at table could enjoy guest artists like Johnny Dankworth and Cleo Lane, George Melly or Winton Marsalis.

Reborn in the 1960s, the 100 Club was home to an emerging British blues scene. Rod Stewart, Long John Baldry, John Mayall's Blues Breakers and the Animals played here, as did the rock 'n' roll legends the Who, the Kinks, the Pretty Things and the Spencer Davis Group. By the late 1970s, the music fashion had switched to punk, and the Sex Pistols, the Clash, the Damned, Siouxsie & the Banshees and the Buzzcocks all debuted here.

Most famous of the basement rock clubs, the Marquee in Wardour Street opened in 1958. The cramped spotlit stage, low-ceilinged dance hall and warehouse vibe attracted the major rock bands of the 1960s. Young fans queued around the block to dance to the Rolling Stones in July 1962 and the Who in November 1964.

The late 1960s saw the emergence of a vibrant counterculture whose roots stretched across the Atlantic to New York's Greenwich Village and San Francisco's hippy heartland Haight-Ashbury. Bands like Lou Reed, the Doors, Soft Machine, Jefferson Airplane, the Jimi Hendrix Experience, the Crazy World of Arthur Brown and Pink Floyd played at 'underground' clubs like UFO, the Roundhouse, Camden Town and Middle Earth at 43 King Street, Covent Garden.

In a strange case of history repeating itself, Middle Earth occupied the epicentre of the early nineteenth-century 'underground' music scene, in the shape of Evans's Song and Supper Rooms. One can only speculate what those early nineteenth-century glee singers would have made of the Doors' lead singer Jim Morrison.

CHINATOWN

A close-knit community was established by Chinese seafarers in the East End who, along with Lascars from the Indian subcontinent, slaved below decks or stoking the boilers of Britain's vast merchant fleet. Limehouse, neighbouring London docks, was the original Chinatown. Brought vividly to life by Charles Dickens and Arthur Conan Doyle for its opium dens and gambling houses, the original Chinatown was no culinary quarter.

London's original Chinatown had been virtually obliterated by German bombing raids during the Second World War. In the early 1950s the Communist Revolution spearheaded by Chairman Mao Tse Tung prompted many Chinese to leave their country and migrate to Britain via Hong Kong. Often poor and ill-educated, opening a restaurant was the obvious employment option.

A second Chinatown sprang up just off Shaftesbury Avenue centred on Gerrard Street, Lisle Street and the lower end of Wardour Street. Among the early restaurants were the Kowloon, the Tailor and Cutter and Lee Ho Fook, all in Gerrard Street, and the Wong Kei in Wardour Street, famed for the rudeness of its waiters. By the 1970s, Chinese restaurants existed cheek by jowl with food and spice importers, gaming clubs, barbers, Chinese beauty parlours, Chinese mini-cabs, accountants, bookshops and libraries, supermarkets, travel agents and gambling clubs. There was even a Chinese chamber of trade.

The steamy windows of these cheap and cheerful eateries were hung with Peking ducks being warmed up ready to serve over a hot grill. Flattened and deboned, the spatchcock birds were glazed bright red with spices. Eating duck torn off the carcase with a huge bowl of boiled rice was an exciting and novel fast-food experience, as was the abrupt customer service.

At the Wong Kei, the insults were part of the experience. I carried out a straw poll among my friends and acquaintances who visited in its heyday. 'You want table? You go there? You want eat? You eat rice? You finish? You pay? You go? That was the standard Wong Kei experience,' recalls Derek Lawson. Sarah Minxy Mann Yeager adds, 'That place was hilarious, they used to scream at you as you walked in "UPSTAIR NOW!"' Journalist Miranda Levy remembers visiting with a gang of friends in her days as an impecunious student. The students were ordered upstairs and told what to eat, but when Levy requested seaweed as a side dish the waiter retorted, 'Seaweed expensive. You cheap!' These were the sort of encounters that elevated the restaurant to unlikely cult status.

Westminster Council officially designated the entire area Chinatown and installed signage. And in 1985, the first organised Chinese New Year celebrations took place. With its traditional 'dragon dance', this street carnival became a major tourist attraction. In 2016, an enormous Chinese carved wooden gateway ornamented with dragons was installed and Gerrard Street was pedestrianised. There are now more than eighty Chinese restaurants in this small area. The West End's Chinatown is today as much of a tourist attraction as its namesake in San Francisco.

FINE DINING

West End fine dining was given a major boost when Albert and Michel Roux Senior opened Le Gavroche at Upper Brook Street in 1967. At the time it was the first restaurant to open in London offering classical French cuisine. Run by Michel Roux Junior since 1991 and offering classical French fine dining, Le Gavroche now has two Michelin stars.

The tradition for exclusive restaurants, which began in the late nineteenth century, can still be experienced as several of the West End's iconic names survive. The Café Royal still trades on its original site and continues to set an international gold standard for luxury. Rebuilt in the mid 1920s when Regent Street was redeveloped by its freeholder Crown Estates, the Café Royal has sadly lost some of its original character and atmosphere.

Rules Restaurant still occupies its original premises at 35 Maiden Lane, just off the Strand. Founded by Thomas Rule in 1798 and serving English fare with emphasis on game, Rules is London's oldest restaurant. Simpson's in the Strand, a former cigar divan and famous for its roast beef carvery, is keeping a Victorian tradition very much alive.

Fashionable with film stars and celebrities from Dustin Hoffman to Mick Jagger, Langan's Brasserie, which opened on Stratton Street, was a partnership between Cockney actor Michael Caine and Irish chef Peter Langan. Sadly, the restaurant closed its doors for the final time in November 2020, a high-profile victim of the Covid pandemic.

A famous name in fine dining, Quaglino's at 16 Bury Street, St James's, was revived by Sir Terence Conran in 1993 and its art deco interiors were brought to life, reflecting the restaurant's 1930s heyday. A number of celebrated high-end restaurants including Leoni's Quo Vadis restaurant in Dean Street, Soho, and the Ivy at 1–5 West Street, Seven Dials, offer exclusive dining clubs and provide an extra level of service.

Owned by Richard Caring, the Ivy has cultivated an exclusive clientele but has decided recently to franchise its name to capture some of the middle ground by establishing 'Ivy Brasseries' in some of the more exclusive London postcodes, as well as in locations like Winchester, Guildford, Oxford, Cambridge and Bath.

CLUBLAND'S SHIFTING AXIS

While traditional members' clubs continued to plough a well-worn furrow, a new post-war generation of clubmen and women looked towards Soho's vibrancy, its cultural diversity and its affordable rents to create exciting new meeting places.

In October 1961, the Establishment Club was formed at 18 Greek Street, Soho, by Peter Cook and Nicholas Luard, two satirists behind the irreverent magazine *Private Eye*. At the time the '*Eye*' was well known for poking fun at Prime Minister Harold Macmillan, an old Etonian and clubman. The Establishment was a nightclub that hosted musicians and comedians. The Dudley Moore trio and stand-up comics Lenny Bruce and Barry Humphries made regular guest appearances. Members included satirists John Bird, John Fortune and Eleanor Bron. The club lasted until 1964.

Most famous of all post-war Soho clubs, the Colony Room Club, was a private drinking club founded in 1948 by Muriel Belcher at 41 Dean Street. Founding members were gay artist Francis Bacon, who walked into the club's tiny first-floor bar the day after it opened, Lucian Freud, George Melly and legendary journalist and drunk Jeffrey Bernard. The club acquired a reputation for tolerance towards the gay community and its mix of alcoholic rabble-rousers and eccentrics welcomed guests including Molly Parkin and the high-living Princess Margaret. The club and its famous dingy green-painted Colony Room finally closed its door for the very last time in 2008.

Wise-cracking comedian Groucho Marx famously said, 'I sent the club a wire stating "please accept my resignation. I don't want to belong to any club that will accept people like me as a member."' In the mid 1980s, a group of publishers, Liz Calder, Carmen Calill, Ed Victor and literary agent Michael Sissons, took inspiration from Groucho's one-liner and launched a club for media types who would have been deemed unclubbable by stuffy St James's members' clubs.

The Groucho Club was launched on 7 May 1985 at 45 Dean Street, Soho, in a restaurant called the Zanzibar, which had an all-day and late-night drinking licence. Kitted out with colourful prints, eccentric decor and comfortable sofas, the Groucho had a bar, restaurant and lounge where publishers and media types could relax and socialise. The dress code was relaxed and women were admitted as members on equal terms.

Within weeks of opening, word had got out that the Groucho was the place to be seen in. Membership was decided by asking a simple question: 'Does anyone know this person and would you like them sitting next to you at the bar?'

Change was on the way. Relaxed attitudes among the baby-boomer generation and the urge to rebel against tradition were making waves in clubland. Traditional members' clubs have tried hard to keep pace with social change. Some of the more progressive clubs have joined schemes like InterClub, a network open to young men and women below the age of 35, giving them a reduced membership fee and access to a wide range of sports and social activities. Determined marketing campaigns have also been launched by clubs like the Reform, the Naval and Military Club and the National Liberal Club, which have enabled them to diversify their membership and boost their intake of women members to over 40 per cent. Traditional clubs like White's, the Travellers and the Garrick steadfastly refuse to accept women members.

Soho House arrived on the scene in 1995. Occupying an entire Georgian townhouse above the Cafe Bohème, 40 Greek Street, Soho House set the scene for a major expansion in luxury clubs catering for niche markets such as media executives, rock stars and new money. In a similar league to the Chelsea Arts Club and Home House, Soho House has expanded rapidly. Today there are twenty-two sister clubs all over the world, with nine in the UK including Shoreditch House, Little House, Electric House, Soho Farmhouse at Chipping Norton, and outposts in Mumbai, Manhattan and Berlin. Members enjoy reciprocal rights to all these clubs.

Businesswomen could soon expect and demand similar facilities as it was recognised that a market existed for women-only clubs. The exclusion of men offered a safe haven from casual sexism and clearly many women found men a distraction or overly competitive. London's first private members' club aimed at providing a space to host brilliant, like-minded women, the AllBright Club in Fitzrovia, is located in a splendid five-storey townhouse just off Oxford Street. A second club in Mayfair's Maddox Street opened in 2019. Meanwhile, Grace of Belgravia, another exclusively female club, echoes the women-only West End clubs of the 1890s and 1900s, such as the Dorothy Club for lady shoppers and the Ladies' Empire Club.

ANNABEL'S – CELEBRITY MEETS ROYALTY

While a new breed of members' clubs has emerged based on business networking, informality and the need to embrace women's interests, some of the most exciting and influential modern institutions have taken the concept of the club back to its aristocratic roots.

The pleasures of gaming, wining, dining and having fun go right back to the Regency and to the heady attractions of the Jazz Age dance clubs. In 1962 John Aspinall founded one of the most exclusive gaming establishments, the Clermont Club at 44 Berkeley Square. Housed in a stunning Queen Anne mansion, originally the property of the 1st Earl of Clermont, the Clermont attracted a group of wealthy playboys and aristocrats. Members including Mark Birley, Ian Fleming, David Stirling, the founder of the SAS, Lord Lucan, the Duke of Devonshire and businessman James Goldsmith were known as 'the Clermont Set'.

A year later, Aspinall's close friend and business associate Mark Birley suggested the pair needed somewhere to party after an evening's gambling. Birley leased the basement and converted it into a nightclub, which he named after his wife, Lady Annabel Vane-Tempest-Stewart, daughter of the 8th Marquess of Londonderry.

Annabel's nightclub attracted debutantes, aristocrats, celebrities, rock legends, Hollywood film stars and junior members of the royal family, including Frank Sinatra, Bond film producer Cubby Broccoli and Prince Michael of Kent. Annabel's quickly proved more profitable than the Clermont Club, which moved to new premises in Mayfair, enabling the club to expand and create ever more luxurious facilities. No expense was spared in installing restaurants, bars and sumptuous club facilities.

Couples were often snapped leaving the club and the reported goings-on fuelled the gossip columns of well-known tabloid newspapers. Sadly, Mark Birley's marriage did not last, and after an amicable divorce, his wife went on to marry Birley's friend, Sir James Goldsmith, in 1976.

Annabel's was famous for its exclusivity and its royal connections, including Lady Diana Spencer, Prince Charles and, more recently, royal princes William and Harry. The queen even visited the club in 2003, and it is thought to be the only nightclub she has ever attended.

Mark Birley's death in 2007 could have spelled an end to Annabel's but the name has lived on under new management and, after more than fifty years in Berkeley Square, the club reopened in 2018, two doors down in a Grade I listed Georgian mansion house. Robin, Mark Birley's son, has built on his father's legacy and opened probably the most exclusive and fashionable private members' club in London. Known simply as 5 Hertford Street, the club feels much like the old Annabel's with its endless Chesterfield sofas, and photos of family members filling fireplaces and walls. Described by *Vogue* in 2016 as the 'loveliest club in London', it is frequented by Hollywood A-listers. Its basement nightclub, Loulou's, is used for after-dinner dancing.

FILM PREMIERES

On 7 July 1964, the London Pavilion rolled out the red carpet for the world premiere of the Beatles' long-awaited film *A Hard Day's Night.* To the Fab Four's fans, the film was a cultural icon. Arriving in a Rolls-Royce, John Lennon, Paul McCartney, George Harrison and Ringo Starr were joined on the red carpet by John's wife Cynthia. For a brief time, Piccadilly Circus was almost brought to a standstill as the paparazzi descended, flashbulbs popping, and crowds of screaming teenage girls had to be held back by a police cordon.

Under an agreement with United Artists, the studio's top films were shown here first before they were released for nationwide distribution. As post-war Britain experienced years of austerity, the London Pavilion remained an affordable luxury as Londoners were always keen to view the latest films. In October 1962 the first James Bond film *Doctor No* was given its public showing.

But even as the cinema was booming, the London Pavilion itself was becoming dilapidated. It had become the victim of a planning blight. For a long time, it looked as though iconic buildings including the London Pavilion would be compulsorily purchased and demolished. The cinema closed on 26 April 1981. Its place as the location for red-carpet film premieres was taken by the Empire, Leicester Square.

In 1986, the interior of the building was gutted and converted into a shopping arcade, preserving only the 1885 facade and the outer walls and roof. Once the last word in luxury, the London Pavilion was rebranded 'the Trocadero Centre' in 2000 and became a shopping mall and exhibition centre, the first being an exhibition of waxworks of famous rock stars and celebrities sponsored by Madame Tussaud's, known as the Rock Circus.

The British Academy of Film and Television Arts (BAFTA) has its head-quarters in Piccadilly, where educational events, film screenings and tribute evenings are held. The charitable organisation has around 6,000 members drawn from the film, TV and video-gaming industries.

BAFTA was created in 1976, but its forerunner was the British Film Academy, founded in 1947 by a group of leading producers including David Lean, Alexander Korda and Carol Reed. Today, BAFTA aims to 'support, develop and promote the art forms of the moving image' and to show-case British-made film and TV drama. It holds an annual awards ceremony for British and international film each February. There are categories for Outstanding British Film and Outstanding Writer, Producer or Director.

Up until 2001 the ceremony was held in April or May but has been brought forward to avoid clashing with the Academy Awards. Originally held at the Empire cinema, Leicester Square, the annual event switched to the Royal Opera House from 2008 to 2016 and, more recently, the Royal Albert Hall.

ANGRY YOUNG MEN

On 8 May 1956, *Look Back in Anger* by new playwright John Osborn opened at the Royal Court Theatre, Sloane Square. Critics were baffled. There was no light-hearted dialogue, no romance and no happy ending. Instead, its actors portrayed angst-ridden characters arguing over the kitchen table of a squalid flat located in a gritty northern city.

The play established Osborn's reputation as one of Britain's brightest new authors, while its central character, Jimmy Porter, became a cult figure for angry young men disillusioned with post-war austerity. The play starred Kenneth Haigh, Mary Ure and Alan Bates. West End theatre would never be the same again. There was even a name coined for this type of play – 'kitchen sink drama'.

In 1958 Shelagh Delaney's *A Taste of Honey*, starring Wendy Craig and Richard Briers, premiered at the Criterion Theatre, Piccadilly Circus. Here was yet another northern working-class drama – this time about a teenage girl made pregnant by her black boyfriend and her unshakeable optimism in resolving all of the issues around her broken home and living on the bread-line. Playwright Shelagh Delaney, a 19-year-old from Lancashire, gave women a much-needed voice.

The new mood of realism was reflected in America where it influenced playwrights like Tennessee Williams, whose plays *Cat on a Hot Tin Roof*, *Suddenly Last Summer* and *A Streetcar Named Desire* were starting to become popular at London's arts theatre clubs.

Gay themes smashed yet another theatrical taboo. While Oscar Wilde kept his sexuality a secret, the openly gay playwright Joe Orton amused audiences with his scandalous comedies. His first stage play, *Entertaining Mr Sloane*, was a huge success while his second, *Loot*, which had transferred to the Criterion Theatre in 1966, won the *Evening Standard* award for Best Play. In August 1967 Orton's lover Kenneth Halliwell, suffering from severe depression, murdered Orton before killing himself.

Post-war theatre set out to break the mould. But the West End was not a place for experimentation. The high overheads of running a central London theatre meant appealing to middle-of-the-road tastes. Agatha Christie's *The Mousetrap*, a murder mystery that opened in 1952 at the Ambassador's Theatre, enjoyed an unbroken run until March 2020 and the start of the Covid pandemic. The unassuming little play eventually enjoyed the status of national treasure.

Meanwhile, plays like Samuel Beckett's *Waiting for Godot* and Harold Pinter's *The Caretaker*, which drew heavily on the French existentialist philosophy, never caught the imagination of West End audiences and instead became a fixture for the subsidised and more highbrow National Theatre, whose brutalist concrete structure opened on the South Bank in 1976.

MUSICALS

Musicals are the mainstay of West End theatre, appealing to tourists and visitors to London looking for a night to remember. Featuring singing stars backed by a huge supporting cast and spectacular stage effects, musicals became the big box-office earners, underpinning London's tourist economy. In 2018 there were more than 15.5 million attendances at West End theatres alone.

There are strong cultural and financial links between the West End and New York's Broadway, with successful musicals often crossing and re-crossing the Atlantic as shows gather popularity. Sometimes appearing simultaneously with different star casts, British musicals have been a major cultural export.

One of the most notable recent examples of the West End–Broadway nexus are the string of hit musicals written by Andrew Lloyd Webber. His musicals *Phantom of the Opera* and *Cats* both transferred from the West End to Broadway, where they enjoyed phenomenal success. By the time it closed in February 2012, *Phantom of the Opera* had run for a record 10,000 shows in America.

Knighted and given a peerage in 1992, Lord Lloyd Webber had his first hit with *Joseph and his Amazing Technicolour Dreamcoat* in 1967, followed by *Jesus Christ Superstar* in 1973, then *Evita*, followed in the 1980s by *Cats*, *Starlight Express* and culminating with *The Phantom of the Opera* in 1986. *Cats*, which closed in 2002, ran for a total of 8,949 performances over twenty-one years. In the tradition of the great West End impresarios, Lord Lloyd Webber owns and manages a number of West End theatres, including the Theatre Royal, Drury Lane, and the London Palladium through his company, the Really Useful Theatre Group.

Successful shows have often been revived many times. The musical *Me and My Girl* was a 1937 smash hit at the Victoria Theatre. Starring and directed by Lupino Lane, the show featured 'The Lambeth Walk', 'Leaning on a Lamp Post' and 'The Sun Has Got its Hat on'. Revived in 1984 for a West End run of eight years, the show transferred to Broadway in 1986, with a tour of the USA the following year.

As I write this history, six long-running musicals were dominating the West End in 2020: *Les Misérables*, *The Phantom of the Opera*, *Mamma Mia!*, *The Lion King* at the Lyceum, *Wicked* at the Victoria Theatre and *Matilda* at the Cambridge Theatre. The longest-running musical in West End history, *Les Misérables*, produced by Cameron Mackintosh, had been running in London at the Sondheim Theatre, Shaftesbury Avenue, since October 1985.

Shuttered theatres tell their own tale of cultural and economic devastation, and none more so than the Sondheim in Shaftesbury Avenue, whose glass-fronted foyer was papered over during the height of the coronavirus pandemic with a massive poster – 'We're Mizzing You, But We'll Be Back Soon'. As this book is being finalised, theatre owners are staking everything on being able to reopen safely and on being able to tap into a pent-up demand for live entertainment. Many measures, such as the wearing of masks, social distancing, temperature checks, one-way routes and a restriction on ordering drinks in the interval, are being suggested as ways to regain the trust of audiences.

Sadly, uneconomic theatres look likely to close and, with the sizable gig economy workforce of freelance lighting technicians, sound engineers and production staff still out of work, any meaningful recovery will have to wait. Meanwhile, fans of 'Les Miz' were treated to an all-star line-up led by Michael Ball, Alfie Boe, Carrie Hope Fletcher and Matt Lucas, together with fifty actors, when coronavirus restrictions were briefly relaxed in December 2020.

GREEN SHOOTS

There are parallels between the early post-war years and the Covid-19 pandemic. As the West End struggles with the many government-imposed restrictions conceived as a response to the pandemic, the belief is that theatres, restaurants and clubs will bounce back. The pleasure principle is so ingrained in all of us that, with a glance at the packed nightclubs of 1920s Piccadilly, the dance restaurants and revues, it is hard to conceive that a few years earlier the world was in the grip of the Spanish influenza epidemic, which killed more people worldwide than the First World War. The human animal is devoted to pleasure and is endlessly creative; we generally find a way round whatever barriers appear for the moment to be insuperable. The devastation of London after the Second World War and the hard slog back to a bearable and then enjoyable reality that followed provides food for thought in the face of the pandemic.

In 2020, the British Government's response to the pandemic was to introduce a range of measures from carefully calibrated restrictions aimed at slowing the spread of the virus to complete lockdown whereby people were told to stay indoors or to work from home if they could. This had the effect of closing theatres and indoor spaces where people would be too close together. This curtailment of the social world also occurred as the war progressed. Although relaxation of the strict pandemic rules over the summer months in 2020 allowed many West End restaurants to reopen, and even prompted some hardy entrepreneurs to open completely new establishments, theatres and concert halls needed to put in place rigorous infection-control regimes. One-way movement and social distancing have created insuperable problems, especially backstage, making theatres and classical concerts unsafe and uneconomic.

By the time the pandemic ends it will have sadly destroyed the viability of large swathes of the West End's hospitality and entertainments sector. But then again, consider the London described by Charles Dickens in *Sketches by Boz*:

> One of our principal amusements is to watch the gradual progress – the rise and fall – of particular shops … We could name off-hand, twenty at least, which we are quite sure have paid no taxes for the last six years. They are never inhabited for more than two months consecutively, and, we verily believe, have witnessed every retail trade in the directory.[1]

The future is very often a replay of the past to different music: the gig economy, the pop-up shop, the famous chef trying his or her hand at street food are not too distant from what Dickens describes and may again come into their own.

But, as history has shown us repeatedly, the West End has had the capacity and imagination to endlessly reinvent itself in response to changing times. Piccadilly has always evolved and will no doubt do so again.

NOTES

Chapter 1

1. John Thomas Smith, *Mendicant Wanderers Through the Streets of London* (Edinburgh: William P. Nimmo, 1883), p.23.
2. Robert Machray, *The Night Side of London* (London: T. Werner Laurie, 1902), p.10.
3. Ibid., pp.9–10.
4. Ibid., pp.15–19.
5. Mrs Robert Henrey (Madeleine Henrey), *A Village in Piccadilly* (London: Dent, 1942), p.1.

Chapter 2

1. William Hone, *Hone's Everyday Book* (London: Hunt and Clarke, 1826), p.572.
2. *The Lady's Magazine*, July 1818.
3. A 'Thais' was a hetaera or courtesan who accompanied Alexander the Great, reputedly most witty and entertaining. Hetaera were famous for their witty conversation, artistic accomplishments and, of course, sexual services provided to patrons.
4. Lord Byron, 28 March 1814, cited in Thomas Moore, *Letters and Journals of Lord Byron*, Vol. 1, p.74.

Chapter 3

1. *London Courier and Evening Gazette*, 7 April 1831.
2. *London Courier and Evening Gazette*, 22 February 1814.
3. Edward Walford, *Old and New London*, Vol. IV (London: Cassell Petter and Galpin, 1878), p.296.
4. Charles Eyre Pascoe, *London of To-Day: An Illustrated Handbook for the Season 1888* (Boston: Roberts Brothers, 1888), p.38.
5. Ibid., p.37.

Chapter 4

1. *The Travel Diary of Zacharias Konrad von Offenbach*, 19 June 1710.
2. John Timbs, *Curiosities of London* (London: David Bogue, 1855), p.268.
3. Ibid., p.267.
4. Ibid.
5. W. MacQueen-Pope, *Goodbye Piccadilly* (London: Michael Joseph, 1960), p.83.

Chapter 5

1. James Laver, *Hatchards of Piccadilly 1797–1947* (London: Hatchards,1947), p.13.
2. *Gentleman's Magazine*, September 1817, p.272.
3. Erika Diane Rappaport, *Shopping for Pleasure: Women and the Making of London's West End* (Princeton: Princeton University Press, 2000), p.156.

Chapter 6

1. Brenda Assael, *The London Restaurant 1840–1914* (Oxford: Oxford University Press, 2018), p.159.
2. Henry Mayhew, *Mayhew's London: Being Selections from 'London Labour and the London Poor'* (London: Spring Books, 1960), p.130.
3. George Augustus Sala, *Twice Round the Clock or The Hours of the Day and Night in London* (London: John and Robert Maxwell, 1880), p.320.
4. Ibid., p.322.
5. Charles Cochran, *Cock-a-Doodle-Do* (London: Methuen,1941), p.265.
6. Machray, *The Night Side of London*, p.17.
7. Extract from *The Era*, 26 October 1901.
8. Guy Deghy, *Paradise in the Strand: The Story of Romano's* (London: Richards Press, 1958), p.21.
9. Machray, *The Night Side of London*, p.14.
10. Assael, *The London Restaurant 1840–1914*, p.159.
11. Lieut Col Nathaniel Newnham-Davis, *Dinners and Diners Where and How to Eat in London* (London: Grant Richards, 1899), p.53.
12. Antony Powell, *Casanova's Chinese Restaurant* (London: William Heinemann, Arrow Books edition, 1967), p.270.
13. MacQueen-Pope, *Goodbye Piccadilly*, p.118.
14. *The Caterer*, 15 July 1895.

Chapter 7

1. Machray, *The Night Side of London*, p.226.
2. J. Ewing Ritchie, *The Night Side of London* (London: Tinsley Brothers, 1869), p.79.
3. Ibid., p.89.
4. Sala, *Twice Round the Clock*, p.341.
5. Cochran, *Cock-a-Doodle-Do*, p.266.
6. 'A London Restaurant by Midnight', *British Journal of Catering*, 1 March 1888, p.189.
7. Cited in Andrew Lownie, *The Mountbattens: Their Lives and Loves* (London: Blink Publishing, 2019), p.88.
8. Ibid., p.89.
9. Reprinted from Mark Tucker and Duke Ellington, *The Duke Ellington Reader* (Oxford: Oxford University Press, 1993), p.73.

10. Judith R. Walkowitz, *Nights Out: Life in Cosmopolitan London* (New Haven: Yale University Press, 2012), p.234.
11. Fanny Burney, *Stage, Screen and Sandwiches: The Remarkable Life of Kenelm Foss* (London: Athena Press, 2007), pp.9–10.

Chapter 8
1. *The British Journal*, 10 June 1726.
2. Dan H. Marek, *Alto: The Voice of Bel Canto* (London: Rowman and Littlefield, 2016), p.84.
3. Jean Benedetti, *David Garrick and the Birth of the Modern Theatre* (London: Methuen, 2001), p.140.
4. James Boswell, *Life of Johnson* (Oxford: Oxford University Press, 1791), p.520.
5. Thomas Grant, *Court Number One The Old Bailey: The Trials and Scandals that Shocked Modern Britain* (London: John Murray, 2019), p.61.
6. *Daily Telegraph*, 18 November 1908.

Chapter 9
1. *The Entr'acte*, 5 December 1885, p.6a.
2. *Ally Sloper's Half Holiday*, 18 August 1888.
3. *The Era*, 1 June 1862.
4. *The Era*, 20 August 1887.
5. James Jupp, *The Gaiety Stage Door* (London: Jonathan Cape, 1923), p.56.
6. Ibid.
7. Cochran, *Cock-a-Doodle-Do*, p.117.
8. James Harding, *Cochran* (London: Methuen, 1988), p.61.
9. Rachel Shteir, *Striptease: The Untold History of the Girlie Show* (Oxford: Oxford University Press, 2004), p.217.

Chapter 10
1. Charles Dickens, *Sketches by Boz* (London: Bradbury and Evans, 1836), p.167.

BIBLIOGRAPHY

Ackroyd, Peter, *Queer City: Gay London from the Romans to the Present Day* (London: Chatto and Windus, 2017)

Almeroth-Williams, Thomas, *City of Beasts: How Animals Shaped Georgian London* (Manchester: Manchester University Press, 2019)

Assael, Brenda, *The London Restaurant 1840–1914* (Oxford: Oxford University Press, 2018)

Avery, Simon and Katherine M. Graham (eds), *Sex, Time and Place: Queer Histories of London c. 1850 to the Present* (London: Bloomsbury, 2016)

Baker, Richard Anthony, *Old-Time Variety: An Illustrated History* (Barnsley: Remember When, 2011)

Beckett, Francis, *Fascist in the Family: The Tragedy of John Beckett M.P.* (London: Routledge, 2017)

Benedetti, Jean, *David Garrick and the Birth of the Modern Theatre* (London: Methuen, 2001)

Birkenhead, Sheila, *Peace in Piccadilly: The Story of Albany* (London: Hamish Hamilton, 1958)

Boswell, James, *Life of Johnson* (Oxford: Oxford University Press, 1791)

Brooker, Peter, *Bohemia in London: The Social Scene of Early Modernism* (Basingstoke: Palgrave Macmillan, 2004)

Burnett, John, *England Eats Out 1830–Present* (Abingdon: Pearson Education, 2004)

Burney, Fanny, *Stage, Screen and Sandwiches: The Remarkable Life of Kenelm Foss* (Twickenham: Athena Press, 2007)

Causton, Richard and Henry (printers), *Kent's Directory for the Year 1801*

Clayton, Anthony, *London's Coffee Houses: A Stimulating Story* (Whitstable: Historical Publications, 2003)

Cochran, Charles, *Cock-a-Doodle-Do* (London: Methuen, 1941)

Corina, Maurice, *Fine Silks and Oak Counter Debenhams 1778–1978* (London: Hutchinson, 1978)

Dasent, Arthur Irwin, *Piccadilly in Three Centuries* (London: Macmillan, 1920)

Deghy, Guy, *Paradise in the Strand: The Story of Romano's* (London: The Richards Press, 1958)

Deghy, Guy and Keith Waterhouse, *Café Royal: Ninety Years of Bohemia* (London: Hutchinson, 1955)

Ellmann, Richard, *Oscar Wilde* (Hamish Hamilton, 1987)

Gill, A.A., *The Ivy: The Restaurant and its Recipes* (London: Hodder and Stoughton, 1997)

Grant, Thomas, *Court Number One The Old Bailey: The Trials and Scandals that Shocked Modern Britain* (London: John Murray, 2019)

Harding, James, *Cochran* (London: Methuen, 1988)

Hoare, Philip, *Noël Coward: A Biography* (London: Sinclair-Stevenson, 1995)

Hone, William, *Hone's Everyday Book* (London: Hunt and Clarke, 1826)

Honeycombe, Gordon, *Selfridges, Seventy-Five Years: The Story of the Store* (London: Park Lane Press, 1984)

Lancaster, Bill, *The Department Store: A Social History* (Leicester: Leicester University Press, 1995)

Laver, James, *Hatchards of Piccadilly 1797–1947: One Hundred and Fifty Years of Bookselling* (London: Hatchards Ltd, 1947)

Jenness, George Arthur, *Maskelyne and Cooke: Egyptian Hall, London 1873–1904* (Middlesex: Jenness, 1967)

Jupp, James, *The Gaiety Stage Door* (London: Jonathan Cape, 1923)

Keeler, Christine and Douglas Thompson, *Secrets and Lies: The Trials of Christine Keeler* (London: John Blake Publishing, 2019)

Linnane, Fergus, *Bawds and Brothel-Keepers of London* (Stroud: Sutton Publishing, 2005)

London, Museum of, *London Eats Out: 500 Years of Capital Dining* (London: Philip Wilson, 1999)

Lownie, Andrew, *The Mountbattens: Their Lives and Loves* (London: Blink Publishing, 2019)

Machray, Robert, *The Night Side of London* (London: T. Werner Laurie, 1901)

MacQueen-Pope, W., *Goodbye Piccadilly* (London: Michael Joseph, 1960)

Marek, Dan H., *Alto: The Voice of Bel Canto* (London: Rowman and Littlefield, 2016)

Mayhew, Henry, *Mayhew's London being Selections from London Labour and the London Poor* (London: Spring Books, 1960)

Moyle, Franny, *The Tragic and Scandalous Life of Constance, Mrs Oscar Wilde* (London: John Murray, 2011)

Newnham-Davis, Nathaniel, *Dinners and Diners: Where and How to Eat in London* (London: Grant Richards, 1899)

Pascoe, Charles Eyre, *London of To-Day: An Illustrated Handbook for the Season 1888* (Boston: Roberts Brothers, 1888)

Rappaport, Erika Diane, *Shopping for Pleasure: Women and the Making of London's West End* (Princeton: Princeton University Press, 2000)

Ritchie, J. Ewing, *The Night Side of London* (Lonodn: Tinsley Brothers, 1869)

Sala, George Augustus, *Twice Round the Clock or The Hours of the Day and Night in London* (London: John and Robert Maxwell, 1880)

Shteir, Rachel, *Striptease: The Untold History of the Girlie Show* (Oxford: Oxford University Press, 2004)

Smith, Richard O., *The Man with his Head in the Clouds: James Sadler the First Englishman to Fly* (Oxford: Signal Books, 2014)

Timbs, John, *Curiosities of London* (London: David Bogue, 1855)

Tucker, Mark and Duke Ellington, *The Duke Ellington Reader* (Oxford: Oxford University Press, 1993)

Wainwright, David, *The British Tradition: Simpson – a World of Style* (Shrewsbury: Quiller Press, 1996)

Walford, Edward, *Old and New London*, Vol. IV (London: Cassell Petter and Galpin, 1878)

Walkowitz, Judith R., *Nights Out: Life in Cosmopolitan London* (New Haven: Yale University Press, 2012)

Willetts, Paul, *Members Only: The Life and Times of Paul Raymond* (London: Serpent's Tail, 2010)

INDEX

43 Club, Gerrard Street 167, 168, 169
100 Club 172, 230

Adam, John (architect) 186
Adam, Robert (architect) 56
Adams, John Quincy 16, 106
Adelphi Theatre 149, 192, 205, 213, 214
advertising hoardings 17, 223–4
Aerated Bread Company 154–5
Aix-la-Chapelle, Treaty of 40
Albany 24–5, 52–5, 58
Albemarle, Duke of 43
Albemarle Club 72
Albery, James 188–9
Albery Theatre 189
Aldwych Theatre 194
Alfred Club 72
Alhambra Palace of Varieties 99, 158–9,
    197, 204, 210, 211
Allan, Maud 190–1
Allbright Club 234
Almon, John (bookseller) 16, 104–6
Ambassador's Theatre 213, 238
Anglo-Boer war 29–30, 206
Annabel's Club 235–6
Anteros, statue of 20, 30, 32, 34, 219, 223
Apollo Theatre 22, 205, 207
Apsley House 24, 55–7, 58
Armitstead, Elizabeth Bridget (née Cane)
    51–2
Armstrong, Louis 170, 213
Ashley Cooper, Anthony, 7th Earl of
    Shaftesbury 20, 22

Asquith, Margot 190
Astley, Philip 80
Astley's Amphitheatre 80–1
Astley's Hippodrome 79–80
Astor Club 167

Baartman, Saartje ('Sarah') 90–1
Bachelors Club 72
BAFTA (British Academy of Film and
    Television Arts) 236–7
Bag o'Nails Club 168
Baker Street and Waterloo Railway 31
Barnum, Phineas T. 16, 92–4
Bath Club 72
Bath Hotel 59, 60, 64, 65
Bazalgette, Joseph 22
Beardsley, Aubrey 146, 148, 190
Beckett, John 193
Bedford Music Hall 199
Bell Savage coaching inn 61
Bellwood, Bessie (Catherine Mahoney)
    149, 199, 202
Bentley, Will 133, 152–3
Bentley's Oyster Bar 133, 152–3
Berkeley, Lord 40, 43
Berkeley House 58
Bernhardt, Sarah 75, 189
Berry Bros & Rudd 103
Biba 222
Bioscope 99
Birley, Mark 235
Birley, Robin 236
Black Bear coaching inn 60, 61, 64

Black Horse Inn 198, 201
Blake, William 44–5
Blitz, the 35–8, 150, 189
Blomfield, Sir Reginald 33
Blue Lagoon Club 16–17, 169, 170–1
Bone, Stephen 32
Bordoni, Faustina 180
Bouillabaisse International Club 171, 172
Bowlly, Al 155, 164–5
Braganza, Catherine of (consort of
    Charles II) 19, 40, 103–4
Brown's Hotel 71
Brummel, Beau 72, 103
Bullock, William 83–4, 85–6, 88, 90, 91
    see also Egyptian Hall
Bullock's Museum 79–80, 83–6, 122
Burlington Arcade 102, 107–9
Burlington House 24–5, 39, 45–8, 58, 105,
    107–8
Burton, Decimus (architect) 57
Byron, Lord 53, 54–5, 72

Café Anglais 142, 163, 165
Café de Paris 36, 163, 164, 166
Café Royal 143, 146–8, 151, 155–6, 175,
    232
Cambridge House 24–5, 72
Cambridge Theatre 197, 239
Campbell, Colen (architect) 45
Canterbury Theatre of Varieties 199
Caravan Club 173–4
Carlton Hotel 74, 75–6
Carnaby Street 168, 170, 222
Cave of the Golden Calf Club 172
Cavendish, Lady Dorothy 46
Cavendish, George, 1st Earl of Burlington
    107–8
Cavendish, William, 5th Duke of
    Devonshire 46, 48
Cavendish Hotel 70, 73–4
Cavendish-Bentinck, William, Duke of
    Portland 46
Chambers, Sir William (architect) 52
Chant, Laura Ormiston 203, 211
Chelsea Arts Club 234
Chez Victor 165–6, 169
Chinatown 231–2
Christy Minstrels 16, 200

Churchill, Winston 34, 37, 38
Cibber, Colley 178
Ciro's Nightclub 119, 161, 163
Clarendon House 42–3, 58
Claridge's Hotel 70, 71, 142
Clermont Club 235
Coal Hole 158
Cochran, C.B. (Charles Blake) 160, 170,
    212–14
Colarossi, Angelo 20
Coliseum 195, 197
Collier, Constance 174, 206, 209
Colony Room Club 233
Comedy Theatre 193
Concord, Temple of 40–1
Cooke, George 96–8, 99, 100
Copland, Alexander 52–3
Cotter O'Brien, Patrick ('The Irish
    Giant') 88
Covent Garden Theatre 179
Coward, Noël 164, 174, 175, 194, 214
Criterion Theatre 23, 25, 61, 141, 144,
    188–9, 201–2, 221, 223, 237, 238
Criterion Theatre Restaurant ('the Cri')
    25, 125, 144, 151, 209
Cruikshank, George 86
Cumberland Hotel 154, 228
Cunard, Nancy 175
Cuzzoni, Francesca 180

Daly's Theatre 211
Dartmouth, Lord 50
Davy, Sir Humphry 82, 87
Debenhams 222–3
Debrett, John 105, 106
Defence of the Realm Act (DORA) 1914
    158, 161, 211
Denham, Sir John 43–4, 45
Devonshire, Dukes of 40, 46, 47, 48, 49,
    235
Devonshire, Georgiana, Duchess of 39–40,
    48–9, 51
Devonshire House 24–5, 33, 40, 46, 48–9,
    58
Dickens, Charles 23, 25, 101, 113, 142,
    231, 240
'Disappearing Lady' (illusion) 97–8
Dixey, Miss Phyllis 216–17

Douglas, Lord Alfred 148, 190
Douglass, Frederick 200
D'Oyly Carte, Richard 75, 183, 193
Dubourg's Mechanical Theatre 95
Durrant's Hotel 70

East India Company 49, 56, 103, 104, 111
Eddystone lighthouse 81–2
Edward, Prince of Wales (later Edward VIII)
    73, 162–3, 164, 165, 166, 213
Edwardes, George 144, 149, 192, 205–7, 209
Egyptian Hall 16, 79–80, 84–6, 88, 90,
    91–2, 93–4, 95, 96, 98, 99, 125
Elgin Marbles 46
Embassy Club 162, 163
Empire Theatre, Leicester Square 99, 158,
    194, 197, 204, 210, 236, 237
Eros News Cinema 36
'Eros', statue of 20
    see also Anteros, statue of
Escoffier, Auguste 75–6
Establishment Club 233
Evans's Song and Supper Rooms 134,
    159–60, 204, 230
Evelyn, John 42

Fanque, Pablo (William Darby) 80
Fifty-Fifty Club 174–5
First World War 32–3, 34, 151, 158, 161,
    206, 211
Foote, Samuel 183–4
Fortnum, Charles 16, 63, 103, 110, 111
Fortnum and Mason 16, 63–4, 100, 101,
    103, 104, 110–15
Fox, Charles James 48–9, 51–2
Fox, Roy 164, 165
Franklin, Benjamin 16, 50, 105

Gaiety Girls 149, 192, 205, 206–10
Gaiety Theatre 144, 149, 183, 197, 204–10
Gargoyle Club 175
Garrick Club 234
Garrick, David 184–6
Gatti, Carlo 151
Gaumont News Theatre 36
Gibbon, Sir Walter 163
Gibbons, Grinling 35, 44
Gibbs, James 45

Gilbert, Alfred 20
Gilbert, W.S. 183, 188
Gill, Eric 172
Gillespie, Dizzy 135, 170, 171, 213
Gloucester Coffee House 23, 62, 65–7
Great Exhibition of 1851 67, 69–70, 115
Great Western Hotel 70–1
Green, Leslie (architect) 31
Grey, Charles, Earl 49, 56
Grillon's Club 72
Grillon's Hotel 70, 71, 72
Groucho Club 233–4
Guards and Cavalry Club 72

Hambone Club 174
Handel, George Frideric 41, 178–9, 180,
    181, 182
Hatch, Ike 169, 213
Hatchard, John 104–5, 106–7
Hatchards Bookshop 106–7, 147
Hatchett's Hotel 60, 67–9
Haydon, Benjamin Robert 92, 93
Haymarket Theatre 183–4
Heaven and Hell Coffee Bar 230
Hefner, Hugh 227
Heidegger, 'Count' John James 181, 182
Henderson, Mrs Laura 214–15
Henrey, Madeleine 36
Hervey, John, 1st Earl of Bristol 40, 209
His Majesty's Theatre 175, 209, 211
Hoey, Mildred 168
Holden, Charles (architect) 32
Holford, Sir William (architect) 220
Holland, Henry (architect) 53
Hollingshead, John 205
Hone, William 41–2, 89
Hope, Thomas 84
'Hottentot Venus' (Saartjie ('Sarah')
    Baartman) 90–1
Houdini Brothers 95–6, 213
Howe, Admiral Earl 49, 50
Howe, Caroline 49–50
Hutchinson, Leslie 'Hutch' 165–6, 169
Hyde, Edward, Earl of Clarendon 42–3

'In and Out' (Naval and Military) club 72
Irving, Sir Henry (John Henry Brodribb)
    186–8

Isow, Jack 169, 213
Italian opera 178–83, 184
Ivy, The 92, 232–3

J. Lyons Corner Houses 131, 153–5, 173, 228
Jackson's of Piccadilly 104
Jellico, Geoffrey 220
Jermyn, Henry, Earl of St Albans 43, 44
Johnson, Ken 'Snakehips' 36, 169
Johnson, Dr Samuel 184, 186
Jupp, James 206, 208

Keeler, Christine 224–5
Kent, William (architect) 48
Kettners Restaurant 144, 151
Kit Kat Club 162, 163, 178

Lackington, George 88, 90, 91–2
Lamb, Sir Peniston, Viscount Melbourne 52
Lambert, Daniel 88
Lane, John (publisher) 190
Langan's Brasserie 232
Le Gavroche 232
Le Méridien Hotel 26, 99, 143
Leno, Dan 192–3
Lewis, Matthew 'Monk' 54, 55
Lewis, Rosa (née Ovenden) 70, 73–4
Liberty, Arthur Lasenby 117
Liberty's 16, 117
Lillywhite's 117
Lloyd Webber, Andrew 238–9
London Building Act 1894 27
London Palladium 197, 214, 239
London Pavilion 22, 25, 27, 61, 100, 126, 165, 194, 197, 198–9, 201–3, 204, 213–14, 221, 224, 236
Lunardi, Vincenzo 47
Lyceum 149, 186, 187, 221, 239
Lyons, Joseph 154
    see also J. Lyons Corner Houses
Lyric Theatre 22, 205

Machray, Robert 28
Madame Tussaud's 82, 236
Mafeking, relief of 29–30
Mallory, George 114–15

Marvell, Andrew 42–3
Maskelyne, Nevil 96–8, 99, 100
Mason, Hugh 16, 110, 111
    see also Fortnum and Mason
masquerade 181, 197
Maxim's 152, 162
May Fair (annual fair) 41–2, 79
Mayfair, The (hotel) 33
Messina, Alfredo 226
Meyrick, Kate ('Ma') 130, 167–9
Middle Earth Club 230
Millar, Gertie 127, 205, 206, 209–10
Mills, Florence 135, 170, 212–13
Mivart's Hotel 70
Monico, The 25, 26, 27, 145–6, 201, 221, 223–4
Monseigneur Club 164–5
Moss, Edward 195
Mountbatten, Lady Edwina 162, 165–6
Mountbatten, Lord Louis ('Dickie') 165, 166
Murray's Jazz and Cabaret Club 137, 161, 167, 224–5
Myrtil, Odette 161

Nash, John 21–2, 25, 58, 80, 122, 182
Naval and Military ('In and Out') Club 72
Neave, Jack 'Ironfoot' 173
New White Horse Cellar 60, 67–9
Newnham-Davis, Nathaniel 76–7, 151–2
Nicols, Daniel (Daniel Nicholas Thenevon) 147–8
Novello, Ivor 174–5

Old Times Brighton stage coach 68–9
Old White Horse Cellar 33, 59, 64–5
Original Dixieland Jazz Band 212
Oxford Music Hall 199

Palace Theatre 22, 99, 190, 197, 212, 213
Palmer, John 61–2
Pantheon, Oxford Street 181–2
penny gaffs 198–9
Perosino, Victor 165, 166
Pettigrew, Thomas 'Mummy' 86–7
Piccadilly Circus 15, 17, 19–38, 60, 128, 136, 145, 160, 197, 201, 220–1, 223–4

Piccadilly Circus Underground Station 31–2, 34, 37, 129
Piccadilly Hotel (now Le Méridien Hotel) 26, 33, 163
Pick, Frank 32, 34
Pitt, William 44–5, 46, 49, 52, 61–2
Pond, Christopher 144
Pratt, Roger 42
Prince of Wales Theatre 190
Profumo, John 225
Pulteney, The 70, 71–2
Pulteney, William, 1st Earl of Bath 40, 43

Quaglino's 151, 232
Quicksilver mail coach 62
Quo Vadis Restaurant 151, 232

Raymond, Paul (Geoff Quinn) 138, 226–8
Raymond's Revuebar 226–7
Regent Palace Hotel 154, 216
Repton, Humphrey 182
Ricci, Sebastiano 45
Rice-Davies, Mandy 224–5
Ritz, César 16, 74–6
Ritz Hotel 16, 33, 60, 64, 74–7
Ritz-Carlton 75, 76
Robert-Houdin, Jean-Eugene 95, 98
Romano, Alfonso Nicolino 148–50
Romano's 139, 143, 148–50, 151, 155–6, 209
Ronnie Scott's jazz club 172, 230
Roux, Michel 232
Royal Albert Potato Can 141
Royal Court Theatre 237
Royal Opera House 183, 221, 237
Royalty Theatre 175, 188
Rules Restaurant 156, 232

Sacqui and Lawrence 25
Sadler, James 46–7
Sage, Letitia (née Hoare) 46
St James's Church, Piccadilly 35, 44–5, 105, 140
St James's Hall, Piccadilly 16, 25–6, 33, 96, 143, 200
    restaurant ('Jimmy's') 25, 29, 33, 143–4, 157, 209
St James's Theatre 95, 189, 190

Sala, George Augustus 141, 142, 160
Salmon and Gluckstein 154
Sandy's Bar 173
Saracen's Head, the 61
Savile Club 33
Savoy Hotel 71, 75, 142, 151
Savoy Operas 75, 149, 183
Savoy Theatre 183, 197
Scott, George Gilbert (architect) 71
Scott, Ronnie 171, 172, 230
Second World War 21, 33–8, 99, 109, 132, 136, 150, 167, 171, 189, 215–16, 219, 231
Selfridge, Gordon 117–18
Seurat, Claude ('The Living Skeleton') 88–9, 124
Shaftesbury Memorial Fountain 20–1, 25, 32, 140
Shaftesbury Theatre 22, 197, 212
Sheridan, Richard Brinsley 178, 181
Sherwood Stratton, Charles (General Tom Thumb) 93–4
Shillibeer, George 24
Shim Sham Club 16–17, 169–70, 172, 213
Siamese Twins 89–90
Silver Slipper Club 167, 168
Simpson, Alec 118–19
Simpson's in the Strand 156, 232
Simpson's of Piccadilly 117, 118–19, 224
Skindles Hotel, Maidenhead 209
Sloan, Sir Hans 82, 84
Smith, Sir Bracewell 33
Soho House 234
Sondheim Theatre 239
Spaghetti House 228–9
Spiers and Pond 144, 151, 154
Stafford Street Club 72
Stockdale, John (bookseller) 104–5
Stoker, Bram 186, 187–8
Strand Palace 154, 228
Strand Theatre 12, 192, 193
Sullivan, Arthur 183
Swan and Edgar 25, 33, 116, 117, 221, 224
Swan with Two Necks, The 62

tableaux vivants 210
Taylor, Sir Robert (architect) 49
Tennant, Stephen and David 175

Terry, Ellen 187, 188
Theatre Royal, Covent Garden 179,
    182–3, 185, 191
Theatre Royal, Drury Lane 177–8, 182,
    183, 184–6, 191, 192, 221, 239
Thesiger, Ernest 174–5
Three Kings coaching inn 60
Tom Thumb, General (Charles Sherwood
    Stratton) 93–4, 123
Tomlins, William 24
Tree, Herbert Beerbohm 175, 209
Tree, Iris 175
Trocadero 22, 154, 155, 173, 197, 236

UFO Club 230
Upson, Jack 164, 165

Van Damm, Vivian 215, 216, 226–7
Vanbrugh, Sir John (architect) 178
Vaudeville Theatre 149
Veeraswamy's 152
Vulliamy, George 22

Walford, Edward 70
Walsingham House Hotel, The 60
Ware, Samuel (architect) 108

Wellesley, Arthur, Duke of Wellington
    55–7, 70, 85, 93
Wellington Arch 55–6, 57–8
Whistler, James McNeill 146, 148, 189
White Bear coaching inn 23, 60–1, 64,
    112, 141
White Horse Cellar 23, 60, 67, 112
White Horse Inn 195
White Swan coaching inn 60
Whitehall Theatre 216, 217, 227
White's gentlemen's club 73, 181, 234
Wilde, Constance 147, 148, 189
Wilde, Oscar 75, 146–7, 148, 173, 175,
    183, 189–91, 238
Wimpy Bar 228
Windmill Theatre 35, 132, 215–17,
    226–7
Winstanley, Henry 81–2
Winstanley's Water Theatre 79–80, 81–2
Wong Kei Restaurant 231
Wren, Sir Christopher 44, 177, 186
Wyatt, Benjamin Dean (architect) 56
Wyndham, Charles 188–9
Wyndham's Theatre 188–9

Zeppelin raids 34